BROTHERS
AND
WIVES

An Affair to Remember: The Remarkable Love Story
of Katharine Hepburn and Spencer Tracy

Jack and Jackie: Portrait of an American Marriage

Young Kate: The Remarkable Hepburns and the Childhood
That Shaped an American Legend

The Best of Everything (with John Marion)

The Serpent's Tooth

The Book of People

Father, the Figure and the Force

The Name Game

BROTHERS AND WIVES

INSIDE THE PRIVATE LIVES OF
WILLIAM, KATE, HARRY, *and* MEGHAN

CHRISTOPHER ANDERSEN

GALLERY BOOKS

New York   London   Toronto   Sydney   New Delhi

Gallery Books
An Imprint of Simon & Schuster, Inc.
1230 Avenue of the Americas
New York, NY 10020

First Gallery Books hardcover edition November 2021

GALLERY BOOKS and colophon are registered trademarks of Simon & Schuster, Inc.

For information about special discounts for bulk purchases, please contact Simon & Schuster Special Sales at 1-866-506-1949 or business@simonandschuster.com.

The Simon & Schuster Speakers Bureau can bring authors to your live event.
For more information or to book an event, contact the Simon & Schuster Speakers Bureau at 1-866-248-3049 or visit our website at www.simonspeakers.com.

Interior design by Davina Mock-Maniscalco

PHOTO CREDITS
Alpha Photo Press: 1
Shutterstock: 2, 3, 4, 5, 6, 7, 8, 9, 10, 11, 12, 13, 14, 15, 16, 17, 18, 19, 20, 21, 22, 23, 24, 25, 26, 27, 28, 29, 30, 31, 33, 34, 35, 36, 37, 38, 39, 40, 41, 42, 43, 44, 45, 46, 47, 48
Zuma Press: 32

Manufactured in the United States of America

10   9   8   7   6   5   4   3   2   1

Library of Congress Cataloging-in-Publication Data has been applied for.

ISBN 978-1-9821-5972-6
ISBN 978-1-9821-5974-0 (ebook)

For my brilliant grandchildren,
Graham, Charlotte, and Teddy

CONTENTS

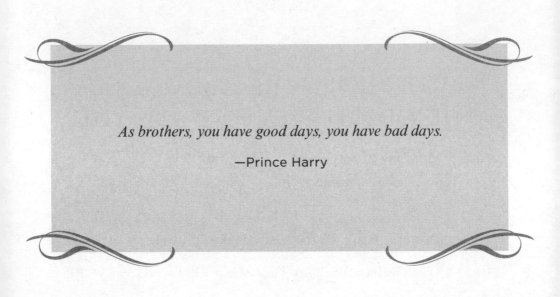

As brothers, you have good days, you have bad days.

—Prince Harry

"BUT I LOVE HIM DEARLY" / "THEY DIDN'T EVEN TELL THE QUEEN" / "WHAT THE F— DOES HE THINK HE'S DOING?"

Sandringham House, Norfolk
Three O'clock, Christmas Day 2019

WILLIAM'S HEART SANK. He was well practiced at not registering true emotion on his face, and with his father, the Prince of Wales, and his grandmother the Queen sitting only a few feet away, it was best for all concerned to simply remain expressionless. Gathered in the cavernous Long Library at Sandringham House, palatial centerpiece of the monarch's 20,000-acre country estate 96 miles north of London, senior members of the family were joining their countrymen in an annual ritual: viewing "Her Majesty's Most Gracious Speech," the Queen's televised Christmas message to her subjects. In her six-minute address, the sovereign pointed to the birth of her great-grandson Archie Mountbatten-Windsor as the one genuinely bright spot in a "quite bumpy year" that included Brexit, Britain's

1

tortured exit from the European Union, as well as an underage sex trafficking scandal that led to second son Prince Andrew's fall from grace, ninety-eight-year-old Prince Philip's brief hospitalization before the holidays, and her new granddaughter-in-law Meghan Markle's difficult—and tabloid-filling—adjustment to her new role as a member of the world's most scrutinized family.

None of this came as news to Prince William, who had a ringside seat to these and other troubling events buffeting the Windsor clan. Yet he was taken aback by the optics of his grandmother's speech—always one of the most watched and overinterpreted events on the royal calendar. The Queen had taped her address days before in Windsor Castle's opulently appointed, damask-walled Green Drawing Room, where Archie had been christened the previous July. Wearing a cobalt-blue dress and the 30-carat sapphire-and-diamond brooch that her great-great-grandfather Prince Albert gave to his bride-to-be, Queen Victoria, on the eve of their wedding in February 1840, Her Majesty sat at a desk alongside several large, framed photographs positioned to be clearly seen by viewers. To the Queen's immediate right was a black-and-white photograph of her father, King George VI, as well as small snapshots of Charles and Camilla and Philip. At twice the size of all the other photographs, a color portrait of the Cambridges—William, Kate, and their joyously rambunctious children George, Charlotte, and Louis—was placed front and center, dominating the shot.

In prior years, Prince Harry had always been included among the snapshots; in 2018 both he and wife, Meghan, were included with the other senior royals in the prominent central photo. But this year, neither the Duke nor the Duchess of Sussex—much less little Archie—was anywhere to be seen. Palace officials would later try to explain that this year's collection of royal family photos merely reflected the direct line of succession, but the damage was done. To the world at large, it appeared that Harry and Meghan, who had loudly voiced complaints about their treatment at the hands of both the press and Buckingham Palace, had been pushed out of the picture altogether—both literally and figuratively.

William, who had spent much of his life shielding his younger brother from hurt feelings, was nevertheless reluctant to bring up the subject of the absent photos—not when everyone seemed to be in such an uncharacteristically ebullient mood. As she did every year, the Queen put considerable time and effort into writing her Christmas address herself. This time she felt she "got it right. Yes, well," Her Majesty said, accepting the usual round of applause from family members after the broadcast concluded, "I was particularly proud of that one." Unwilling to put a damper on the proceedings, William pulled his wife, Kate, aside and whispered to her that Harry was likely to be "terribly upset" that the Sussexes had been plucked from the usual lineup of royals flanking the Queen.

Kate agreed, but she cautioned her husband to keep his concerns to himself—at least for the moment. Besides, she reminded William, Harry was undoubtedly still asleep and blissfully unaware of any perceived slights or insults directed at him and his family. Indeed, nearly 4,700 miles away in British Columbia, the brother to whom William was psychically tethered would soon awaken to experience a Christmas unlike any he had ever known—a distinctly American Christmas. Rather than spend the holidays with the rest of the royal family at Sandringham—as the couple had done the previous two years (and as Harry, up until then, had done for all but two of his thirty-five years, in 2007 and 2012, while serving in Afghanistan as an officer in the British Army)—they decided to celebrate Thanksgiving straight through Christmas and the start of the New Year at a $16 million beachfront hideaway on Vancouver Island with Archie and with Meghan's mother, Doria Ragland. Fleet Street pilloried the Sussexes when they decided not to show up for Christmas at Sandringham, but it was a departure from tradition that the Queen had already come to terms with in 2012 and 2016 when William and Kate celebrated the holiday with Kate's parents, the Middletons, at their home in West Berkshire.

An immutable and highly structured ritual for the royals, Christmas at Sandringham began with everyone gathering on Christmas Eve to put the finishing touches on the twenty-foot tree that had been chopped down on the grounds of the estate and set up in the White Drawing Room. Later that afternoon, William and his Windsor relatives opened the wrapped gifts that had been spread out on trestle tables; following the German tradition of their ancestors, the descendants of Victoria and Albert always opened their presents on Christmas Eve. That evening, everyone donned formal attire for cocktails, followed by a holiday dinner menu that never varied over the decades: roast turkey with either sage and onion or chestnut stuffing, mashed and roasted potatoes, Brussels sprouts and parsnips, and Christmas pudding for dessert. The meal ended when the Queen finished eating, like clockwork, precisely at ten o'clock.

The next morning, after indulging in a full English breakfast, everyone, with the exception of the Queen and Prince Philip, headed off on foot for the church on the grounds of Sandringham, St. Mary Magdalene. This year, Harry missed the debut appearance of Prince George and Princess Charlotte at Christmas Day church services and the walkabout among awestruck local folk that followed—a rite of passage experienced by every royal child, not to mention an important opportunity for the royal family to connect with the common man.

On Vancouver Island, Harry, Meghan, and Archie awoke Christmas morning 2019 to discover overstuffed stockings hanging from the fireplace mantel and a small mountain of presents beneath the tree waiting to be unwrapped. With eight-month-old Archie perched in Grandma Doria's lap, everyone tore open the packages and tossed the paper aside with abandon—just the way Meghan did when she was a little girl growing up in Los Angeles. Midmorning, Harry paused to look at his phone and check on the Queen's speech. Meghan watched as his mood shifted in an instant from surprise, to confusion, to simmering rage.

Erased. That was the first word that came to mind. "He felt," said one of his oldest confidantes, "as if he, Meghan, and Archie were being erased from the family." Erased—and punished. Over the previous few months, Harry had spoken to his father and the Queen—and equally important, courtiers who pull the levers of power within the monarchy—about the Sussexes' desire to carve out a new and largely independent role for themselves. A large part of the plan involved dividing their time between the United Kingdom and North America, where they could live something approaching a normal family life away from the prying eyes of Britain's relentless tabloid press. Just before Christmas, Harry and Meghan felt confident enough to email the Queen and the Prince of Wales directly to say that they had had made up their minds: they wanted to pursue their own interests without interference from the powers-that-be at the Palace and, at the same time, fulfill their obligations to the Crown. Now the young prince needed to know if he and Meghan had overplayed their hand.

Harry called Buckingham Palace directly and asked for a face-to-face meeting with the Queen as soon as the Sussexes returned to London on January 6, only to be rebuffed by Her Majesty's handlers. The sover-

eign's calendar was packed, Harry was told by her assistant private secretary, and he would simply have to wait until January 29 to see his
grandmother—and even then, only for a few minutes. Harry dug in,
explaining that he and Meghan would be in England for only a short
time; they planned to return to Vancouver Island, where they'd left
Archie in the care of his nanny, as soon as possible.

No matter. Even after Prince Charles's office interceded on their behalf, the Sussexes were told they would have to wait. Yet time was running out. Until now, the Windsors had managed to keep the ongoing
negotiations between Harry and the rest of the royals top secret; it was
only a matter of time before the story was leaked to an enterprising reporter. With four royal protection officers in tow, Harry and Meghan
boarded a nonstop Air Canada flight on the afternoon of January 5 and
arrived at Heathrow Airport late the next morning. Rather than make a
bold attempt to drive straight to Sandringham and see the Queen without an appointment—flouting protocol and, in the process, alienating
her senior aides—Harry and Meghan instead headed for Frogmore
Cottage, their modest nineteenth-century four-bedroom residence near
Windsor Castle.

In the past, Harry would have automatically reached out to his older
brother for support and guidance at a time like this; William had been
Harry's emotional anchor for as long as either could remember, going all
the way back to what Highgrove housekeeper Wendy Berry called the
"sheer bedlam" of their childhood—including pitched battles between
the parents that their nanny Jessie Webb described as "barking mad—the
both of them." But the brotherly bond between the young princes was
now strained to the breaking point, something Harry had acknowledged
publicly in a documentary about the Sussexes' African charity work that
aired the previous October on both British and American television.

"This family, being under the pressure that it's under, inevitably stuff happens," he said in *Harry and Meghan: An African Journey*. "But, look, we're brothers, we'll always be brothers, and we're certainly on different paths at the moment, but I will always be there for him, as I know he will always be there for me. We don't see each other as much as we used to because we're so busy. But I love him dearly."

At the time, William was miffed at his brother for deigning to discuss their relationship in the press, much less concede that they were now to some extent estranged. Since then, they had not communicated at all. Indeed, Harry had no idea that William was so disturbed by the Sussexes' exclusion from the lineup of royal photos displayed on the Queen's desk that he spoke with their father about it. The Prince of Wales waved off his eldest son's concerns; if Harry and Meghan wished to separate themselves from the rest of the family, he reasoned, then the optics of the Queen's Christmas speech shouldn't bother them.

Now, with the press breathing down their necks, Harry and Meghan needed some sort of guarantee that their decision to forge a new and largely separate life for themselves was being taken seriously. Once ensconced at Frogmore, Harry shot off another email directly to the woman he called "Granny." (The Queen has had her own email address since 2007.) In response, Her Majesty agreed to issue a joint statement at some point in the near future—enough reassurance from the Crown that their bid for freedom would soon be sprung upon an unsuspecting public.

Feeling confident that their new life was at last on the horizon, Harry and Meghan appeared hand in hand the next day at Canada House in London, Canada's diplomatic mission to the United Kingdom. There they viewed works by Mohawk multimedia artist Skawennati, had tea with the high commissioner, Janice Charette, and posed for photographs with two hundred starstruck commission staffers. After thanking their Canadian hosts for the hospitality shown them during their stay with Archie in British Columbia ("What a beautiful place you live in!" Harry gushed), the couple climbed into their Land Rover for the ride back to Frogmore Cottage.

They were only minutes outside central London when they learned the news: enterprising reporters for the *Sun* ferreted out just enough information to post a story on the paper's website about the couple's break with the royal family. There would be some debate about whether the Palace had leaked the information, or the Sussexes did it themselves to force the issue, but the results were the same. Within minutes, royal offices were swamped with calls from media outlets seeking clarification.

"Damn it!" Harry said, turning to Meghan as their Land Rover raced toward Windsor and Frogmore Cottage. "What do we do now?" He would later recount to a friend his wife's characteristically clarifying response. "Well, Harry," she replied almost matter-of-factly, "I don't really think we have a choice, do you?"

January 8, 2020

A personal message from the Duke and Duchess of Sussex:

After many months of reflection and internal discussions, we have chosen to make a transition this year in starting to carve out a progressive new role within this institution.

We intend to step back as "senior" members of the royal family and work to become financially independent, while continuing to fully support Her Majesty the Queen.

It is with your encouragement, particularly over the last few years, that we feel prepared to make this adjustment.

We now plan to balance our time between the United Kingdom and North America, continuing to honour our duty to the Queen, the Commonwealth, and our patronages.

This geographic balance will enable us to raise our son with an appreciation for the royal tradition into which he was born, while also providing our family with the space to focus on the next chapter, including the launch of our new charitable entity.

We look forward to sharing the full details of this exciting next step in due course, as we continue to collaborate with Her Majesty the Queen, the Prince of Wales, the Duke of Cambridge, and all relevant parties.

Until then, please accept our deepest thanks for your continued support.

The following morning at Sandringham, the Queen paused to survey the usual breakfast spread—one soft-boiled egg, crustless whole wheat toast with a round of butter and orange marmalade, cornflakes brought to the table in a Tupperware container, small bowls of apricots, macadamia nuts, and prunes—then moved on to a side table piled with the morning papers. Normally, the horse-obsessed monarch would start with her favorite publication, the *Racing Post*, and then pore over *Thoroughbred Owner and Breeder*. But not today. On this rainy Thursday, Her Majesty swept the racing results and tip sheets aside and stared down at the blur of red, yellow, blue, and purple tabloid headlines that all seemed to be screaming directly at her.

Having learned the news on television the night before, Her Majesty was not surprised at what the newspapers had to say and how they would say it. She herself had, after all, spent a mostly sleepless night trying to process it all. "Queen's Fury as Harry and Meghan Say: We Quit!" shrieked the *Daily Mail*, while the *Daily Telegraph*, referring to George VI's statement that the royals are "not a family, we're a firm," proclaimed "Harry and Meghan Quit The Firm." Even the stuffily venerable *Times* of London devoted virtually its entire front page to the story, announcing, "Harry and Meghan Quit Roles Amid Palace Split." The *Sun* took the prize for creativity, coining the term that with a brevity bordering on genius so perfectly described the latest ordnance to rock the royal House of Windsor: "Megxit."

Yet for all the cleverness of the *Sun*'s headline writers, it was the front-page banner in the *Daily Mirror* that struck at the heart of the monarch: "They Didn't Even Tell the Queen." "Angela, why do you suppose they did it?" Elizabeth sighed to her longtime dresser and trusted confidante Angela Kelly, the Liverpool dockworker's daughter whose official title now was Personal Assistant, Advisor, and Curator to the Queen. Kelly was well aware that informal discussions had been going on with the Sussexes for months and that the Queen was sympathetic to their frustrations and desires. But too many questions about the future of Harry and Meghan remained unsettled—most glaringly, how much they would be allowed to capitalize on their titles and position in the royal family to build a "brand" of their own. Kelly wondered aloud if perhaps Prince William had the answer. While the Queen had fully embraced social media as a powerful tool to promote the monarchy, Kelly noted that William and Kate would certainly know more about the finer points of Instagram.

Yet, just two miles to the east at Anmer Hall, the Duke and Duchess of Cambridge's eighteenth-century redbrick Georgian manse on the grounds of Sandringham Estate, William was equally dumbfounded by his brother's actions. "What the fuck do Harry and Meghan think they're doing?" the prince blurted out as staff huddled nervously in a hallway. "My father will be furious."

"Not to mention your grandparents," chimed in Kate, who, along with the rest of the world, had seen the photos of a beaming Harry and an equally radiant Meghan at Canada House taken just hours before the release of their bombshell Instagram announcement. "What a lovely outfit," Kate remarked as she stared at newspaper photos of Meghan in a tight brown sweater, ankle-length satin skirt, and matching stiletto heels. "Duchess Meghan and Prince Look Happier Than Ever" blared the headline in *Closer* magazine. "Well," the Duchess of Cambridge said, "they certainly do *look* happy."

Kate was right about the boys' grandparents—particularly Prince Philip, whose penchant for making blunt and often cringe-inducing remarks had intensified with age; at ninety-eight, he was already the oldest male in the history of Britain's royal family. Philip knew nothing of

Instagram, but when he was told about the Sussexes' unilateral declaration of independence, the Duke of Edinburgh was, said an aide, "furious, deeply hurt, spitting blood"—and went straight to the Queen's side to let her know how angry he was. "This shows a complete lack of respect," stated Philip, who, like Prince Charles and other senior royals, had formed a warm relationship with Meghan but now viewed her as a twenty-first-century Wallis Simpson. "It appears as if," Philip told one of his closest aides, "we were wrong about her all along."

For her part, the Queen was more bewildered and hurt than angry. She was, after all, accustomed to grappling with the public relations fallout from countless family scandals, not the least of which were the latest and most scandalous revelations concerning her son Andrew's yearslong friendship with Jeffrey Epstein, the well-connected American financier who hanged himself in his prison cell following his arrest on charges of running a child sex ring. After Prince Andrew appeared on BBC-TV's *Newsnight* in November 2019 to deny—unconvincingly—that he had abused one of Epstein's underage "sex slaves," an enraged Charles urged his mother to take decisive action against the errant prince. Four days after the disastrous TV interview aired, Buckingham Palace announced that Prince Andrew was suspending all his royal duties "for the foreseeable future." (Within months, Andrew permanently resigned from all his public duties as a *Newsweek* poll showed that a majority of Britons wanted him stripped of his titles and extradited to the United States for questioning.)

As painful as it had been for the Queen to effectively force her own son into early retirement, it was only the latest step in a scandal that had been dragging along in one form or another for nine years. The Sussexes' explosive announcement was unexpected. The Queen and Prince Philip—he had attended Harry's wedding to Meghan Markle in May

2018 despite having cracked a rib in a bathroom fall the night before—harbored a special affection for Harry that transcended their feelings for their own children, and Megxit had come with all the shock and awe of a thunderclap. "What Harry and Meghan did was a terrible blow," said Her Majesty's longtime press spokesman Dickie Arbiter. "The Queen is feeling very let down—more disappointed than she felt after Andrew's terrible BBC interview."

For all the Sturm und Drang to the south, none compared with the torrent of epithets unleashed by the Prince of Wales at Birkhall, Charles and Camilla's retreat just an eighteen-minute drive alongside the River Dee from the Queen's beloved Balmoral Castle. The heir to the throne was known for his Vesuvian temper—on not one but two occasions, he had yanked a bathroom sink off its base in a fit of pique—and staffers at Balmoral described Charles's reaction to the Sussexes' surprise announcement as "frightening." In his study cluttered with books and photographs, the Prince of Wales at one point grabbed a carved wooden floor lamp that stood behind his desk—a particular favorite because of its hand-painted shade depicting a seventeenth-century British galleon on the high seas—and stopped just short of hurling it across the room. "I have seen him that angry before," Camilla told a Highgrove neighbor later, "but rarely."

Harry and Meghan were initially "nothing short of stunned," as one friend put it, by the uproar their Instagram posting had caused—especially among members of the royal family, who'd known already that the Sussexes were in the process of making a major change. Yet the fact remained that they had committed one of The Firm's cardinal sins: doing virtually anything of significance without the Queen's express consent. "We wanted to get out ahead of it and control the narrative," Harry explained over the phone to Charles. Thwarted in their attempts to warn the Queen, Harry and Meghan had no choice but to go ahead and announce the news themselves.

According to a senior member of the Prince of Wales's staff, Charles was having none of it. "You couldn't have simply picked up the phone and called me? Or called the Queen?" Charles asked, the anger in his voice escalating with every syllable. "Really, Harry, this is completely unacceptable. You must apologize to your grandmother immediately. You must try and fix this."

It would not be so easy. Her Majesty was variously described as "terribly disappointed," "devastated," and "heartbroken" at what senior courtiers described as an act of "outright betrayal." The Instagram statement, which took the senior staffs of all the royal palaces by complete surprise—including Harry and Meghan's own team of seasoned royal operatives—wasn't the only thing that rubbed Buckingham Palace's Old Guard the wrong way. In tandem with their Instagram post, Meghan and Harry spelled out the details of their plan to become financially independent—and thereby free from the constraints and press intrusions that came with being on the public dole—on their shiny new SussexRoyal.com website.

The Queen's private secretary, Sir Edward Young, was particularly chagrined. At fifty-three, Young was scarcely a hidebound traditionalist; in 2012 it fell to him to convince the Queen to take part with James Bond actor Daniel Craig in a staged parachute jump that kicked off the London Olympics. But ambushing the Crown in this manner, spelling out their ambitious and unprecedented plan for partial independence to the world at large before consulting the Queen and obtaining her necessary approval—this was, as one courtier put it, "more than an unforgivable breach of etiquette. It is a brutal slap in the face to the entire royal family, but most especially for the Queen."

In fact, Her Majesty understood the Sussexes' desire to spend more time in Canada, closer to Doria Ragland and Meghan's American roots. She also understood Harry's deeply felt hatred of the British press, which he had always blamed for literally chasing his mother, Diana, Princess of Wales, to her violent death at the age of thirty-six. Looking ahead to Charles's blueprint for a streamlined, trimmed-down version of the monarchy—one in which Harry saw himself playing a minor supporting role at best—the Queen even understood that it made sense for a young man of action to at least try to shape his own destiny apart from the Windsors.

What neither the Queen nor anyone else in her inner circle could comprehend was how, given the weight of centuries-old tradition and the Palace power structure that enforced it, Harry and Meghan would possibly pull it off. The royal imprimatur had long been used to raise funds for a wide range of charities and causes, but this was different. The notion of becoming financially independent—of actually pursuing various moneymaking schemes that could conceivably yield tens or even hundreds of millions of dollars of personal income—while still representing the Crown on a part-time basis was fraught with potential obstacles. There were also the obvious security issues: Where would the money come from to protect the sixth in line to the throne and his family? How would taxes, travel, and living expenses be paid? Surely the idea of Harry and Meghan exploiting the Sussex name, their titles, and their connection to the House of Windsor ruffled feathers both inside and outside palace walls. According to one veteran member of the communications staff at Buckingham Palace, Prince Philip called the concept nothing less than "repugnant."

These were all complicated matters that would take time to unravel. In the short term, all the Queen could do to tamp down worldwide hysteria was make some sort of pro forma response. "Discussions with the Duke and Duchess of Sussex are at an early stage," read the official Palace statement, issued fifteen minutes after William and Harry posted their megaton announcement on Instagram. "We understand their desire to take a different approach, but these are complicated issues that will take time to work through."

The terse Palace reply, issued beneath the Queen's official red letterhead bearing the royal coat of arms, left little doubt that the Palace felt it had been blindsided. For William, Charles, and the Queen in particular, the Sussexes' unilateral action had been nothing less than, as the Prince of Wales put it, "a bolt from the blue." With the pandemonium outside palace walls persisting and the press clamoring for answers, the Palace issued its second statement in less than twenty-four hours. The Queen had ordered all four royal households—the Queen, Charles, the Cambridges, and the Sussexes—to find "workable solutions," it read, and the final decision regarding Harry and Meghan's future would be arrived at "within days, not weeks."

For the next three days, all four principals and their staffs scrambled to come up with some sort of strategy for moving forward. In the end, Her Majesty decided that the entire matter had to be worked out by the principals, face-to-face. Still ensconced for the season at her estate in Norfolk—along with Balmoral the only piece of real estate owned personally by her and not by the Crown—Elizabeth II summoned Charles and his sons to a closed emergency meeting at Sandringham on the afternoon of Monday, January 13, 2020. In addition to Charles, William, and Harry—Meghan was already back in Canada and initially given the option of listening in on speakerphone—a number of key aides would be in attendance, including Sir Edward Young; Charles's private secretary, Clive Alderton; William's top advisor, Simon

Case; and Harry's newly appointed private secretary, Fiona Mcilwham. With the world press still hyperventilating over the Sussexes' surprise statement, the meeting was quickly billed on front pages everywhere as "the Sandringham Summit."

For her part, the Queen was eager to resolve the issue quickly. Sandringham was normally her safe haven during the holidays, a place where, despite its undeniable grandeur and household staff of thirty-five, the atmosphere could be described as family oriented and—well, by royal standards anyway—informal. She would remain here, and the elaborate Christmas decorations would stay up until February 6, the anniversary of her father, King George VI's, death in 1952 and the day she became Queen.

In the meantime, weekend shooting parties, during which guests bagged thousands of game birds, were held at Sandringham throughout the winter months. This weekend's host, William and Harry's cousin Peter Phillips, was given the unenviable task of sending his friends packing a day early. Escorting his grandmother to Sunday church service the day before the summit, Phillips, whose mother, Princess Anne, was described by a fellow riding enthusiast as "absolutely seething with rage" about the release of the Sussexes' statement, was asked by a fellow worshipper how the Queen was bearing up under the strain of another crisis in the House of Windsor. "All right," was his curt reply.

Harry knew that Granny was anything but "all right" and that he would have to speak to her alone—away from his father and brother and what he viewed as the meddlesome bureaucrats who stood in the way of progress—if he was ever to smooth things over with the Queen. The ground rules were firmly set: Everyone would arrive at two o'clock for lunch in the dining room, followed by the meeting itself in the Long Library. Everything was to be wrapped up so as not to interfere with one of Her Majesty's most sacrosanct daily rituals: tea at precisely five.

Sandringham held mostly warm memories for the monarch—mostly, but not all. It was here, after all, that William and Harry's mother, just four months into her first pregnancy, stood at the top of the stairs in the main hallway and threatened to kill herself if Charles left for a rendezvous with his mistress, Camilla Parker Bowles. It was not an idle threat: as Charles headed out the door, the Queen looked on in horror as Princess Diana hurled herself down the stairs, landing at her shocked mother-in-law's feet. That day, Princess Margaret joined her sister in rushing to Diana's aid and summoning help.

Fortunately for William and Harry, there were no such unforgettably shocking moments to tarnish their childhood memories. It was at Sandringham where they spent nearly every Christmas as far back as they could remember, where they played with their cousins, took lessons in horsemanship from the Queen, and were taught to shoot by their marksman grandfather. The Long Library, where the bulk of the Sandringham summit was to take place, was situated right next to the billiard room and had actually been a bowling alley prior to the short reign of Edward VII. It was in this room that, once they'd turned five and were considered old enough to comport themselves properly, Diana's sons and their cousins were permitted to take part in the afternoon ritual of high tea—"sucking down great amounts of clotted cream and jam," William recalled, "while the adults ate watercress sandwiches."

It was also at Sandringham that William first realized his grandmother was quite unlike any other person in the world. Watching how very important-looking people not only paid her more respect than anyone else but also seemed to be genuinely awestruck in her presence, it suddenly dawned on seven-year-old William what it meant to be Queen. "It was as if the world we lived in revolved around her," he later observed, "and of course, in a very real sense it does."

For William, the trip from Anmer Hall to Sandringham took a mere five minutes—less than three miles straight west along tree-lined King's Road. Harry, on the other hand, had a two-and-a-half-hour trip ahead of him—125 miles due north from London on the A10. Worried that William, his father, and their respective advisors—all of whom he now viewed as hostile to the Sussexes' desire for semi-autonomy—would arrive before him, Harry wanted to get his grandmother alone before the meeting so that he could make his case without interference. "The Queen has always had a very soft spot in her heart for Harry," Elizabeth's cousin Margaret Rhodes once observed. "She'll forgive him almost anything."

Harry was counting on it. At nine thirty on the morning of January 13, he climbed behind the wheel of his gunmetal-gray Land Rover and started off for Norfolk, determined to arrive at Sandringham a full two hours before the summit was scheduled to start. His private secretary and two royal protection officers accompanied him, but this time there was virtually none of the friendly banter that usually went on between the self-effacing young prince and the people who worked for him.

At about the same time, Prince Philip, still fuming over the Sussexes' abrupt decision to exit the royal family, climbed into the front passenger seat of another Land Rover and departed Sandringham with his longtime companion, Countess Mountbatten, at the wheel. The former Penelope Romsey was thirty-two years younger than Philip and for decades had been rumored to be his lover. Still, she could be counted on to keep the obstreperous duke's formidable temper in check during trying times such as these. Whatever the nature of their relationship over the years, Queen Elizabeth now counted on Countess Mountbatten to essentially watch over her husband. "The Queen," her cousin observed, "is just happy to have Penny Romsey around." When Angela Kelly told the Queen of Philip's hasty exit, she nodded in agreement. "I think it's a very good idea, yes," Her Majesty remarked. "Prince Philip is so angry as it is; having him here will just make matters worse."

As he sped toward Sandringham, Harry knew he faced a Herculean task. First, he had to make amends for disobeying the established rules of protocol and essentially ambushing his grandmother. All members of the royal family had been brought up with the understanding that essentially nothing of significance could be done without the sovereign's express approval. Period.

But Harry knew that he had done more than merely break the rules. He had been told by his outraged father in no uncertain terms that the famously inscrutable Queen had been brought to the brink of tears by the Sussexes' unilateral announcement. At the age of ninety-three, she was still haunted by the memory of another member of the royal family—her uncle Edward VIII, whose abdication in 1936 after less than a year as king triggered a series of events that eventually catapulted her onto the throne. Nor was it possible for the Queen to ignore the fact that both the Duke of Windsor's exit from the royal family to marry Wallis Simpson and the one now called Megxit would never have happened had it not been for women—both glamorous American divorcées.

Harry later told one of his oldest friends that, as he drove to Sandringham that day, he felt "truly apart" from the rest of the Windsors—

especially from the one person he could always count on: William. That morning, the minds of both brothers drifted back, as they did so often, to a time when they truly needed each other—a singular moment in modern history that they could never escape, and one that set them on the path to the men they would become.

It's hard, and it will continue to be hard.
There's not a day that William and I don't wish she was still around.

—Harry

The shock is the biggest thing, and I still feel it. The trauma
of that day has lived with me for twenty years . . . like a weight.
People think shock can't last that long, but it does.

—William

I thought that was where tradition
went too far against human nature.

—Diana's brother Charles Spencer (titled 9th Earl Spencer),
on William and Harry being forced to walk behind
their mother's coffin

TWO

~

"MUMMY, LOOK! IT'S THE BOX WITH THE PRINCESS!"

London
Saturday, September 6, 1997

WILLIAM AND HARRY weren't entirely certain that they had actually heard the little girl say it at the time, or if they simply read about it later. It scarcely mattered. "Mummy, Mummy, look!" she said, pulling at her mother's sleeve with one hand and pointing to the coffin carrying the most celebrated woman in the world with the other. "It's the box with the princess!" Diana's casket, borne on a carriage pulled by six black horses from the Royal Horse Artillery, had just pulled in front of the forbidding, fortress-like north gate main entrance to St. James's Palace. There the men of Windsor—William, Harry, Charles, and Philip—waited with Diana's brother Earl Spencer to join the funeral cortege as it made its way through the streets of London to Westminster Abbey.

Just one week earlier, Diana's sons and the rest of the world awoke to the news that the Princess of Wales had been killed with her lover Dodi Fayed in a senseless car crash in Paris. The brothers, who were vacationing with their father and their grandparents at Balmoral Castle, had spoken with their mother just hours before her death. William took the phone first. As it did so often, the conversation revolved around his concern for his little brother's feelings. A photo op had been scheduled for William's return to one of the world's most elite prep schools, Eton College, and the heir to the throne once again worried about eclipsing "the Spare." They also discussed the Sony PlayStation Diana had purchased in Paris and was bringing home to give Harry for his thirteenth birthday on September 15.

Both William and Harry would look back at that final phone call with deep regret. Eager to get back to playing with their cousins Peter and Zara Phillips in the gardens of Balmoral, Diana's sons were in "a desperate rush to say good-bye," William recalled. "If I'd known what was going to happen, I wouldn't have been so blasé about it. But that phone call sticks in my mind, quite heavily."

It became an even heavier burden for Harry, who, during the course of his parents' separation and divorce, had come to resent communicating with one parent over the phone while staying with the other. "The two of us bouncing between them," Harry said. "We never saw our mother enough, and we never saw our father enough." When Diana called that final time in August 1997, "William went to go and speak with her, and then 'Harry, Harry, Mummy's on the phone.' Right, my turn, off I go, you know, pick up the phone, and it was her speaking from Paris," Harry later said. "I can't really remember what I said—it is probably, you know, regretting for the rest of my life how short the phone call was. And if I'd known that that was the last time I was going to speak to my mother, things that I would have said to her. Looking back on it now," Harry continued, "it's incredibly hard. I have to deal with that for the rest of my life. If I had even the slightest inkling that her life was going to be taken that night . . ."

It fell to Charles to break the news of their mother's death to the boys. "One of the hardest things for a parent to have to do is to tell your children that your other parent has died," Harry reflected. "How you deal with that, I don't know, but, you know, he was there for us." Father and sons clung to one another figuratively and literally as, for hundreds of millions of people around the world, shock and disbelief turned to overwhelming sadness. Floral tributes had turned London, the emotional epicenter of this unprecedented outpouring of sorrow, into a sea of riotous color; waist-high waves of flowers lapped at the gates of all the royal palaces and public buildings, and the cards that accompanied them bid tearful farewells to the woman who was denied a crown but chose instead to reign as Britain's "Queen of Hearts."

On the eve of their mother's funeral, the brothers stopped outside Kensington Palace to look over the flowers and cards and personally thank some of the people who had come to pay their respects. It was a solemn moment, and while for the most part a respectful silence prevailed, occasionally it was punctuated by an anguished wail of grief. Several people in the crowd burst into tears as the boys approached. When they reached out to greet well-wishers, William and Harry were surprised that many of the outstretched hands they shook were wet from tears they had just wiped from red and swollen eyes.

The princes were taken aback by the "very, very strange outpouring of love from so many people," Harry said. "How is it," he thought to himself at the time, "that so many people that never met this woman— my mother . . . can be crying and showing more emotion than I actually am feeling?" William admitted to being "very touched by it, but none of it sank in. . . . All I cared about was, I'd lost my mother, and I didn't want to be where I was. . . . But we have to put on a game face, and you have to be quite strong about it because otherwise you're a walking mess." Harry called it an "out-of-body experience. I wasn't there. I was still in shock."

That first Saturday in September 1997—the day of Diana's funeral—more than a million clogged the streets of central London to honor "the People's Princess." Another two and a half billion around the world—at that time by far the largest audience in history—watched the events in London unfold live on television.

The former wife of the Prince of Wales did not technically rate a full-fledged state funeral, but there was no denying that the Queen's tepid reaction to Diana's death had placed the institution of the monarchy in jeopardy. Britain's leading newspapers demanded that the Union Jack over Buckingham Palace be lowered to half-mast and that the Queen, who seemed reluctant to cut short her annual summer vacation at Balmoral, pack up and return to London. Harry and his brother, shielded from the angry headlines and still in what William called "a kind of daze," had no idea they would soon be enlisted as pawns in the Palace's effort to placate the British people.

Right up until the morning of the funeral, there was heated debate among Palace officials and Prime Minister Tony Blair's government about whether William and Harry should even be asked to walk behind the horse-drawn wagon carrying Diana's casket. "There was doubt as to whether the boys would feel able to do it, up to do it, whether they should do it," said Blair's spokesman Alastair Campbell. Another of Blair's aides made what she called "an intervention" on Harry's behalf. "How can he, at twelve, walk behind his mother's coffin?"

At the time Diana's brother, Earl Spencer, felt it was "terribly cruel" to ask either boy, but especially "tiny Harry," to undertake such an emotionally wrenching task. "I was just so worried—what a trauma for a little chap to walk behind his mum's body," Spencer said. "It's just awful. And, actually, I tried to stop that happening, to be honest. . . . I genuinely felt that Diana would not have wanted them to have done it."

Earl Spencer withdrew his objections when he was told that his nephews had both wanted to make the gesture—"a lie, of course; I was tricked into going along." What Diana's brother didn't realize was that the Duke of Edinburgh had taken matters into his own hands. Convinced that the monarchy would benefit from such an obviously moving show of solidarity, Prince Philip stepped up to his grandsons and said, "If I do it, will you do it?" Neither William nor Harry was in the habit of contradicting their elders, and the boys lined up obediently alongside their father, grandfather, and uncle.

Palace officials told William and Harry to look straight ahead as they made the thirty-minute walk to Westminster Abbey. As the cortege passed in front of St. James's Palace, William hitched up his trousers, and the five men walked slowly toward the back of the coffin. In the slanting late-summer sunlight, even Harry, though dwarfed by his towering relatives, cast a looming shadow.

"It was the most horrifying half an hour of my life. It was just ghastly," Spencer recalled. "But, of course, it was a million times worse for them . . . two boys who were massively grieving their mother." Diana's brother also used the word "bizarre" to describe the orders they had received to stare straight ahead, which only magnified "the feeling, the sort of crashing tidal wave of grief coming at you as you went down this tunnel of deep emotion, all hammering in on you. It was really harrowing, actually, and I still have nightmares about it now."

For most spectators, it was simply too painful to look directly at the boys. But even then, many who averted their eyes from William and Harry were moved to tears by the card placed atop Diana's coffin. Clearly visible was the word "Mummy" printed in Harry's twelve-year-old hand. Occasionally, someone would break down. William coped by tilting his head down and allowing his blond hair to cover his eyes—"hiding behind my fringe," he said. "It was kind of a safety blanket, if you like." Acknowledging that this approach "sounds ridiculous now," the Heir explained that if he looked at the ground and his hair came down over his eyes, "nobody could see me." This trick, he said, made it possible for him to simply "get through the day."

William would say later that this "very long, lonely walk" was "the hardest thing" he had ever done or ever would do. As he remembered how he was thinking at the time, William struggled to strike a balance "between me being Prince William and having to do my bit versus the private William who just wanted to go into a room and cry, who'd lost his mother." It was that "balance between duty and family, and that's what we had to do." Harry recalled that it "felt like my mother was almost walking along beside us, to get us through it."

Harry, whose red hair was cut short, fixed his eyes on the pavement in front of him, his fists clenched as he vowed to himself not to break down, not to cry. As the gun wagon bearing Diana's flag-draped casket passed by Buckingham Palace, both brothers looked up to see their grandmother bow her head—a carefully orchestrated gesture of obeisance that, coming after her hastily thrown-together televised tribute to Diana, was a transparent attempt to further assuage an angry public.

The grim procession would be relived in the minds of both brothers "a thousand times," William said, and twenty years later, Harry confessed that he and his brother were still dealing with the psychic aftermath of that long walk behind Diana's coffin. "I don't think any child should be asked to do that under any circumstances," he said. "I don't think it would happen today."

When they arrived at the abbey, a spray of thirty-six white lilies was placed on the casket—one for each year of Diana's short life. William continued to look at his feet, reaching up only once to wipe away a tear; Harry, conversely, now looked up and stared straight ahead, fixing his gaze on the flowers that now cradled his handwritten card—lilies had been his mother's favorite.

Inside sat more than two thousand mourners, including famous faces from the worlds of music, film, art, fashion, and politics as well as cancer survivors, abused spouses, and land mine victims. All watched, pain etched on their faces, as Diana's casket was carried to the center of the nave. As they took their seats, William and Harry glanced in the direction of their ninety-seven-year-old great-grandmother, the Queen Mother, who smiled at them comfortingly. She would later tell one of her ladies-in-waiting that seeing the boys at their mother's funeral was "a heartbreak, and I have had more than my share."

Perhaps no one in the abbey knew Diana better than William, who from the age of eight had been both her comforter and counselor—even to the point of the princess sharing with him the most intimate details of her love life. "There were some things that were just not appropriate for a boy his age," a friend recalled, "or for a mother to be discussing with her son at all." It had also fallen on William to routinely comfort her when she came home in tears after visits to child cancer wards, battered women's shelters, and AIDS clinics. Her elder son "was the one person she most counted on," Diana's close friend Rosa Monckton observed. "She expected a great deal from Prince William, and he did not hesitate to give it."

Even in death, Diana relied on William to make sure her funeral was conducted in accordance with her wishes. He selected the first hymn—the timber-rattling "I Vow to Thee My Country"—because he knew it had been a favorite of Diana's since she was a young girl. He also overrode the objections of Palace officials who believed it inappropriate for a pop star to perform at a royal funeral. Elton John managed to hold back his tears only by playing "Candle in the Wind 1997" with his eyes closed. The song, a 1973 tribute to Marilyn Monroe reworked by lyricist Bernie Taupin as an homage to Diana, became the biggest-selling pop single of all time. The muffled sobs of mourners could be heard throughout the service, but William and Harry held it together until John sang the last line of the chorus: "Your candle's burned out long before your legend ever will." With that, the brothers burst into tears.

"It is impossible to describe the level of tension, the depth of feeling and loss," said Mary Robertson, a New Jersey businesswoman living in London who in 1980 hired a nineteen-year-old Diana Spencer to take care of her infant son, Patrick, for $5 an hour. Over the years, Robertson and Diana had remained friends. "Sitting there, I kept thinking about the wonderful young girl she was. . . . I could never have guessed back then that she would become this iconic figure. But she never changed, not really."

Unbelievably, the crescendo of emotion was yet to come. In his soaring eulogy, Earl Spencer accused the press of hounding his sister to her grave, and then, within feet of the monarch, leveled a broadside at the royal family. In a reference to the fact that the Queen took away the princess's Royal Highness status after her divorce from Charles, Spencer praised Diana as someone who "needed no royal title to continue to generate her particular brand of magic." He then promised Diana that the Spencers would not permit her sons "to suffer the anguish that used regularly to drive you to tearful despair." Then he promised that the boys' "blood family"—although the Windsors were obviously no less "blood" than the Spencers—would "continue the imaginative way in which you were steering these two exceptional young men so that their souls are not immersed by duty and tradition but can sing openly, as you planned."

Despite the intentionally provocative tone of his speech, Spencer did acknowledge "the heritage into which they have both been born. We will always respect and encourage them in their royal role. But," he continued, "we recognize the need for them to experience as many different aspects of life as possible to arm them spiritually and emotionally for the years ahead."

Spencer then turned to lock eyes with his nephews. "William and Harry, we all care desperately for you today," he said. "We are all chewed up at the sadness of the loss of a woman who was not even our mother. How great your suffering is, we cannot even imagine."

When Spencer ended with his famous line giving thanks for "the unique, the complex, the extraordinary and irreplaceable Diana, whose beauty—both internal and external—will never be extinguished from our minds," the hundreds of thousands of people watching the service on giant screens outside erupted in thunderous applause. William and Harry joined in like everyone else inside the abbey, with the exception of the other royals who were seething over Spencer's blunt remarks.

Three hours later, the brothers stood next to each other at Althorp, the sprawling Spencer family seat, heads bowed in silence, weeping openly as their mother's coffin was lowered into the ground. In what would be another clear and lasting memory, the dark clouds that had been gathering all afternoon parted just enough to allow a ray of sunlight to fall on Diana's grave.

William and Harry had nothing to do with the decision to bury the most celebrated woman of the twentieth century on a secluded 75-foot-by-180-foot island in the middle of a small ornamental lake known as the Round Oval. Frances Shand Kydd, fearing that gawping tourists would turn her daughter's gravesite into another Graceland, overruled plans to bury her daughter with nineteen other generations of Spencers interred in the family plot at the nearby Church of St. Mary. Instead, Shand Kydd wanted Diana to at last be granted the sanctuary she was denied in life.

It was no small irony that the estate's current owner, her brother Earl Spencer, had once offered Diana the four-bedroom Garden House at Althorp in hopes she might be better protected from the ravenous tabloid press after her split from Charles. "At long last," she said when it appeared Spencer was willing to let her live on the estate, "I can make a cozy nest of my own." But, having other needs for the cottage and fearing the disruption it would inevitably cause, Diana's brother ultimately reneged. Crestfallen, Diana wrote a letter to her brother and begged him to reconsider. While Spencer asked her to consider other family-owned properties, the princess did not feel they could provide her what Althorp could. Adding to the irony, Earl Spencer himself would soon turn this corner of the estate into the sort of shrine Shand Kydd had disdained so vocally. Althorp, which had been open to the public for years to defray costs, was soon inviting tourists to gaze at Diana's lonely island grave from across the banks of the Round Oval, and to peruse exhibits that included intimate family photographs and several of the princess's gowns—all for the modest price of admission.

Diana's sons voiced no objection to burying their mother here; she had often spoken of chasing butterflies and feeding the ducks with her younger brother on the sylvan grounds of Althorp—a handful of fond memories that stood in stark contrast to the rest of her childhood. Diana was only six when her mother walked out on the family, leaving her youngest daughter and little brother Charles in the care of a succession of nannies. One took obvious pleasure in beating Diana with a wooden spoon. Another made a practice of banging Diana's and Charles's heads together when they stepped out of line. In short, said her friend Peter Janson, Diana's childhood was "hell. Her parents hated, despised each other. She grew up under that."

Diana would convince herself that her unhappy childhood in the end made her "a better person. I can appreciate other people's pain because I've experienced it. But," she continued, "it also made me a stronger person. I had to be strong to survive my childhood."

Sadly, at least in terms of their own parents' highly combustible marriage, William and Harry wound up suffering much the same fate. Just as Diana cupped her hands over her brother's ears so he wouldn't hear their parents screaming at each other, the princes were caught in the crossfire between Mummy and Papa. William not only tried to shield his brother from the mayhem, but also hurried to his mother's side whenever Charles reduced to her tears. When Diana retreated to the bathroom, as she so often did, William would slide tissues beneath the locked door. Even when she rushed to comfort her children—for example, when the lurid details of her affair with the boys' riding instructor, James Hewitt, became public in October 1994—it was twelve-year-old William who presented her with a box of chocolates. "Mummy, I think you've been hurt," he said. "These will make you smile again."

William was not born with this profound sense of empathy. His arrival on June 21, 1982, was heralded with booming cannons, royal proclamations, and fireworks—and the little prince seemed determined from the outset to maintain that high level of excitement. William was scarcely nine months old when he embarked with his parents on their first royal tour as a family, to Australia and New Zealand. The Queen did not object to having William tag along; she wasn't given the opportunity. "We never even asked her," Diana said, conceding what was a clear breach of royal protocol. "We just did it."

As expected, the press Down Under could not get enough of the cherub-cheeked toddler who had yet to take his first steps. But behind the scenes, his eager parents had their hands full trying to control "Willy Wombat," as he soon came to be known. During the last two weeks of their tour the Waleses visited New Zealand, where they holed up at Government House in Wellington, official residence of the Queen's principal representative, the governor-general. Diana remembered her son "crawling about, knocking everything off the tables and causing unbelievable destruction."

No sooner did they return home than Charles and Diana were once again dispatched abroad—this time on a two-week tour of Canada without William. At just fifteen months, he somehow managed to find and push a panic button at Balmoral that resulted in police cars racing to the castle and security guards scrambling to seal off the grounds. Soon he was careening around Kensington Palace, knocking over vases, sticking his tongue out at footmen, and wailing loudly when he didn't get his way.

Kevin Shanley, one of Diana's hairdressers, remembered having to drop everything and rescue the toddler from a Kensington Palace windowsill. "You couldn't keep your eyes off Wills for a second," he said. Indeed, on several occasions, William tried to flush his booties down the toilet—as well as his father's John Lobb bespoke black Oxford shoes. He also developed a knack for, as Charles put it, "running around smashing things." By the time he turned two, and despite being constantly under the watchful eyes of his two nannies, Barbara Barnes and Olga Powell, William chewed and tore his way through several of the centuries-old leatherbound volumes in Charles's private library. William's abashed mother began calling him "my mini-tornado."

Kensington Palace staff members were the first to concede that, even compared to his rowdy cousins, William's wild streak was extraordinary—and concerning. They chalked it up to not only the perpetual swirl of activity that seemed to surround the Prince and Princess of Wales, but also the palpable tension between them. It did not help that Diana was battling both anorexia and bulimia—twin disorders triggered shortly before her wedding day when Charles pinched her waist and sniggered, "A bit chubby here, aren't we?"

Ironically, tensions had in fact eased during the few months prior to the birth of William's only sibling. Indeed, Diana acknowledged that, given all she was going through in her marriage, it was a wonder that she became pregnant at all. "Harry appeared," she later said mysteriously, "as if by a miracle." By the time they presented William with an electric-powered mini version of a Jaguar XJS for his second birthday, Diana had begun to convince herself that perhaps Charles did in fact love her. "We were blissfully happy," Diana later said of that brief time in the royal marriage. "Charles was overjoyed about the new baby, very tender and caring—and genuinely concerned about me in a way that he hadn't been for a long time. I didn't want it to end."

The reason for their newfound harmony was simple: Charles had wanted a girl to round out the family and was so resolute in his belief that he was about to become the father of a princess that he simply refused to look at any sonograms. Diana did look, however. "I knew it was a boy," she later said, "and I didn't tell him."

Privately, Diana was irked by any talk of gender preference. Following the births of Diana's sisters Jane and Sarah—and the arrival of a son who lived only ten hours—the senior Earl Spencer and his wife were so convinced their fourth child would be a boy that they didn't even trouble themselves to pick out a name for a girl. It was a full week before the Spencers decided to name their third daughter Diana Frances. As a result, Diana grew up feeling "unloved and unwanted"—words she often used to describe the feelings of self-doubt that would gnaw at her throughout her life.

Still, Diana told friends that she didn't "want to spoil" the newfound sense of mutual love and respect that had suddenly and unexpectedly taken hold of the Waleses. It had happened once before; there had been a similar thaw in their relationship in the few months before William's arrival. "Fantastic, beautiful," Charles had said to Diana just moments after William's birth. "You are a darling." But it was not long before Charles closed himself off emotionally once again. "Maybe this time," she remembered telling herself, "we'll be able to keep the magic going." And not just for their sake. Diana actively worried along with his nannies that William's hyperkinetic, destructive streak was due at least in part to all the anger that surrounded him on a daily basis.

"We were very, very close to each other the six weeks before Harry was born," Diana would recall. "The closest we've ever, ever been and ever will be." The Heir stayed home at Kensington Palace when, on the morning of September 15, 1984, Charles and Diana returned to the same suite in the Lindo Wing of St. Mary's Hospital, where she had given birth to William. "I was full of hope," she remembered, "but, of course, that didn't last."

Late that afternoon, Diana gave birth to a six-pound, fourteen-ounce boy. Charles's reaction was immediate—and, for Diana, devastating. "Oh, God," he blurted out disdainfully, much to the astonishment of the doctors and nurses in the room, "it's a boy. And he even has red hair."

In that moment, said Diana, "it just went bang, our marriage. The whole thing went down the drain. Something inside me closed off." It didn't help matters when the princess learned, in the days just prior to Harry's birth, that Charles had resumed his affair with the very married Camilla Parker Bowles. "By then," she said, "I knew Charles had gone back to his lady."

Charles would double down on his criticism of Harry at the baby's christening, focusing on the boy's gender and—perhaps most tellingly— on the color of his hair. He complained not once but several times that Harry was not only "another boy" but also that he had "rusty" hair. The prince's dismissive remarks did not sit well with Diana's mother, Frances Shand Kydd, who scolded her son-in-law for not simply being grateful that the child was healthy. Besides, she reminded him that many members of the Spencer clan, including all three of Diana's living siblings, had rusty hair.

Charles's reaction may have had less to do with Harry's gender and appearance than with his own suspicions about the baby's paternity. Although Diana's affair with Captain James Hewitt would not be revealed until the 1994 publication of the international bestseller *Princess in Love* by British author Anna Pasternak—and Diana would insist she did not even meet Hewitt until 1986, two years after Harry's birth—by 1982, Charles was already well aware of rumors that his wife was infatuated with the handsome, young, redheaded cavalry officer.

In fact, Hewitt stated in his memoirs that he actually first spotted Lady Diana Spencer six weeks prior to her marriage to Prince Charles, at a polo match in Tidworth, Wiltshire, in June 1981. The captain was playing for the army team, Charles for the navy. "She was fun, charming, and flirtatious," Hewitt recalled of that first meeting. "Tall, willowy, strikingly beautiful—and utterly adorable." According to Hewitt, several days later, she invited him to dinner at the London home of mutual friends. It was there that, while sitting next to each other on the sofa, she stole a kiss from Hewitt when their hosts weren't looking. She also told him that, even though she was going ahead with her marriage to the Prince of Wales, she knew Charles didn't love her.

The relationship continued to simmer until the fall of 1982, when, not long after William was born, Hewitt was smuggled into Kensington Palace in the trunk of a car, and the couple consummated their affair. There were reputable eyewitnesses to the simple fact that, contrary to Palace spin aimed at averting scandal and ensuring Harry's place in the line of royal succession, Diana and Hewitt had definitely known each other well in advance of Harry's birth. Journalist Nicholas Davies spotted the couple "out riding together one morning in Windsor Great Park in the early 1980s, and they were kissing. It was plain that they were lovers." Ronald Lewis, who for years served as one of Prince Charles's closest and most trusted aides—his "Traveling Yeoman and Baggage Master"—conceded that Hewitt was frequently seen in the company of the princess at Kensington Palace in 1983 and 1984.

The couple often rendezvoused at a small cottage in Devon owned by Hewitt's mother. Diana "was happiest there," remembered the officer, who said she often fantasized about settling down as his "army wife. She thought she'd make a very good army wife. It wasn't possible to do that. I think it was a dream."

Things turned more serious in early 1984, when Diana told Hewitt she was pregnant. "She was part anxious and part matter-of-fact," Hewitt recalled of that moment. She told him she was happy about the pregnancy, and that it was too early to determine the baby's sex, but she hoped she was having a girl. Throughout the remainder of her pregnancy, they refrained from having intercourse ("It seemed more respectful," he said), and when Diana called him from the hospital just hours after giving birth, Hewitt told her—in stark contrast to Charles's reaction—that Harry's arrival was "wonderful, happy news."

Perhaps, but Hewitt also suspected he knew why Charles was so upset about the newborn's rusty hair. He also knew of the possible consequences if word of his clandestine romance with the princess was ever leaked to the press. Clearly, the lovers' attempts at subterfuge had not proved entirely successful; Hewitt had already received anonymous phone calls warning that it would be "healthier" for him if he stopped seeing the Princess of Wales. But neither he nor Diana was willing to walk away, and, within weeks, they resumed their affair with a renewed passion.

After several tension-filled months, Hewitt sought advice from one of Britain's most flamboyant and successful publicists on how to keep a lid on the affair. Max Clifford concocted what he saw as a foolproof scheme: simply start giving Diana riding lessons. The ploy worked, and, in the guise of being riding instructor to the Princess of Wales and her children, Hewitt became a fixture in the lives of both William and Harry. ("People came to me and asked me to keep quiet about it," said Clifford, who, like Hewitt, felt pressure from the Palace. "But the affair went on a lot longer than people realize.")

Not that everybody was fooled. No sooner did he sign on as Diana's bodyguard than Ken Wharfe was informed by his predecessor, Inspector Graham "Smudger" Smith, that Captain Hewitt of the Household Cavalry was the boss's lover. Moreover, Diana made it clear to Wharfe and others that her marriage to the Prince of Wales was a sham. "After Harry was born, my marriage to Charles just died," she told Wharfe in conspiratorial tones. "I tried, I honestly tried, but he just did not want me. We haven't slept in the same bed for two years." She also shared with the newly arrived protection officer details of her numerous suicide attempts. "It was a cry for help," she said, "but nobody ever listened."

Diana went out of her way to describe the first time she met the dashing young officer—supposedly at a party thrown by her lady-in-waiting Hazel West in early 1986. In typical fashion, the misleading cover story she shared with Wharfe and others never varied in the slightest detail from telling to telling—the princess was clearly less concerned about word of the affair getting out than having Harry's paternity called into question.

The ruse may have worked with some, but not with the one person who mattered most. Early on in the relationship, Her Majesty was made aware of Diana's affair with Hewitt—a situation that seemed to explain Charles's seeming obsession with Harry's hair color, his mother-in-law's angry response to Charles's comments at Harry's christening, and the total breakdown of the marriage coinciding with Harry's birth.

The brothers were too young to realize it, of course, but from the very beginning the contours of their relationship would be shaped not simply by their difference in rank within the monarchy, but also by the simmering tensions in their parents' turbulent marriage and even by the women in their lives. While never addressed publicly by the Crown, which covertly perpetuated the myth that James Hewitt and the Princess of Wales met after Harry was born, the question of the prince's paternity remained unresolved—a ticking time bomb with the potential, said one courtier, "to blow the monarchy to kingdom come."

EVEN EARLY IN THEIR lives, William and Harry would be buffeted by scandal, intrigue, anger, and betrayal. Their mother knew intuitively that, if her boys were ever to emerge from the royal maelstrom with their emotions intact, theirs would have to be a brotherly bond like no other. Harry was just hours old when Charles brought William from Kensington Palace to the hospital to meet the newest Windsor. As father and son came down the corridor, Diana scrambled out of bed, swept up the baby, and stood in the doorway. Drawing on her own experience as a part-time nanny, the princess believed it was important that, as she told her nurses at the time, "the first time William sees his brother, I'm holding him in my arms."

William was fascinated with little Harry—perhaps a bit too fascinated. Left unattended in the Kensington Palace nursery for just a few moments, William decided his brother needed some fresh air and was dangling the infant from a third-story window when a staffer spotted the boys and pulled them both back to safety. "William loves Harry," Diana told her mother. "We just have to make sure he doesn't love him to death."

Granny took William's exhausting exuberance in stride. When the prince took a tumble at Buckingham Palace and began crying for "Gary, Gary," a member of the household staff asked if anyone knew who Gary was. "I'm Gary," Her Majesty explained. "He hasn't learned to say Granny yet."

Diana was, in fact, focusing all her attention on "mah boys," as she liked to call them in an ersatz southern drawl. Charles had made it clear from the moment he set eyes on Harry that whatever feelings for each other he and Diana might have salvaged were irretrievably lost. For his part, Charles would eventually become a loving and attentive father to both his sons. But for now, he made no attempt to mask his anger toward

Diana—nor his resentment toward the newest member of the family. No sooner did he drive Diana and his sons from the hospital to Kensington Palace than he jumped back behind the wheel of his cobalt-blue Jaguar sedan and sped off to a polo match at Windsor.

From the standpoint of those around her, Diana reveled in the duties and responsibilities of motherhood. "I do love having children around me," she said at the time. "It gives life to a house." Yet, if anything, Harry's arrival seemed to have triggered even more misbehavior on the part of his big brother. At Harry's Windsor Castle christening, William ricocheted around the room, barking like a dog as he ran circles around the archbishop of Canterbury. Later, he managed to wreak even more havoc during a family get-together at Birkhall, the Queen Mother's residence on the grounds of Balmoral. Charles and Diana both decided something had to be done after William committed the one unforgivable sin: he was rude to the servants, at one point repeatedly kicking at a hapless footman.

Charles suggested hiring a stern governess to take the boy in hand, but Diana came up with another, distinctly more modern solution. Her husband had often complained that his isolation as a child made him anxious and socially awkward—a gnawing awareness of always being the outsider that followed him into adulthood. The former kindergarten teacher was convinced that William was already feeling the effects of leading what she saw as a suffocating, isolated life behind palace walls. On the rare occasions he was around children of his own age, William had no idea how to join in the fun—he merely stood on the sidelines and watched the others.

Convinced that her son needed to "mix it up" with other children, Diana enrolled him in Mrs. Mynors' Nursery School, a prekindergarten situated only a few minutes from Kensington Palace in Notting Hill. In no time at all, William was cutting in line, shoving other students, and, in his capacity as the future king, threatening to have students, staff, and teachers alike arrested or worse. Fleet Street was soon churning out front-page stories about the naughty-boy antics of "the Basher," as William quickly came to be known. On British TV's *Spitting Image*, a wildly satirical series that poked fun at the famous and powerful—most notably, the royal family—using hysterically malformed puppet likenesses, William was portrayed in combat fatigues, menacing his hapless brother with a machete.

Diana, now under the care of a squadron of psychiatrists and downing large amounts of the powerful tranquilizer Valium, was too preoccupied with trying to pry her husband away from his mistress to notice what a handful William had become. "He's just spirited," she told her longtime friend and confidante Lady Elsa Bowker. "They [the royal family] can't bear that, even in a child."

As long as the Queen seemed unfazed by her grandson's antics, William continued to run roughshod over schoolmates, teachers, and members of the royal household. That ended during his uncle Andrew's wedding to Sarah Ferguson in July 1986, where William was a standout amidst the otherwise scrupulously well-behaved flower girls and page boys included in the wedding party. Among other things, he stuck out his tongue at spectators repeatedly, nearly tripped over the bridal gown's seventeen-foot-long train, and used his rolled-up wedding program as a trumpet during the most solemn moments of the ceremony.

The Queen suggested that a new nanny be hired—one with a firmer hand than the boys' devoted and sweetly indulgent Nanny Barnes. Up until this point, "Baba," as the little princes called her, filled the giant void left by Charles and Diana as they fulfilled their royal responsibilities away from Kensington Palace. In fact, the only time the boys could count on seeing Papa and Mummy was at six thirty, when they sat on the edge of their beds waiting eagerly for their parents to share a few words with them and then tuck them in.

Diana had brushed off any criticism of William's behavior, but what did rankle her was the notion that she had effectively been replaced in her own children's lives by Nanny Barnes. On the day that five-year-old William started at Wetherby, a prekindergarten located at nearby Nottingham Gate, the brothers' beloved Baba was dismissed—news that prompted a flood of tears from both of them. Within weeks, Barnes was replaced by Ruth Wallace, former nanny to the children of William's godfather, King Constantine II of Greece. Fair but firm "Nanny Roof" was given the one power that had been denied her predecessor: when warranted, she was permitted to spank the boys.

Still, William persisted. "No one was spared," confessed a teacher who watched him shove a little girl in class and then throw a tantrum when he was reprimanded. "He threatened to have his knights chop all our heads off." While the public was still unaware of the friction in the royal marriage, by this time Charles had essentially moved out of Kensington Palace and into Highgrove House, his country home two hours due west and a proverbial stone's throw from the woman the Prince of Wales's staff referred to as "Mrs. PB"—his mistress, Camilla Parker Bowles.

During the week, all was relatively tranquil as the boys stayed with Mummy and Nanny Roof at Kensington Palace. But during their weekend visits to Highgrove, nothing could shield them from the sound of voices raised in anger and muffled sobs coming from down the hall. "William was obviously hurting," said Highgrove housekeeper Wendy Berry. "If your parents are going at it tooth and nail, you're going to act out in some way."

Harry, who mimicked his brother's every gesture and move, was soon "crashing about and carrying on," said Olga Powell, who had been hired to share nanny duties with Barnes and then with Ruth Wallace. But Powell, who would remain a fixture in the boys' lives for fifteen years, joined the rest of the staff in doting on the baby of the family—favoritism that would ultimately lead to a simmering rivalry between the princes. "One cause of William's unease as a boy growing up was that the attention from a lot of the staff was centered on Harry, and not on him," recounted Diana's longtime bodyguard Ken Wharfe. By way of retaliation, William used to steal or break something and then attempt to pin it on his brother. "William would hide his cereal bowl, and when I asked where it went, he'd point to poor Harry," remembered Powell, who often told William, "I love you—but I don't like you."

Expecting the worst from the Basher's little brother, the staff at Mrs. Mynors' Nursery School braced themselves for Harry's arrival in the fall of 1987. Although he often tried to live up to William's terrible example on his home turf, Harry was so quiet and withdrawn around other children that one teacher worried that he was "suffocating in his brother's shadow. He may have been the baby of the family at home, just smothered with love, but strangers were obviously much more interested in Prince William." Indeed, that was painfully clear when Harry arrived for his first day of school and had to be coaxed out of the car. Once the three-year-old was at the front door, Mrs. Mynors went out of her way to greet William instead.

From toddlerhood on, it was clear to Charles that "William is a strong personality. Harry is the one with the gentle nature." While William was rarely absent from school—even if he spent much of the school day sulking or complaining—Harry often invented reasons to stay home. "He used to come down with coughs and colds," remembered Simone Simmons, a spiritual healer who visited Diana at Kensington Palace once a week. "But I think he just wanted to stay home with Mummy. He loved having her to himself and not having to compete with William."

At age four, Harry was already painfully aware of where he stood in the royal pecking order. One Friday night on their weekly ride from London to Highgrove, Diana was sitting in the front passenger seat and, as was usually the case, the boys were roughhousing in the backseat. When Olga Powell told them to settle down, William refused. "Don't be rude," Powell replied, but Harry told her not to bother. "It doesn't matter anyway," he explained, "because William is going to be king. I'm not going to be king so I will be able to do whatever I like!"

"All the adults in the car looked at each other and thought, where the hell did that come from?" recalled Wharfe, who was driving the car that evening. "There was a sense that from a very young age Harry thought he could do whatever he wanted, while his brother had to shoulder all the responsibility." Not long after, William said he wanted to be a policeman so he could "look after Mummy." Harry shot back: "Oh, no you can't. You've got to be king!" Wharfe called the Spare's grasp of the situation "extraordinary. Even at that age, Harry knew."

Harry quickly became a downstairs favorite, each day venturing alone into the kitchen or onto the palace grounds to chat with the chefs, gardeners, chauffeurs, footmen, and maids, all of whom he called by their first names. "He knew everyone—the flower man, the butcher," Wharfe said. "And everyone adored him; he was a very funny little boy."

While Harry was coming out of his shell, William was gradually awakening to the fact that other people had feelings, too—an important first step. "Now, William, imagine how you would feel if someone said that to you?" Diana asked her son after he'd reduced a little girl at school to tears. "You would want to cry, wouldn't you?" That, coupled with Ruth Wallace's instructions on the proper way to behave toward adults—including members of the household staff—soon had William proudly saying please and thank you, shaking hands, opening doors for the ladies, and making polite conversation. "I think a switch went off inside his head," Wallace said. "A lot of it had to do with what his mother said to him, I think. But all of a sudden, William was quite earnest about how he treated other people. He turned into an exceptional little gentleman." Not surprisingly, William's teachers at Wetherby were delighted. "Night and day," said one. "The bullying stopped, he started taking a real interest in the other children, and, before long, he really was our most well-liked student. As you can imagine, everyone was thrilled."

Not everyone. Newfound manners aside, William had not shed his bossy streak—especially when it came to Harry. The Heir barked orders at the Spare incessantly: "Now, Harry, stop sticking your tongue out at the photographers! It's very naughty!" But he also took charge whenever he was around his Windsor and Spencer cousins. "William tells them where to stand and what to do," said Diana, "and, for some reason, they all listen to him. Now I call him Mr. Bossy Boots."

The princes still had their moments, however. At Highgrove and Balmoral, they ambushed visitors with water pistols (and even mistakenly squirted the Queen, once), gargled with Jell-O at the dinner table, and, when no one was looking, even gave their minders the slip. Both boys were required to carry cell phones with transponders at all times, and when Wharfe realized Harry had vanished from Kensington Palace, he frantically called the boy. "Where are you, Harry?" Wharfe asked, trying to remain calm. Harry told him he was standing outside Tower Records, four blocks away on Kensington High Street. "I've never run so fast in my life," Wharfe said. "It was classic Harry."

Just as Althorp lived on in Diana's memory as a place of childhood wonder, the brothers would remember Highgrove—and to a lesser extent, Balmoral—as a kind of paradise. Situated on 350 acres in the picturesque Cotswolds, the nineteenth-century three-story manor house with a façade of gray stone had been Charles's cherished country refuge since he shelled out $1.75 million for it in 1980. Here he could indulge his love of organic gardening, landscaping, farming, and animal husbandry—all passions he hoped to instill in his sons. Toward that end, Papa set aside two separate plots of land, purchased child-sized spades, hoes, and gardening gloves, and urged his sons to dig alongside him. In the end, neither took to gardening. But they did raise guinea pigs and rabbits, dutifully cleaning their cages and feeding them the lettuce and carrots Diana chopped up in the kitchen.

Much to their father's unalloyed delight, both boys would embrace the country pursuits that Charles felt were an essential part of every English gentleman's life. Although they would not be taught how to use a firearm until they were ten years of age, both William and Harry were only four when they were allowed to take their toy guns along on shoots at Sandringham. It would not be long before William and Harry took aim at much larger targets; each would claim the distinction of being "blooded," having shot their first stag, before they turned fourteen. Whether at Sandringham or Balmoral, the boys were always accompanied by Charles's beloved Jack Russell terrier Tigga—the name inspired by A. A. Milne's *Winnie the Pooh* character Tigger—and Tigga's puppy, Roo. (Eventually the boys persuaded Charles to change Roo's name to Pooh.)

Highgrove also boasted an elaborate treehouse, and a woodshed that had been converted into a ball pit that the princes hurled themselves into with relish. Usually wearing the child-sized military uniforms made especially for them by James Hewitt, William and Harry took to ambushing the Highgrove staff with their squirt guns, then daring their drenched victims to toss them headlong into the pit. Nearly everyone—including their royal protection officers and even the housekeeper—obliged happily.

Given the Windsors' obsession with equine pursuits—from the Queen's fascination with thoroughbred racing to Philip's and Charles's testosterone-fueled love of take-no-prisoners polo to Princess Anne's Olympic-caliber dressage—it came as no surprise when both the Heir and the Spare also excelled on horseback. William was still terrorizing the other children at Mrs. Mynors' Nursery School when he first began riding his pony Trigger bareback. At four, Harry was entered into a riding competition under the name "Harry Cox" and won first prize. The following year, he leapt onto his father's frisky gelding, Centennial, and took home another ribbon.

According to a former Balmoral groom, "William was just amazing on a horse, from the very beginning. But Harry was definitely the better of the two. William was very methodical, very deliberate, and he would practice and practice until he got it right. But Harry just threw himself into it. He was a faster learner, I think, and he was definitely willing to take more chances. We were all especially impressed by Harry."

Even the royal family's premier equestrian, the Princess Royal, noted Harry's riding prowess early on. Aunt Anne even predicted that he would follow her lead and compete in the Olympics. But the one person whose opinion counted most paid scant attention to the Spare's accomplishments, athletic or otherwise. Instead, the Queen made a point of heaping praise on the brother destined to one day sit on the throne. With obvious pride, Her Majesty told guests at a picnic lunch that William not only had a superb "seat"—equestrian lingo for riding posture—but also that he commanded such total control of Trigger that she was almost pitched off her horse into a ditch trying to keep up.

Yet another horse-obsessed member of the family, the Queen Mother, also doted on William. So much so that, whenever the two boys were invited for tea at their great-grandmother's residence, Clarence House, Elizabeth the Queen Mother sat chatting with William at one end of the drawing room while Harry sat in a chair thirty feet away. More than once, sandwiches would be served to the Queen Mother and William—but not to Harry, who would be "totally forgotten—as if he wasn't even in the room," said Olga Powell. "He'd try not to cry or make a fuss, but it hurt his feelings every time."

In truth, little effort was made to conceal the fact that William would always be the center of royal attention. Not long after his fifth birthday, William started joining the Queen at Buckingham Palace or Windsor Castle for a private tea—a weekly ritual that would, in essence, constitute a master class in kingship. Over the years, Her Majesty would use this time to monitor William's progress: to learn all she could about his studies, friends, and interests, but also to offer words of support and encouragement whenever necessary. She might even slip in a history lesson now and then, showing him a rare manuscript signed by King Henry VIII or allowing him to flip through one of her prized possessions: the red leather–bound royal stamp collection, considered to be the finest in the world.

But most of all, the Queen wanted to make sure the little boy who would one day hold the fate of the monarchy in his hands was all right. "Like any grandmother, she wanted to know he was happy," said the

Queen's cousin, Margaret Rhodes. "She was especially concerned about what effect the mayhem of his parents' marriage was having."

That concern did not seem to spill over to Harry. "Harry was never on the Queen's mind the way William was," said one of Charles's deputy private secretaries. "It was just understood that William was going to be king, and he was the one who mattered. Harry was always left on the sidelines." According to Diana's friend Lady Elsa Bowker, these slights chipped away at Harry's confidence and "deeply hurt his feelings. I felt so sorry for poor Harry, but Diana did too, and she tried very hard to make sure that he never felt unwanted or unloved, as she had been as a small child."

Still, Diana realized that Harry's position in the family had its advantages. "Royal firstborns may get all the glory," she said, "but second-borns enjoy more freedom. Only when Harry is a lot older will he realize how lucky he is not to have been the eldest." In the meantime, however, she was determined to treat her sons equally, at least to the extent that such a thing was possible. With the exception of William's private tête-à-têtes with the Queen—command performances that sometimes immediately preceded or followed Her Majesty's weekly audience with the current prime minister—Diana never spent time with one son at the exclusion of the other.

The Princess of Wales was also determined to give them the kind of education no one inside the royal family had ever received—to expose them to what everyday life was really like for the vast majority of Britons. She put on a dark wig and sunglasses to take them to McDonald's or Kentucky Fried Chicken (hands down the princess's favorite fast-food chain), made them stand in line at the movie theater like everyone else, and raced alongside them at a popular London go-kart track. Diana and her sons watched the finals of the British Open from the royal box at Wimbledon, but they also went to amusement parks, miniature golf courses, and bowling alleys.

Determined that they would love her favorite sport as much as she did, Diana often took William and Harry swimming—either at one of the gyms she belonged to in London or to the pool King George VI had built on the grounds of Buckingham Palace in 1939 as a surprise for his daughters, Elizabeth and Margaret. Harry took to the water "as if he had gills," Diana once observed, although even the Spare would come to concede that William, who went on to captain his water polo team at college, was always the superior swimmer. "Because he was born to be number two," Olga Powell observed, "Harry tried to be number one in other ways." Jessie Webb remembered that "the competition between them was always fierce. They loved each other and watched out for each other, but they also both hated to lose."

For a time, Diana enlisted a personal trainer to put her through her paces Rollerblading and power walking on the grounds of Kensington Palace. "William and Harry often joined in," recalled trainer Jenni Rivett. "Sometimes she'd get genuinely annoyed when they didn't take it seriously, but that didn't last for long." Often they mimicked their mother's arm-swinging power-walk technique—which "she tried desperately to ignore, but, of course, couldn't." In one instance, the princess tore after them on Rollerblades, stumbled and fell, then dissolved in laughter. "It was obvious to anyone who saw them together," said Rivett, "that the boys were her whole world."

It was the larger world, in fact, that Diana wanted her sons to know, and in a way that no other members of the royal family had. From an early age, she took them to visit AIDS patients, homeless shelters, and children battling cancer. "We all know the Queen and Prince Charles and the rest of them visited hospitals," Elsa Bowker said. "But it was all very stiff and formal. They were cold; there was no feeling."

But Diana's outings with the boys served another, less selfless purpose. The public simply never got to see Charles's interactions with William and Harry, or the undisputed depth of affection between father and sons. The game of Big Bad Wolf that sent the boys into hysterics as they tried frantically to escape their huffing and puffing dad, the fierce pillow fights that churned up massive clouds of feathers, the wrestling matches and tickle fights—even the days spent fishing in the Scottish countryside and the long walks at Sandringham with Tigger and Roo—all took place far from the prying lenses of the indefatigable paparazzi.

Conversely, Diana made certain there was no doubt in the public mind who was the more loving and attentive parent. Not only in Britain but around the globe, newspapers and magazines brimmed with pictures of the young princess and her children riding bikes, taking to the ski slopes in Austria, Jet Skiing, cavorting on the beach on the Caribbean island of Barbuda, screaming with laughter as they were soaked plummeting down an amusement park flume ride. "Diana was a genius at manipulating public opinion," said British journalist James Whitaker. "Even if they weren't doing anything particularly exciting, she made certain there were plenty of shots of her hugging and kissing the boys. The message was terribly clear: 'Charles is a terrible father, and I'm the only parent these boys really have.'"

Admittedly, Charles gave Diana plenty to work with. When three-year-old Harry needed surgery to correct a hernia, the princess canceled her engagements and slept on the floor of his hospital room so that she would be there when he woke up. Meanwhile, Charles, who was vacationing alone in Italy, checked in on Harry via telephone but saw no reason to cut short his holiday. Had they known that Charles's Italian idyll was being shared with Camilla, who was conveniently stashed away in a villa not far from the prince's, Britons would have been more than just mildly perturbed by his decision not to rush to his ailing son's hospital bedside.

But, of course, Diana knew, and in desperation she took her case straight to "the Top Lady," one of her pet nicknames (along with "the Boss") for the Queen. With William and Harry both deposited safely at Wetherby for the day, she drove herself the six minutes from Kensington Palace to Buckingham Palace and pleaded tearfully with the sovereign to intercede and save her marriage. Diana told her mother-in-law that she had overheard Charles having a torrid phone conversation with Camilla while he soaked in the tub, and that he exploded when she begged him to stop seeing the woman Diana now called "the Rottweiler."

"I refuse," he shouted back, "to be the only Prince of Wales who never had a mistress!"

"What do I do?" Diana sobbed to the Queen. "I'm coming to you. What do I do?"

Her Majesty, seldom confronted with such displays of emotion, was clearly shaken. "She cried nonstop," the Queen later told Diana's butler, Paul Burrell. "Nonstop!" The Queen was also sympathetic, but nevertheless insisted to her daughter-in-law that there was nothing she could do. Her son refused to budge on the issue of Camilla. "I don't know what you should do," Elizabeth told Diana with a shrug. "Charles is hopeless."

It was left to the princess to take matters into her own hands. After she tucked William and Harry into bed at Kensington Palace, Diana ("I was feeling frightfully brave and bold") surprised Charles by deciding to accompany him in February 1989 to a fortieth birthday party for Camilla's younger sister, Annabel. During the thirty-five-minute drive to Richmond, one of London's most affluent buroughs, Charles "needled, needled, needled" her, Diana recalled. "Why are you coming tonight?" he demanded. "What do you think you're doing?" Once they arrived, everyone else at the party could not conceal their shock. "Nobody expected me to turn up," said Diana, who made the conscious decision "not to kiss Camilla hello anymore. I was going to shake hands with her instead. This was my big step." When she stuck out her hand to Camilla, it was a defining moment. "Phew," Diana later recalled thinking at the time, "well, I've got over that."

After dinner, Diana went searching for her husband, who had disappeared downstairs with his mistress and another male guest. "Okay, boys," she told the men as they returned to the party, "I'm just going to have a quick word with Camilla—I'll be up in a minute." Charles was ashen faced. "They shot upstairs like chickens with no heads," Diana said, "and I could feel upstairs all hell breaking loose. 'What's she going to do?'"

What she did was confront Camilla, who at first denied that anything was going on—"I don't know what you're talking about!"—and then shrugged that her affair with Charles was common knowledge and "not a cloak-and-dagger situation." Camilla then went on the offensive by complaining that Diana kept Charles from seeing his own sons.

Diana wasn't buying that argument. She told her rival that Charles knew exactly where his sons were at all times, and was always free to spend time with them—if he really wanted to. "Camilla," Diana said flatly, "the children are either at Highgrove or in London." Looking back on that exchange two years later, the princess claimed "Charles's biggest fault" was that "he never sees the children. But I never take them away. The other day, for instance, William said, 'Papa, will you play with us?' Charles's response: 'Oh, I don't know if I have time.' Always happens. So, he can't gripe about that."

Camilla was far from apologetic. Once again she brought up William and Harry. "You've got everything you ever wanted," she told Diana. "You've got all the men in the world falling in love with you, and you've got two beautiful children. What more could you want?"

"I want my husband!" Diana shot back. "I'm sorry I'm in the way. It must be hell for both of you, but I do know what is going on. Don't treat me like an idiot."

Once the party broke up, a livid Charles headed for Highgrove while Diana returned to their children and "cried and cried and cried like I've never cried before" into her pillow. Three days later, she explained to Charles that she had done "nothing wrong. I just said I loved you. . . . I've got nothing to hide. I'm your wife and the mother of your children."

Diana knew what she was doing when she brought up William and Harry. "That always makes Charles slightly twitch, when I say 'mother of your children,'" the princess observed. "He hates being made aware of it."

The seemingly never-ending war between their parents—the hurled insults, screaming matches, and crying fits—left both sons with indelible psychological scars. "Those boys," said Jessie Webb, the straight-talking Cockney hired to replace the retiring Ruth Wallace in July 1990, "are going to need a lot of help." Like the nannies who went before her, Webb spent far more time with William and Harry than their busy, preoccupied parents did—hours during the day when they were not exposed to the epic, window-rattling donnybrooks that characterized the Waleses' catastrophic marriage. "Those times when they could be with the nanny and not Prince Charles and the Princess," said Wendy Berry, "I mean, at least they had that escape route that other children don't have."

For eight-year-old William, however, that escape route would soon be closed off. In September 1990 he was enrolled at Ludgrove, an elite boarding school located a half hour's drive from London in the Berkshire town of Wokingham. Diana, who felt abandoned when she was sent to boarding school at the same age, pleaded with her husband not to send their son away. "He's just a little boy, Charles," she said after watching him pack his small suitcase for school. Among the cherished items he included was his favorite stuffed animal: a rainbow-colored parrot. "He doesn't show it, but I'm sure he's terrified," Diana said. "It's just cruel to send a small child away from his mother and father."

On this issue, Charles refused to budge. He, too, had hated boarding school life. Bullied relentlessly, shunned by peers who resented the fact that he would someday be king, Charles nevertheless clung to the conviction that somehow such soul-crushing abuse was character building. Diana claimed later that she managed to "keep cool and stay steady" when she and Charles dropped William off at school that first day, but once she was back home she collapsed in tears. "I buried my head in my pillow and wept for hours," she told Elsa Bowker. "I will never, ever forgive Charles for that. Never."

To be sure, William had less reason to be homesick than most of the other boarders. He had grown close to his royal protection officers at Kensington Palace, and one, the memorably named Graham Craker, was now assigned to watch over him at Ludgrove; Craker even slept in a room next to William's. Headmaster Gerald Barber and his wife, Janet, also took it upon themselves to look after the future monarch, checking in on him personally, consulting staff and teachers about his progress and state of mind, and having him to their residence on campus at least once a week for tea.

Initially, none of it mattered. Desperately homesick, William was quiet and withdrawn during his first month at Ludgrove. When he was allowed to visit Highgrove for the first time, Diana was waiting at the front door to smother him with kisses. Charles, however, was nowhere to be found; rather than wait to spend time with his son, he decided to go fishing at Balmoral. Crushed, William ran to his room, slammed the door behind him, and wept.

No one was more thrilled to see William than Harry, who had been left alone to bear the emotional weight of his parents' disintegrating marriage. "William was very protective of Harry," Jessie Webb said. "When his parents were shrieking at each other, he would try to distract him with play or tell him that everything would be fine. It broke my heart, because you could see it was such a very heavy burden for both of them."

Even at this stage, the general public was unaware of the havoc being wrought inside Charles and Diana's marriage, not to mention the emotional toll it was taking on the little princes. It wasn't until May 1991 that British tabloids finally picked up on the curious coincidence that Charles and Mrs. Parker Bowles both happened to be on holiday in Florence sans their spouses. By contrast, Diana made a point of being photographed everywhere with her sons: skiing at Lech, the exclusive Austrian resort; doffing her shoes to run a footrace against other mothers during sports day at Harry's school; taking both boys to a Royal Air Force base and a safari park.

If she hadn't established herself already as the more caring parent of the two, Diana clinched the title on June 3, 1991. The princess was lunching with a friend in the upscale Knightsbridge area of London when her bodyguard informed her that William had been whisked by ambulance to Royal Berkshire Hospital with blood gushing from a severe head injury. Apparently, one of his Ludgrove classmates had been horsing around with a golf club and inadvertently clocked the prince just above his left eye, knocking him cold. Diana wasted no time racing to the hospital, where she and Charles, who had been spending time at Highgrove with Camilla, rushed to William's bedside.

Worried doctors immediately transferred the boy to Great Ormond Street Hospital in London, where specialists quickly determined that he would need emergency exploratory brain surgery to look for infection, bone fragments, and the possibility that he had suffered brain damage. Shaken, Diana paced the waiting room during the seventy-five-minute procedure and remained there until William regained consciousness several hours later.

The Prince of Wales was not so inclined. His parents never altered their schedules when he fell seriously ill as a child—not even when Charles underwent an emergency appendectomy at thirteen—so he went ahead with plans to attend a performance of Puccini's opera *Tosca* at Covent Garden. Informed that the operation had been a success and satisfied that William would make a complete recovery, Charles saw no reason to go to the hospital. Instead, he went straight from the opera to the luxuriously appointed royal train for a five-hour overnight trip to North Yorkshire, where he was scheduled to speak at a symposium on the environment. Charles returned to London the following day to briefly check in on his oldest son at the hospital, then rejoined Camilla at Highgrove.

Conversely, Diana left William's side only long enough to fetch Harry and bring him back for a quick visit; William's little brother had heard the distress in his nanny's voice when news of the accident was relayed to Kensington Palace, and the grave expressions on the faces of his schoolteachers were giving the younger prince cause for concern. "There is a deep, deep love between those boys," said Powell, who, like so many others, noticed that William was becoming "more serious and more thoughtful about things. They look out for each other and rely on each other, but, of course, Harry relies on William more."

Fleet Street's reaction to Charles's seeming indifference was immediate—and withering. "What Kind of Dad Are You?" asked the *Sun*'s front-page headline. The *Daily Express* struck the same tone, beginning its equally damning indictment of Charles with "What Sort of Father . . . ?"

For Diana, it was another victory in her ongoing campaign to portray Charles—and, by extension, the rest of the royal family—as aloof and unfeeling. But the victory was pyrrhic at best. Charles, fuming over now being widely depicted as a coldly indifferent dad, lashed out even more frequently at his wife, and vice versa. William and Harry, deeply devoted to both parents, had somehow managed to avoid taking sides even as domestic warfare raged around them. But now they could no longer ignore the toll it was taking on their mother. Even though it would take William seven weeks to bounce back fully from the blow to his skull and the subsequent emergency brain operation, he often seemed more concerned with his mother's well-being than with his own.

At one point, with Harry looking on, William confronted his father after Charles and Diana had lit into each other in the servants' quarters at Highgrove. "I hate you, Papa!" he shouted at the Prince of Wales while his mother sobbed. "I hate you so much! Why do you make Mummy cry all the time?" Neither William nor Harry waited for an answer, and it was just as well. "There wasn't really anything for him to say, now, was there?" observed Nanny Webb, who pointed out that "there was never really a civil word between the prince and the princess. If they were all together, they only talked to the boys. Even if they were standing right there, Charles and Diana would not speak directly to each other unless it was to argue. It was just such a terrible shame."

The royal marriage continued to unravel through 1991. Charles and Diana no longer made even the slightest attempt to be cordial in public, even as press photographers snapped away. "They never smile, laugh, or do anything together," royal protection officer Andrew Jacques said. "They seem to want as little contact as possible."

In February 1992 Diana and Charles said good-bye to their children and departed together on an official six-day tour of India. Veteran journalist James Whitaker, who accompanied them on the trip, said that "suddenly no one was pretending anymore. The signs of hostility between Charles and Diana were just right out in the open." When Charles stayed in Bangalore to address businessmen rather than accompany his wife to the Taj Mahal in Agra, it became glaringly obvious that the marriage was in trouble—and that he had once again committed a huge public relations gaffe. Photographs of Diana looking downcast as she sat alone on a bench in front of the world's most famous monument to love were splashed across the front pages of newspapers from Berlin to Beijing. "That was a defining moment," said Whitaker. "Prince Charles tried to shrug it off, but Diana was making a very strong statement that she was basically unhappy and quite alone. It was brilliant, really."

During the same trip—and, fittingly, just before Valentine's Day—Charles leaned in to kiss his wife as they watched a polo match in Jaipur. At the last minute, she turned away, leaving the prince to collide with her right ear—another painfully awkward image that spoke volumes. "The body language between Charles and Diana was so frosty," said the Queen's longtime press secretary Dickie Arbiter, "you could have driven an icebreaker between the two of them and not cracked the ice."

Back in England, the boys eagerly kept track of their parents' travels and pretended not to notice that the world was now abuzz with rumors about Mummy and Papa. At Ludgrove and Wetherby, teachers and staff were asked not to bring newspapers to school, to refrain from turning on radios or televisions and, of course, to avoid any discussion about Charles and Diana.

For the more outgoing, happy-go-lucky Harry, school and his friends there provided another lifeline—an avenue of escape from the bedlam that surrounded him at home. William was another matter. At Ludgrove, he excelled at his studies and at sports, was well liked by his peers, and already exhibited a kind of natural charm and charisma not unlike his mother's. But he was also extraordinarily sensitive, given to long, thought-filled silences and dark moods.

According to a longtime member of the household staff at Highgrove, "William worried about everyone: Harry, Prince Charles, even me if I got into the middle of one of their screaming fights. But the person he worried most about was his mother. Princess Diana knew this better than anyone, but, in a way, she needed him to worry about her. It was not a healthy situation."

Indeed, Diana often boasted that William was really "a wise old man in child's clothing," an "old soul," and "my deep thinker." By the time he was ten, she was consulting him on everything from her hair and wardrobe to what projects she should pursue and which charities to support. "She'd ask him what he thought of this person or that person," recalled a former Highgrove staff member, "or whether he thought someone on the staff was doing a good job." Another friend, the American journalist and celebrity speech coach Richard Greene, believed Diana "valued William's opinion over everyone else's. They were on the same wavelength spiritually, emotionally. She trusted him implicitly." Soon, following the breakup of his parents' marriage, William would find himself in the strange position of being called on to both comfort his mother and offer her dating advice. "William's role was more that of alternative husband than son," Greene continued. "It was a heavy burden for anyone, but especially someone so young." This role reversal did not sit well with many who watched both Diana and Charles use the boys as frontline soldiers in their divorce wars. "William was having to comfort his mother, when she should have been looking after him," veteran BBC royal correspondent Jennie Bond said. "He was just a little boy."

In many ways, Greene said, Diana "felt like William was a male version of her." The princess often proclaimed, to the exclusion of Harry, that she and William were "two peas in a pod. . . . I worry that he's just like me. He's too sensitive. He feels everything too much." Elsa Bowker agreed. She remembered that around this time William became "more quiet, far too quiet. . . . For the first time, you could see suspicion in his eyes when he looked at people."

For all his innate sensitivity and precociousness, William was not above throttling Harry when the situation called for it. Like brothers everywhere, the two at various times punched, slapped, tackled, jabbed, and tripped each other whenever they thought adults were looking the other way. The Heir could be particularly rough to settle a point and establish his seniority, but the Spare gave back as good as he got. "I have many memories," William said, "of fighting Harry in the back of the Land Rover."

Unfortunately for both William and Harry, by early 1992 Diana had embarked on an undercover mission to tell her side of the story to the British people. Toward that end, she unloaded into a tape recorder that she then had smuggled by her friend Dr. James Colthurst to journalist Andrew Morton. While this cloak-and-dagger process was still under way, the six-year marriage of Prince Andrew to Sarah Ferguson imploded in a fashion that was, even by royal standards, unseemly in the extreme.

Diana and Fergie had bonded instantly over their shared status as family outsiders and, for a time, were inseparable—regarded by the public at large as two down-to-earth, at times charmingly unruly young women who were breathing new life into the staid and musty institution of the monarchy. Like Diana, the Duchess of York had even developed an eating disorder after being mocked in the press as the "Duchess of Pork." But now Diana could only watch in horror as Fergie self-destructed in slow motion.

First, the publication of photos showing Fergie cavorting on the Côte d'Azur with Texas oil tycoon Steve Wyatt were sufficient for the Palace to announce the royal couple's separation. Since her daughters Beatrice and Eugenie were, at the time, fifth and sixth in line to the throne, respectively, the duchess was still permitted to participate in royal life. That ended when she returned to the beach to sunbathe topless, this time with her American "financial advisor," thirty-seven-year-old John Bryan. Once the preternaturally serene Queen Elizabeth was shown tabloid photos of Bryan sucking her daughter-in-law's toes, the monarch lit into Fergie as the entire family, gathered at Balmoral for the summer holiday, squirmed. From that point on, the duchess was essentially persona non grata.

Squeezed in between the oil tycoon and the toe sucker was by far the biggest scandal of the year: the June 1992 publication of Morton's blockbuster *Diana: Her True Story*. Not only did the book take 174 pages to describe in unsettling detail Diana's struggle with suicidal depression brought on by her husband's obsession with another woman, but it unleashed a series of scandals that sent the Queen and the Palace's string-pulling Men in Gray reeling. That summer, transcripts of intercepted torrid, profanity-laced phone conversations between the Princess of Wales and her friend James Gilbey found their way into the hands of tabloid editors. He repeatedly called Diana "Squidgy"—providing this particular peccadillo its distinctively silly handle—and "Darling," disturbingly no fewer than fifty times. (Several months later, the tables would turn dramatically when a transcript of one of Charles's steamy phone conversations with Camilla was also published. Among their many stomach-churning declarations: that he wanted to be reincarnated as one of Camilla's tampons, and she wanted him "desperately, desperately, desperately.")

WITHIN THE YEAR THAT she would call her annus horribilis, the Queen witnessed not only the mortifying collapse of Prince Andrew's marriage to Sarah Ferguson, but also the end of Princess Anne's stormy nineteen-year union with Captain Mark Phillips. Although the public was far too distracted by the Yorks and the Waleses to notice, it turned out that both Anne and Phillips had been unfaithful to each other, and Phillips even fathered a child with another woman. Toward year's end, Her Majesty would stand in a driving rain and watch her beloved Windsor Castle all but burn to the ground.

For the moment, however, the Queen was focused on the marriage of her oldest child. The cavalcade of sordid headlines notwithstanding, she clung—naively, as it would turn out—to the belief that somehow the Waleses' marriage could be salvaged. With the specter of Edward VIII's earth-shattering 1936 abdication to marry Wallis Simpson still hanging over the royal family, there was no way of telling what damage divorce might do to Charles's reputation in particular and the monarchy in general. She confided to the archbishop of Canterbury, George Carey, that she feared Charles might have to relinquish his claim to the throne if he divorced the mother of his children and married Camilla. The Queen was, said Carey, "in despair. She thought Charles was in danger of throwing everything out the window."

IN SEPTEMBER 1992 CHARLES and Diana both managed to show up for eight-year-old Harry's first day of school at Ludgrove, where the Barbers now faced the unenviable task of protecting both princes from the number one story of the day: the breakup of their parents' marriage. Although the brothers slept in separate residence halls, William popped in on Harry at least once or twice a day, as he told Headmaster Barber, "just to make sure he doesn't get too homesick. I'm sure he misses Mummy." It was William, however, who borrowed the cell phones of visiting parents to get around rules preventing students from calling home more than once a week. "He was obviously very worried, especially about his mother," said Diana's butler and confidante, Paul Burrell. "The entire world was consumed with what was going on inside their parents' marriage." William, agreed her close friend Lucia Flecha de Lima, "was Diana's greatest ally and comforter, always. She needed him, and he knew she needed him."

The princess decided to make it up to her sons that October, when she bought them their own go-karts and encouraged them to tear around the grounds at Highgrove at breakneck speed. Until this point, with the exception of looking the other way when William and Harry urinated on the primroses from their favorite spot atop a haystack, Diana had always refrained from doing anything to harm Charles's treasured Highgrove gardens. Now, when the boys' go-karts periodically strayed from the drive and into Papa's meticulously attended-to plantings and hedgerows, she made little effort to disguise her unabashed glee.

Charles chose not to respond but instead bided his time, waiting for the last weekend of November, when William and Harry would join him for the Windsors' annual shooting party at Sandringham—one of the Prince of Wales's favorite dates on the royal calendar. In the meantime, there was yet another fire to be put out.

On the morning of November 20, 1992, William's and Harry's grandmother stood outside Windsor in a hooded macintosh and Wellington boots, watching in gape-mouthed horror as scores of firemen battled a raging conflagration that swept through the nearly one-thousand-year-old castle—all caused by a spotlight that had been left on too close to a curtain in the private chapel. By the time the fire was finally brought under control, it had destroyed more than one hundred rooms and caused the roof over the state apartments to collapse.

The ruins were still smoldering when Charles phoned his mother to tell her he had finally reached the breaking point with Diana. On November 28 the prince was informed that his sons would not be joining him at Sandringham for the annual shooting party after all. Diana had canceled at the very last minute, taking William and Harry to Highgrove instead.

For years now, the Queen had struggled to convince Charles and Diana to somehow make a go of it, if only for the children and appearances' sake. Now, exhausted and dispirited in the wake of the Windsor fire, she consulted with Prime Minister John Major, Archbishop Carey, the foreign secretary, and the lord chancellor—all of whom now agreed cautiously that even if Charles divorced, modern standards were such that that alone would not prevent him from wearing the crown.

Before the world was told the stunning news, Diana dashed straight to Ludgrove to prepare the boys. Sitting beside them on a couch in the headmaster's office, the princess started to tell William and Harry about the impending announcement when William blurted out, "Is it because of the other lady?"

Taken aback for a moment, Diana took a deep breath and tried to explain. "Well, there were three of us in this marriage," she said, "and all the stories in the newspapers and on television—the two together made it very difficult. But I still love Papa. I still love him, but we just can't live together under the same roof."

At that moment, Harry did not fully appreciate what was happening. In fact, more than a year later when Camilla's name was mentioned during a documentary on the royals, he would ask, "Who's that?"

But William took it hard. Brushing away his tears, he hugged his mother and said, "I hope you'll both be happier now."

Diana was convinced she and Charles were doing the right thing. "Everything," she told herself as she drove back to Kensington Palace, "will turn out much better for the boys in the end." Six days later, on December 19, 1992, John Major stood up in the House of Commons to formally announce the separation of the Prince and Princess of Wales. In its carefully worded statement, the Palace insisted that both parties had reached the decision to part ways "amicably," and that Charles and Diana would both "continue to participate fully in the upbringing of their children." The Queen and Prince Philip were "saddened" by the turn of events, Major continued, but hoped the "intrusions into the privacy of the Prince and Princess may now cease. They believe that a degree of privacy and understanding is essential if Their Royal Highness are to provide a happy and secure upbringing for their children."

Diana later said that she reacted with "deep, deep, profound sadness" to the separation. "Because we had struggled to keep it going, but obviously we'd both run out of steam." And there was something else. Although she felt that somehow her boys were insulated from all the publicity surrounding the announcement ("The children were very much out of it, in the sense that they were tucked away at school"), she also worried about the long-term impact of the split. "I come from a divorced background," she remarked, "and I didn't want to go into that one again. . . . I know the pain it causes."

In reality, very little changed. As they had been doing for years, the brothers split their weekends and holidays between their mother in London and Charles at Highgrove and various royal residences. And, like so many children of divorce, the princes benefited from each parent's desire to top the other in the fun department. With Papa, they enjoyed shooting parties at Sandringham, fishing on the banks of the River Dee on the grounds of Balmoral, and polo lessons at the Beaufort Club, located just two miles down a narrow road from Highgrove. They also cruised the Greek isles aboard the *Alexander*, the four-hundred-foot yacht owned by Charles's good friend John Latsis. Not to be outdone, Diana took the boys to Disney World in Orlando, Florida, and on several vacations to the Caribbean, including two trips to Necker Island, billionaire Richard Branson's private getaway in the British Virgin Islands.

There was one notable difference in the young princes' lives postseparation: since they were rarely in the company of both parents at the same time, William and Harry were no longer subject to the withering torrent of verbal abuse Charles and Diana routinely aimed at each other. Yet the acrimony was still there, and it bubbled to the surface when Diana learned that Charles had hired an attractive, twenty-eight-year-old brunette to serve as the boys' nanny when they were not in the care of Olga Powell at Kensington Palace. Alexandra "Tiggy" Legge-Bourke was technically hired as an assistant to the Prince of Wales's private secretary, Richard Aylard. But her real job, it was explained to Diana, was that of "surrogate mother" to eleven-year-old William and his nine-year-old brother.

Not surprisingly, Diana did not take Tiggy's arrival on the scene well. "I don't need a substitute father for the boys when they're with me," the princess objected. "So why does Charles need a substitute mother when they are with him?" According to Diana's private secretary, Patrick Jephson, the hapless Ms. Legge-Bourke quickly became a central focus of resentment and suspicion for the princess, who almost immediately began spreading the unfounded rumor that Tiggy and Charles were having an affair.

Oblivious to the ticking time bomb in their midst, William and Harry instantly took to the fun-loving, down-to-earth Tiggy. Unlike any of their previous nannies—all of whom would be remembered fondly by the princes throughout their lives—Tiggy was more of a big sister than the surrogate mother Diana feared. The daughter of a wealthy merchant banker and a Welsh aristocrat, Tiggy grew up on the two-thousand-acre Legge-Bourke family estate, Glanusk Park. Like Diana, Legge-Bourke was tall, athletic, outgoing, and extremely affectionate. With the obvious exception of Diana herself, Rosa Monckton said, "no one hugged and kissed those boys more than she did." Also like Diana, Legge-Bourke had been a kindergarten teacher, and had even started her own nursery school in central London: Mrs. Tiggy-Winkle, after the hedgehog in Beatrix Potter's *The Tale of Mrs. Tiggy-Winkle*. Alexandra quickly became "Tiggy" to students and parents, and the name stuck.

DESPITE THE BARBERS' BEST efforts to shield them from scorching tabloid headlines when they were at Ludgrove, William and Harry rode an emotional roller coaster over the next two years. As Diana continued to win over the public with her visits to AIDS clinics, homeless shelters, pediatric cancer wards, and halfway houses for victims of domestic abuse, Charles agreed to gin up interest in his forthcoming authorized biography by doing a rare, two-and-a-half-hour prime-time television interview with the book's author, Jonathan Dimbleby. Apparently not completely satisfied with the final product, producers persuaded the Prince of Wales to go back before the cameras and confess that he had committed adultery. "Somebody convinced him, 'Look, sir, this is going to come out sooner or later; wouldn't it be better if it comes out in a sympathetic form, in sympathetic hands?'" said journalist Sir Max Hastings. "And he fell for it."

The televised confessional aired on June 29, 1994, sparking outrage across the political spectrum. Conservative and left-leaning publications alike denounced the Prince of Wales for cheating on his wife with his still-married mistress. Although during the interview he had tried to explain that he strayed only after his marriage "became irretrievably broken down," Charles now put his own claim to the throne in jeopardy. Millions shared the sentiment expressed on the front page of the *Daily Mirror*: "Not Fit to Reign."

If there was any doubt who won this round in their ongoing slugfest, the same papers that denounced Charles on their front pages also ran photos of the Princess of Wales beaming as she swept into a charity event at London's Serpentine Gallery on the same night her husband's disastrous interview aired. The black chiffon off-the-shoulder cocktail outfit she wore that night was calculated to make a splash—Diana was originally going to wear something less daring but changed when she realized what Charles had done. (Three years later, at William's urging, Diana would include her famous "revenge dress" in an auction benefiting cancer- and AIDS-related charities. It sold for $65,000.)

William and Harry were still processing what Papa's confession meant when the focus shifted to Mummy's infidelity—specifically, her affair with millionaire art dealer and married father of three Oliver Hoare. Late one evening, after something set off the smoke detectors at Kensington Palace, Diana's longtime bodyguard Ken Wharfe discovered Hoare crouching half naked behind a potted bay tree in a corridor, smoking a cigar. The next morning, Wharfe quipped to the princess that perhaps they'd been playing strip poker. "She blushed crossly," Wharfe later recalled of his attempt at humor, "and I knew I'd overstepped the mark."

That October, the publication of *Princess in Love* left the boys reeling again. Now they and the world at large were being told for the first time that the family friend they knew as "Uncle James"—their riding instructor Captain James Hewitt and the figure arguably most responsible for their early love of the army—had been their mother's lover for five years. When Hewitt was serving in the Gulf War, Diana wrote sixty-four plaintive love letters (she called them "blueys" and signed them "Julia") in which she complained bitterly about her treatment at the hands of palace operatives, the heartlessness of the royal family, and Camilla's iron grip on the Prince of Wales's affections. The book also described in smoldering detail her sexual encounters with the dashing cavalry officer. Among the many news-making revelations: that Diana and Hewitt made love in her four-poster at Highgrove with William and Harry asleep in the next room.

Astonishingly, it would be years before it was revealed that Diana, convinced that the affair was about to be exposed anyway, actually encouraged Hewitt to go public about their romance. "She insisted to Hewitt that if the world could see that their love was genuine," recalled author Anna Pasternak, "and could understand why she turned to him in the face of Charles's rejection, they would not condemn her." Although the explosive book was instantly denounced as "tawdry, grubby, and worthless" by Buckingham Palace, no one questioned its accuracy. "He treated me like a sex slave," Diana admitted to her friend Simone Simmons. But at this critical juncture in her life, Hewitt was far more than just a boy toy for the complicated, embattled Princess of Wales. Pasternak insisted that the Queen "should have been grateful" to the man quickly branded "the Love Rat" by Fleet Street, since Hewitt "loved and listened to Diana when they wouldn't. At her most unstable, in the grip of bulimia—he was her mainstay."

Diana once again wasted no time dashing to Ludgrove to try to soften the blow for her sons. She breathed a sigh of relief when William greeted her with words of sympathy. As they had so many times before, the boys chose to believe what they were told by the adults around them—that whatever was written about their parents' marriage amounted to nothing more than lies. "William and Harry were told to ignore all the stories in the papers," Wendy Berry said. "But they saw so much going on between their parents with their own eyes, they had to begin to wonder . . ."

Yet for the time being, with the public unaware of her role in the publication of *Princess in Love*, Diana again cast herself in the role of victim—a trusting young woman betrayed by yet another cad, only this time for money. It was a role she reprised two weeks later, when Dimbleby's *The Prince of Wales: A Biography* finally landed on bookstore shelves. In the book, Charles excoriated his parents, claiming that he had been ignored by his mother and bullied by his callous, intimidating father. More important from William's and Harry's perspectives, Charles accused Prince Philip of forcing him to marry Diana—and that he never loved her in the first place.

The book both wounded and enraged Charles's parents, who were about to embark on a state visit to Moscow. Under other circumstances, Diana would have reveled in the prospect of watching Charles scramble to explain himself to Prince Philip and the Queen. Instead, she worried what impact this latest batch of headlines would have on their sons. The princess dashed back to Ludgrove, this time to find that the young princes were equally distraught about what Charles was quoted as saying in the book. "Is it true that Papa never loved you?" William asked his mother point-blank as Harry looked on. Diana tried to reassure them that she and Charles did love each other in the beginning. But Diana said later she "could see in their eyes" that they didn't believe her. The moment, she added, "pierced my heart like a dagger. I just wanted to cry."

The following day, Charles stood motionless as twelve-year-old William ran up to him at Highgrove. "Why, Papa?" he asked. "Why did you do it?" The Prince of Wales, stunned, remained silent as his son ran out of the room.

Harry, at ten still not quite able to grasp what was going on, stood quietly in the corner before being whisked off by one of the household staff to help with chores in the kitchen. "We spent a lot of time distracting William and Harry from what was going on between the prince and princess," said Olga Powell, who divided nanny duties with

Tiggy Legge-Bourke. "Everyone became expert at finding excuses to pick them up and move them out of harm's way." Another Kensington Palace staff member remembered how Harry "always looked to Prince William for cues on how to react to things. Most of the time, the prince was very much in control of his emotions, very calm and collected—mature for someone his age. But as things between their mum and dad got worse, William became more confused and angry, and that obviously frightened Harry."

Things deteriorated further in the coming months, when Diana was linked in the press to a number of men. Among them: rugby star Will Carling, whose wife publicly accused the princess of ruining her marriage; British property developer Christopher Whalley; telecommunications mogul Gulu Lalvani; Canadian rock star Bryan Adams; and the American billionaire, philanthropist, and playboy Theodore "Teddy" Forstmann. In each case, Diana once again turned to William for advice. "Diana told William anything and everything that popped into her head," one of her closest friends said. "There were some things that were just not appropriate for a boy his age—or for a mother to be discussing with her son at all." Diana's friend Vivienne Parry was equally blunt: "Children don't want to know that their parents are doing it. It's out of the question. So when it's obvious that your parents *are* doing it—and with different people—it's a bit disturbing."

Mercifully, Diana kept Harry decidedly out of the loop. "I want them to be protected," she said of the princes, "but William just has so much wisdom for someone his age." Richard Greene agreed that "as far as the emotional scars were concerned—and they had to be pretty deep—William especially seemed to be a happy, well-adjusted kid." No one was the wiser when William, looking poised and upbeat with both of his parents gazing over his shoulder, enrolled at Eton on September 6,

1995. It scarcely mattered to the assembled pack of photographers that William signed his name in the wrong place in the entrance book and had to ask his father what religion he was—a startling question from the future head of the Church of England.

No matter. The Queen was overjoyed that her favorite grandchild would now be living seven days a week at Eton. Unquestionably the world's most elite prep school (history was decided on its playing fields, wrote George Orwell), Eton was conveniently situated directly across from Windsor Castle. Not only could Her Majesty pick up her binoculars and watch William play rugby from the comfort of her sitting room, but also now the tutorials in "kinging" that had taken place at Buckingham Palace for years were shifted to what she regarded as the homier environs of Windsor.

Each Sunday at 3:50, William left Eton's redbrick Tudor campus and made the brief trek on foot across the stone bridge that connected the villages of Eton and Windsor. Seven minutes later, he arrived at the castle and went straight to the Oak Drawing Room for tea with the Queen. There they discussed everything from foreign affairs and the environment to sports, movies, and even rap music. (The Queen Mother made both William and Harry double over with laughter when she did her dead-on impression of would-be rap icon Ali G, portrayed on TV by comic actor Sacha Baron Cohen.)

At Eton, William appeared to succeed at everything he attempted. Unlike most of his Windsor and Spencer relatives, the Heir was a gifted student who excelled in all his classes. He was also an exceptional athlete—a star swimmer and rower, as well as a natural on the rugby field. William's true passion was water polo, which Diana suggested was his way of pleasing both his mother and his polo-loving papa.

On the surface, it appeared that William had made a smooth adjustment to life among the "F-Tits" (first-year students)—a transition made all the easier by a built-in support group that included lifelong pals Lord Frederick "Freddie" Windsor, son of Prince and Princess Michael of Kent, and the late Lord Mountbatten's grandson Nicholas Knatchbull—both distant cousins of William's. For guidance and moral support, the future king could also lean on his master at Manor House, Andrew Gailey; Gailey's wife, Shauna; and Elizabeth Heathcote, the dormitory's "dame," or matron.

Along with his 1,300 fellow Etonians, William was required each morning to don what was rather casually referred to as "school dress": black pin-striped trousers, black waistcoat (always worn with the bottom button undone, in the style of Edward VIII), black tailcoat, highly polished black shoes, white tunic shirt, cuff links, Arundel collar, and white tie. Not that the future monarch could ever blend in entirely with the other boys who flooded the cobblestone-paved quadrangle as they rushed from class to class. Like his brother, who would follow him into Eton three years later, William arrived with his own tracking device and a nineteen-man plainclothes security force armed with 9-millimeter Glock pistols.

"Of course, we've got lots of these famous people's children," said Eton faculty member Dr. M. J. Atkinson, "but once they're in the school environment, that doesn't seem to matter. They're just Fred, Joe, John, et cetera. Their parents can be all over the papers, but it's as if their lives are separate from their parents and it doesn't matter here." Nevertheless, it was only a matter of months before Sky Television aired a fawning documentary about William's arrival at the school. "The importance of the next five years is unequivocal," intoned the narrator over footage of William, smiling convincingly as he emerged from class to a blinding fusillade of flashing cameras. "School is the time in which boys mature into men." After five years at Eton, he continued, William's strength of character "should be sufficient, we hope, to withstand some of the pressures that most thirteen-year-old boys are never required to undergo." Predictably, a mortified William begged his fellow F-Tits not to watch.

His relentlessly cheery façade notwithstanding, William was still called upon to act as his mother's lifeline and sounding board. By the fall of 1995, William was being called by Diana several times a week for advice on how to handle her newest love affair—this time with the man she categorically referred to as "The One": thirty-nine-year-old Pakistani heart surgeon Hasnat "Natty" Khan. Diana met the pudgy, taciturn, mustachioed Muslim while visiting a friend recovering from surgery at Royal Brompton Hospital in London's borough of Chelsea and was instantly smitten. For the next twenty months, the mercurial Dr. Khan would be the focus of Diana's romantic life and one of the principal topics in countless private conversations with William. By design, Harry remained blissfully unaware of Khan's existence.

Diana was so obsessed with Khan that she wore glasses and a wig to the hospital, was allowed into the operating theater using the alias "Dr. Allegra," then donned scrubs and a surgical mask to watch him perform heart surgery. Conversely, on numerous occasions, Khan was smuggled into Kensington Palace hiding under a blanket in the backseat of a car driven by the princess's butler, Paul Burrell. More determined than ever to marry Khan, Diana at one point was spending two hours a day studying the Koran so that she might convert—until she realized any such marriage might in some way threaten William's status as heir to the throne. Without bothering to inform Hasnat, she then flew to Pakistan to ask his parents if they would welcome her—a non-Muslim—into the family. As it happened, they eagerly replied that they would.

At about the same time she began dating Khan, Diana pursued a top secret relationship of a very different sort, with a then largely unknown BBC correspondent named Martin Bashir. Over the course of several conversations, Bashir—whom Diana referred to by the code name "Dr. Jarman"—established a friendly rapport with the princess. Armed with forged documents and a host of outlandish conspiracy theories, he convinced Diana that all her worst fears were true—that her most trusted aides and bodyguards were being paid to spy on her, and that British intelligence services were bugging her car, Kensington Palace, and the gym she belonged to. Bashir even claimed that the new Swatch watch William had been given by his father contained a hidden recording device—all part of a plot by MI6 (Britain's equivalent of the US Central Intelligence Agency) to keep tabs on the princess. (Diana's fears were not entirely unfounded. Following her death, Britain's intelligence agencies and the CIA admitted that they had indeed been spying on her for years. The National Security Agency in Washington declined to formally explain why it had amassed a file on Diana consisting of 1,056 pages of classified information.) Allegedly, Bashir's most outrageous claim was the one that finally nudged the princess over the edge: that Tiggy, whom Diana had long suspected was having an affair with Charles, had become pregnant by him and had had an abortion.

The princess, now convinced that her security detail could no longer be trusted, decided to forgo protection. While driving alone through central London a few months later, Diana approached an intersection and was nearly broadsided by another car when her brakes failed. "The brakes of my car have been tampered with," she wrote to several of her closest friends. "If something does happen to me, it will be MI5 or MI6." Diana was soon floating an entirely new conspiracy theory: that both she and Camilla, who had taken to calling Diana "Barbie" behind her back, would both be "set aside" by assassins to clear the way for Charles to marry Tiggy.

Diana went so far as to share these concerns with her solicitor, Lord Mishcon. "I could not believe what I was hearing," he later said. Another of Diana's lawyers, Maggie Rae, said it was "very clear that Princess Diana thought she was going to be killed"—probably, she added portentously, in a staged car crash. Fearing that the Palace would use this information to brand the princess as seriously unbalanced, Mishcon and Rae said nothing. "It seemed incredible, fantastic, that she could even be thinking such a thing," Lord Mishcon said. "We didn't want Prince Charles or the Queen to think the princess was delusional."

William and Harry knew nothing of their mother's suspicions, of course. But the Heir still harbored fears about his mother's safety. Starting when he was the clench-fisted toddler referred to as Willy Wombat—snarling at photographers who crowded his space—William bore a deep resentment of the press. There were countless moments—on ski slopes in Austria, on beaches in the Caribbean, or simply walking through London's Hyde Park—when Diana would plead with photographers to back off, if only for a little while.

Not unexpectedly, the princess's entreaties were completely ignored. Throughout the princes' entire childhood, the onslaught was ceaseless whenever William and Harry ventured out into the world with their mother. The boys also saw the toll it took behind palace walls, when Diana was driven to tears by an embarrassing shot of her exercising in the supposed privacy of her gym or came home shaken after a particu-

larly harrowing encounter with what she called a "pap" (for "paparazzi")
on the street.

During one unreported incident on Kensington High Street, two
paps leapt out from behind parked cars as she left the luxury department store Harvey Nichols, chasing her down the street and into a cab.
When the taxi stopped at an intersection, the men flung upon the passenger door to see Diana with her head down between her knees, sobbing. "Lift your fucking head!" one of the photographers yelled at her.
"I've got a mortgage and a baby to support!" Diana told William that
she never looked up, and on the entire ride back to the palace was "crying, crying, crying."

Incidents like these often never made it into the papers, but Diana,
sometimes still shaking from the experience, nearly always shared the
troubling details with her older son. Because she did not confide in
Harry, the Spare would have to wait until he was similarly pilloried in
the press before he could appreciate fully the pain Fleet Street had inflicted on his mother. But for William, that knowledge was firmly
rooted in early childhood and would fester into a visceral, pure hatred
of Britain's rapacious tabloids. "William had the best teacher when it
came to handling the media," said Alan Hamilton, the *Times* of London's longtime royal correspondent. "Diana was an absolute magician
in that department, and he watched and learned from her." Hamilton
remembered that even as a small boy, William "could be charming beyond belief. But there's no question that long before his mother died, he
hated the press, or a lot of people in the press, for ruining his mother's
life."

In the fall of 1995 Diana found herself for the first time losing
ground to Charles in the court of public opinion. The media-wise princess had taken a drubbing in the press for her dalliances with married

men such as Gilbey, Hoare, and Carling, and now she felt the time was ripe for a sneak attack on her enemies inside Buckingham Palace. Besides, she had yet to take revenge on Charles for his damning Jonathan Dimbleby interview the year before. Like Khan, Bashir was smuggled into Kensington Palace hiding beneath a blanket in the back of Burrell's car. A cameraman and a producer for BBC's premiere current affairs program *Panorama* were also sneaked into the palace and set up the equipment, which had been delivered days earlier under the guise of setting up a new stereo system.

Diana's *Panorama* interview aired on November 20, 1995—the forty-eighth anniversary of the Queen and Prince Philip's wedding—sending shock waves around the globe. For fifty-five minutes (pared down from three hours), the Princess of Wales looked at Bashir with huge, doleful eyes as she discussed everything from her affair with James Hewitt ("Yes, I adored him. Yes, I was in love with him") and her suicidal depression, to Camilla ("There were three of us in this marriage"), the callousness of the royal family, and her devout hope that William—not Charles—would become the next monarch.

At Ludgrove, the Barbers were still shielding Harry from potentially upsetting media coverage of his parents' disastrous marriage. It would be years before he actually screened the *Panorama* interview that had much of the planet in an uproar. William, however, was left alone in Housemaster Andrew Gailey's study to watch the entire program as it aired. When Gailey returned to fetch the prince, William's eyes were red and swollen from crying. The day before, Diana had driven to Eton and warned him that there might be some upsetting things in the interview, but none of what she said prepared him for this.

An hour after the broadcast ended, Diana phoned William, but he refused to take her call. She tried again the next day, and once again he refused. According to Simone Simmons, William was "absolutely livid. He was the most angry I had seen him at his mother." At Eton, the other boys did not hesitate to tease him and make "rude comments about his mother." William was sympathetic and wanted to defend her on one level, but, in the end, he "felt she had made a fool of herself—and of him."

William stonewalled his mother for the next five days. When he returned to Kensington Palace that weekend, he rushed straight into Diana's sitting room, slamming the door behind him so forcefully that a framed photo on a side table fell to the floor. Shouting at the princess through his tears, William accused her of betraying both Harry and himself by talking about their father and about Hewitt. "How could you say things like that?" he demanded. "Don't you know how that makes us *feel*?"

Diana tried to explain that she had to go on the offensive to counter the Palace's attempt to portray her as "unstable, sick—an embarrassment to be put in a home of some sort." Now weeping herself, the princess tried to put her arms around her son. Instead, he pushed her away. It was a grudge that William was determined to keep for months, and for the first time, the Princess of Wales seriously feared that she had lost her son forever. "William is going to hate me for the rest of his life," Diana told Simmons, who recalled "the look of hopelessness" on her face. "What have I done? What have I done? What have I done to my children?"

Twenty years later, William would say that he understood her decision to do the *Panorama* interview "because having sometimes been in those situations, you feel incredibly desperate, and it is very unfair that things are being said that are untrue." In hindsight, he could see why his mother would "just go to the media herself. Open that door. But once you've opened it, you can never close it again." Diana's sister, Lady Sarah McCorquodale, agreed, saying, "She had run out of options. She didn't know what else to do."

William and Harry weren't the only family members enraged by the interview at the time. While polls showed that more than eight in ten Britons approved of the interview and nearly half now believed Charles was "unfit" to be king, the Queen was not among them. In fact, a senior advisor said she was "seething with anger" as she and Prince Philip watched the program at Buckingham Palace.

As much as Diana regretted the emotional wound she had inflicted on her boys—William in particular—she was elated by the outpouring of support that followed her televised tell-all. After flying to New York to accept an award as Humanitarian of the Year, Diana returned to London for the annual Christmas lunch she and Charles threw for staff members. Still emboldened by what appeared by all accounts to be a public relations masterstroke, Diana took the opportunity to sidle up to Tiggy Legge-Bourke. "So sorry," Diana told the nanny, softly but just loud enough for other guests to hear, "about the baby." Tiggy, understanding full well the totally unfounded implication that she had aborted Charles's child, ran from the room in tears. Patrick Jephson was so shocked that Diana "had exulted in accusing Legge-Bourke of having an abortion" that he resigned as the princess's private secretary.

The day after confronting Tiggy, Diana received two letters: one from Legge-Bourke's lawyers demanding a public apology, and another, more ominous-looking envelope delivered by a liveried messenger from Buckingham Palace. In a handwritten letter sent to both Charles and Diana, the Queen instructed them to proceed—"in the best interests of the country"—with a quick divorce.

Finally, it dawned on the headstrong Princess of Wales that the

Panorama interview had been a grave miscalculation. "Diana was crushed," her friend Lady Elsa Bowker said. "She did not want a divorce. She viewed the Queen as a friend, but the Queen had had enough of scandal."

Under the circumstances, Diana canceled her plans to join the rest of the royal family at Sandringham for the Christmas holidays the following week. So, while William and Harry helped decorate Sandringham's twenty-foot-tall Norman fir Christmas tree, opened gifts, joined in singing carols, and played with their cousins, Diana spent the holidays alone at Kensington Palace. "Diana fell apart," Simmons said. "She was constantly in tears, reflecting over and over again on what might have been."

Once the holidays were over, Diana escorted William directly back to Eton and embarked with Harry on a ski trip to Klosters, Switzerland. "William was still angry with her," Bowker said. "She also worried that William was the focus of too much attention. She did not want Harry to feel pushed aside, left out of the picture." Incredibly, Diana maintained her friendship with Martin Bashir for months afterward, never suspecting that the forged documents he had used to convince her to agree to the disastrous *Panorama* interview were anything but authentic.

Over the next three months, the Princess of Wales and the Crown were immersed in intense negotiations that would determine the details of a final divorce settlement. Diana demanded the right to continue living at Kensington Palace, share custody of the children, and maintain access to all the perks that went with being a member of the royal family—including use of the royal fleet of cars and aircraft, and a staff commensurate with her status as the mother of a future king. All this, and $70 million.

Needless to say, the boys knew nothing of this at the time—nor the fact that the Queen, fed up with both their parents, met with Diana to assuage her concerns as best she could. Diana worried that Charles would now be free to marry Camilla—something that the Queen insisted would not happen, given constraints on remarriage imposed by the Church of England. "Charles will never remarry," she stated flatly. "He can't. He'll be head of the Church of England, and as long as you're alive, he can't marry anyone." Diana wanted and got the Queen's assurance that she would prohibit Charles and William from flying together, her reasoning being that "If something happened, then Harry would become king, and it would crush him."

When the dust finally cleared after nine months of haggling, Diana was allowed to remain at Kensington Palace with an annual allowance of $600,000 and would share custody of William and Harry with Charles. She also received a lump sum payment of $22.5 million. Yet on the issue of Diana's royal status, the Queen would not budge. While she would henceforth be known as Diana, Princess of Wales, and keep her lesser titles (Duchess of Cornwall, Duchess of Rothesay, Countess of Chester, Countess of Carrick, Baroness Renfrew), she would no longer be entitled to be called "Her Royal Highness."

By this point, William had come to terms with his mother's soul-bearing *Panorama* interview, though he convinced her to finally cut off contact with Martin Bashir. "The boys were central to everything she did," said Hasnat Khan, who remembered William bluntly telling Diana that Bashir "is not a good person." William also appreciated how fiercely his mother fought for what she believed was a fair and equitable divorce settlement. She was particularly delighted that Charles had to dig deep into his own pockets to come up with the $22.5 million in cash. But the Queen's decision to strip her of her

HRH rank cut deep. "I think everyone agrees I've earned it," Diana said, adding that, as the mother of a future king, she should still be considered a full-fledged member of the family.

William called her from Eton to offer words of comfort, as he had countless times before. "I don't mind what you're called," he told her. "You're still Mummy." None of this really mattered anyway, he reassured her. William promised that, as soon as he became king, he would reinstate Diana's HRH title. "So you see," he added, "it's silly to cry."

Unfortunately, Diana cried anyway—over her foundering romance with the man she called "Mr. Wonderful." Khan, intensely private, was horrified at the prospect of being hounded by the paparazzi. When reports of their affair began surfacing in the press, Mr. Wonderful accused Diana of leaking the items and broke off their relationship. Within days, though, he was back, pleading with Diana to forgive him.

Throughout this on-again, off-again affair, William continued to provide Diana a shoulder to cry on while Harry remained happily free to live the life of an eleven-year-old. "All his life, William had to navigate around all the drama just for his own emotional survival," Diana's hairdresser Natalie Symonds said. "So he could see things from a very levelheaded, adult perspective."

The Heir's ability to cope with his own stardom—and his newfound status as a bona fide teen idol—was another matter entirely. When the tousle-haired prince attended his first dance as an Etonian— the infamous Toff's Ball in London—he was instantly mobbed by screaming girls who, said one royal bodyguard, had to be "peeled off like you were peeling a banana. Some of them held on for dear life." It came as no surprise to Diana when tabloids christened her elder son "Dreamboat Willie." She was already referring to William, who was already nearing his full height of six feet three inches, as "DDG"—for Drop-Dead Gorgeous. "Isn't he superb?" Diana rhapsodized. "And he's so tall, too!"

Editors of the British teen magazine *Smash Hits* knew a rising sex symbol when they saw one. Their tasteful centerfold pullout of a blazer-clad William flew off the newsstands. At the same time, the young prince was taping torrid eight-by-tens of supermodels Cindy Crawford and Claudia Schiffer to the inside of his locker. Diana took special delight in arranging for William to meet not only Crawford and Schiffer at Kensington Palace, but also Christy Turlington and Naomi Campbell.

But outside of school, William divided his time between counseling his mother and fretting about Harry. On the Diana front, he concocted a scheme to sell off her dresses to raise money for Royal Marsden Hospital Cancer Research Fund and the AIDS Crisis Trust. The auction, held at Christie's in New York, raked in a total of $3.26 million. "He is brilliant," she said as the gavel came down for the final time. "Three million for some old frocks!"

William also pressed his mother to step outside her comfort zone to pursue another, even more daring project to raise money for her favorite charities. When, at Sarah Ferguson's request, actor Kevin Costner initially called and offered the princess $10 million to star in the sequel to his 1992 blockbuster *The Bodyguard*—the movie that turned singer Whitney Houston into a major box office star—Diana politely but firmly declined. "Sorry, I can't act," she told him. "Don't worry," Costner replied. "I'll teach you."

At first, according to Paul Burrell, Diana was "rolling around on the floor, giggling" at the prospect of starring in a film. The princess had identified with Houston's paparazzi-plagued character in the original, but for the mother of England's future king to act in a Hollywood movie seemed, in two words, wildly inappropriate. She changed her mind, however, after William pointed to Costner's repeated assurances that she would be required to spend only a few days in front of the cameras. She made it clear to the big-screen star that she was willing to go ahead for one reason and one reason only: "Because William thinks it's a good idea." (A first script for the project, a love story that begins with a princess's bodyguard protecting her from paparazzi and stalkers, landed on Costner's desk the day before Diana was killed.)

At the time of Costner's offer, William also felt it was a good idea for Diana to take on a more serious role, as a crusader for the abolition of land mines. He urged her to accept an invitation from the Red Cross to fly to Angola and comfort the horribly maimed victims of unexploded munitions just as she had comforted AIDS victims, cancer patients, and victims of domestic violence. But when Harry and William saw video of their mother taking a death-defying stroll through a minefield wearing a flak jacket and surrounded by flags bearing a skull and crossbones, they panicked. "Please, Mummy," William pleaded over the phone. "What you're doing is important, but don't take chances like that." Diana, in turn, emptied her heart out to William as she always did, describing how she'd had to bite her lip to keep from crying while she cradled children who'd had an arm or leg blown off. Diana would make a similar trip to Bosnia later that year and be credited as the person most responsible for an international agreement to ban land mines ultimately signed by 164 countries.

ON THE BROTHER FRONT, William, who at one point during his Ludgrove years allegedly reacted to one student's rude comments about his mother by dunking the boy's head in a toilet, actively worried that the Spare experienced taunting from classmates every time Mummy or Papa made headlines. Just to satisfy himself that Harry was coping, William called him two or three times a week. "William has always believed he is Harry's protector," Diana told her friend Lucia Flecha de Lima. "But things don't bother Harry the way they bother William."

As it turned out, Harry was no longer the quiet, somewhat shy and reticent little boy who seemed destined to wilt in the Heir's history-shaping shadow. Over his years at Ludgrove, Harry proved not to be the stellar academic his brother was. But in the realm of athletics, he not only matched but also often exceeded William's accomplishments. Harry also quickly became one of the school's most popular students, not because he shared his brother's leadership qualities but because he was a fearless practical joker—the kind of unflappable prankster who was far more likely to do the teasing than be a victim of it. "Setting off stink bombs and debagging; you know, sneaking up and pulling down the other chap's pants," a Ludgrove classmate recalled. "That's the sort of thing our group did." During one visit that Charles and Diana paid to the school, several boys mooned the assembled press—a stunt that Harry insisted, somewhat unconvincingly, that he was not a part of.

The younger brother's rebellious side came as no surprise to those inside the family. "The press have always written up William as the terror and Harry as a rather quiet second son," Earl Spencer said. "In fact, William is a very self-possessed, intelligent, and mature boy, and quite shy. He is quite formal and stiff, actually—particularly when he answers the phone." By contrast, their uncle insisted, Harry "is a loveable scamp."

Their evolving personalities aside, William and Harry were pleased to notice a sudden and wholly unexpected thaw in their parents' normally icy relationship. By early 1997, it had become clear that Diana's affair with Hasnat Khan was having a strangely positive impact on her once-toxic relationship with her ex-spouse. Despite Khan's ambivalence, the princess's devotion to the Pakistani heart surgeon at least enabled her to understand Charles's unwavering loyalty to Camilla. "We all have that one person we're meant for," she told Natalie Symonds and Tess Rock, another one of her hair stylists, "and obviously Camilla is the one meant for Charles."

For the first time, fifteen-year-old William found himself on the receiving end of some serious romantic advice from Mummy. Incredibly, she now held up Charles and Camilla as a shining example of true love. "When you find a true, deep love like that," she told William, "it's a precious thing. You've got to hold on tight to it."

Diana was not feeling quite so charitable toward the boys' "surrogate mother," however. The princess grew agitated every time photos ran in the newspaper of Tiggy out and about with her charges, "behaving like she's their mum. It is just ridiculous," Diana said. "Charles had better do something."

Tiggy had always shrugged off the warnings. "I'm just the nursery maid, guv," she liked to say when told that Diana bitterly resented her presence in the brothers' lives. But when Tiggy defiantly drew up a guest list for William's March 1997 confirmation at Windsor Castle that gave short shrift to the Spencer side of the family, Charles felt he had no choice but to let the nanny go.

Legge-Bourke would soon play an even larger role in William's and Harry's lives, but for now her status was strictly that of family friend. In the meantime, William invited Tiggy to parents' day at Eton but explicitly excluded both Charles and Diana. Their presence, he said, would turn the event into a media circus. "If you come," William told his parents, "it will be unbearable."

It wasn't long before Diana did some excluding of her own—this time declining to invite a single Windsor to a fifteenth birthday party she was throwing for William at Kensington Palace. It became clear why when the palace chef rolled out a birthday cake decorated with a half dozen bare-breasted women—Diana's tongue-in-cheek gift to her supermodel-crazed son.

William and Harry had never seen their parents treat each other with such warmth and respect. When Fleet Street savaged Diana for taking the boys to see the action thriller *The Devil's Own*, starring Brad Pitt and Harrison Ford—a film that was slammed in Britain for glamorizing the Irish Republican Army—she immediately called Charles to apologize. The Prince of Wales, whom Diana had in the past derided as "the Boy Wonder" and "the Great White Hope," told his ex-wife to think nothing of it. "In the past," observed one courtier, "Prince Charles would never have forgiven her, and the princess wouldn't have apologized in the first place."

One of the things Diana was most grateful for was the fact that Charles refrained from introducing Camilla to William and Harry. Unlike Tiggy, Charles's mistress never had a particular interest in children, despite having a son and a daughter of her own. Mrs. PB's approach to parenthood, in stark contrast to Diana's, was distinctly laissez-faire. That didn't mean, however, that Charles intended for Camilla to dwell in the shadows forever, especially after she divorced her husband of twenty-two years, army officer Andrew Parker Bowles, in 1995. When Diana learned that Charles was planning to throw a fiftieth birthday bash for Camilla at Highgrove—against the express wishes of the Queen—the princess became, as she put it, "cross. Very cross. *Really* cross." At the same time, she reveled in the thought that the affair would not only anger the Queen but the public in general. "Wouldn't it be funny if I jumped out of the cake in a bathing suit?" she joked.

Complicating matters was Hasnat Khan's intransigence. Diana pushed the envelope, going so far as to have Paul Burrell line up a Roman Catholic priest to secretly marry them—a scheme that had William's seal of approval. When she presented Khan with her plan, he dismissed the idea as "absurd." Off he stormed again, only to call back and apologize.

"Hasnat was a decent, intensely private man from a traditional, conservative Pakistani family," Diana's friend Jemima Khan (no relation to Hasnat) explained, "and he was worried about how it would work. He hated the thought of being in the glare of publicity for the rest of his life."

At wits' end, Diana fled to the one place in the world where she felt truly appreciated. In Washington, she breakfasted with First Lady Hillary Clinton and was the star guest at an eightieth birthday party for legendary *Washington Post* publisher Katharine Graham. Then the princess was off to New York, where, among other, fancier engagements, she reunited for what would be the last time with her friend Mother Teresa at an AIDS hospice in a very gritty section of the Bronx. (Diana had first met the Calcutta-based nun, who was destined to become a Roman Catholic saint, in 1992 and the two instantly bonded over their mutual dedication to helping the poor and the sick. Ironically, Mother Theresa died of natural causes just six days after Diana, at the age of eighty-seven.)

Diana often said she felt "completely at home" in the United States, in large part because the press was not as intrusive, and because, quite simply, "Americans understand me. It's friendly territory." Indeed, Americans were far less likely to view the princess as difficult and demanding, and more inclined to regard her as warm and down-to-earth—both a rule-shattering rebel and the victim of a cheating husband and his conniving mistress. It didn't hurt that Diana was also gorgeous, witty, and impossibly stylish. Not since the late Jackie Kennedy Onassis, whose charismatic son, John Jr., Diana hoped William would emulate, had there been a woman who so totally captured the public imagination.

William traced his own fondness for America back to 1992 when, as his parents' marriage collapsed, Diana sent him along with his security detail to the E-Bar-L dude ranch near Missoula, Montana. Shy at first, the ten-year-old quickly came out of his shell, wearing a cowboy hat tipped back on his forehead and venturing out into Big Sky country to ride, fish, and shoot with the ranch hands. William "excelled at all of it," said Paul Beban, a Yale University undergraduate who was working at the E-Bar-L at the time. "He dove into daily life at the ranch, helping to milk cows and mend fences. He also eagerly competed in old-timey contests, such as plunging his face in water before trying to gobble crackers—using only his mouth, no hands allowed—off a table covered in flour. He danced, he sang, he made friends."

Perhaps the high point of that first trip to the United States came when William dared him to follow through on a threat to hang the prince by a nail and douse him with water. Beban promptly obliged, hammering a nail high into a cottonwood tree, then hanging William by his shorts and spraying "the dusty, tired, happy young heir to the British throne" with a garden hose. "At his request, remember!" added Beban.

The following year, eight-year-old Harry got his first taste of life across the pond when he joined his mother and William on a trip to Disney World. In short order, the Windsors took in the Country Bear Jamboree, Jungle Cruise, and Big Thunder Mountain Railroad rides before being photographed screaming as they plunged down the Splash Mountain log flume. "It's one of my very, very happy memories, of going to Disney World with my mum," Harry said more than two decades later. "I went on Space Mountain fourteen times. I was like, 'This is absolutely fantastic. This is the best thing ever.'"

Once she returned to the United Kingdom, Diana resumed her campaign to win over Hasnat, going so far as to host his mother when she visited with some of his young cousins from Pakistan. The princess even took them to the supermarket and pushed them around in her shopping cart, where the cousins told stunned shoppers that their friend's name was "Sharon." No matter. Khan still blew up whenever she even hinted at the possibility of marriage.

As always, Diana sought William's counsel, knowing that he was particularly fond of her Pakistani lover. But this time she rejected his advice that she simply wear down Khan over time. Instead, she hatched a scheme to make the surgeon jealous. On July 11, 1997, Diana and her sons flew to Nice, France, on an Executive Gulfstream IV jet belonging to Mohamed Al Fayed, the flamboyant Egyptian billionaire who was shunned by British society despite owning, among other iconic institutions, Harrods department store in London and the Ritz Hotel in Paris. Once in Nice, they boarded Al Fayed's 195-foot yacht, *Jonikal*, and began the five-hour journey to their host's $17 million villa in Saint-Tropez.

No sooner did Diana and the boys arrive with their royal bodyguards than they were joined by a small flotilla of press boats anchored just off the beach. While William and Harry zipped about on Jet Skis, Diana commandeered one of Al Fayed's powerboats and zoomed off to confront the gape-mouthed paparazzi. "How long do you plan to keep this up?" she demanded, adding that their interest in her family was "obsessive. William is freaked out. He's worried about the family's safety."

Diana's pleas, not altogether surprisingly, fell on deaf ears. William's solution was simply to make it easy for the photographers rather than ruin their vacation. "Give them what they want," he said. "They'll get tired of it soon enough." Of course, they never did, and papers around the world were chockablock with photos of the princess frolicking with her sons in the Mediterranean sun.

Several days into their trip, they were joined by Al Fayed's forty-two-year-old playboy son, Dodi, an occasional movie producer whose credits included *F/X*, *Hook*, and the Academy Award–winning *Chariots of Fire*. Over a quiet candlelit dinner aboard the *Jonikal*, Diana and Dodi clicked immediately, and their playful banter soon escalated into a full-fledged food fight. "They were chasing each other and laughing and giggling like a couple of kids," recalled the yacht's chief stewardess, Debbie Gribble.

For the next several days, Dodi and Diana did not leave each other's side. Nor did the paparazzi, who chronicled their blossoming love affair from small boats and even Jet Skis that circled the *Jonikal* like a pack of hungry sharks. Not only did Dodi focus all his attention on her in laser-like fashion, but also, unlike the infuriatingly secretive Hasnat Khan, he clearly had no intention of disguising the depth of his feelings toward Diana. For Diana, Dodi's open intentions served two main purposes: they shored up her badly battered ego ("Why am I always unwanted?" she had often asked) and they would serve to make the all too overconfident Natty squirm.

William and Harry bonded instantly with the gregarious, fatally charming, fun-loving Dodi. Delighted to see their mother laugh again, the princes suggested that maybe Dodi Fayed—and not the serious, mercurial Dr. Khan—was really "The One." Diana was still weighing her options when her close friend, the iconic fashion designer Gianni Versace, was shot to death in front of Casa Casuarina, his Miami Beach mansion. Once again William provided a shoulder to cry on—only now both Hasnat Khan and Dodi were also there to listen while Diana poured her heart out over the phone.

This time Diana had to do her share of comforting as well. Versace's senseless murder, committed by spree killer Andrew Cunanan in broad daylight, threw Harry and especially William into a panic. They knew that by dismissing her royal protection officers the year before, Diana had left herself wide open to just this kind of mindless attack. Fortunately, or at least it seemed so at the time, Dodi stepped up and offered to protect the princess with his own private security force of more than twenty armed bodyguards. William's concern for his mother's safety was palpable, and Dodi's gesture went a long way toward allaying his fears.

Determined to let the world at large—and Hasnat Khan in particular—know that she was getting on with her life, Diana quietly turned to Versace's onetime personal photographer, Mario Brenna, for help in creating an appropriately sexy tableau. "I don't trust the other paps to get it right," said the princess, who saw to it that Brenna was tipped off in advance to their appearance on the top deck of the *Jonikal*. "I want Mario to take the photos. The rest of them always show bulges and bumps."

The very next day, July 22, the princess flew to Milan to attend Versace's funeral. At William's urging, she used the occasion to patch up her fractured relationship with one of the other mourners, Sir Elton John. Ironically, the brief falling-out between Diana and Elton had to do with *Rock and Royalty*, a book that Versace and the rocker worked on to benefit John's AIDS Foundation; Diana had agreed to write the book's foreword but backed out when she got a look at the racy photographs inside.

Not long after Versace's funeral, Diana rendezvoused with Dodi secretly in Paris. When Khan called her there, he could sense "something is not right—and that is exactly how I felt when I spoke to her." On July 27 Diana returned to London and arranged for a clandestine rendezvous with Khan in Battersea Park. When he asked her if she was involved with someone else, Diana denied it. "She was not herself," Khan said years later. "I knew there was someone."

They met again the next day at Kensington Palace, but this time Diana was direct. "We are through," she told him. "It's all over between us."

Khan looked at her for a moment, realizing that indeed she had fallen for someone in Mohamed Al Fayed's circle. "You're dead," said Khan, meaning that any involvement with the notorious Egyptian would kill her reputation. The remark—which Khan quickly regretted—would turn out to be sadly prescient.

Soon the world knew that Diana had made her choice. Brenna's photos of the princess and her Egyptian boyfriend slathering each other with suntan lotion and embracing passionately on the deck of the *Jonikal* were splashed across ten pages of London's *Sunday Mirror*. The tabloid had anted up $400,000 for the privilege of being the first publication to run photos of Dodi and Diana under the banner headline "The Kiss." In the end, Brenna would rake in more than $3 million in licensing fees for the images.

As was her usual practice, Diana warned William and Harry about the photos well in advance. But they were not prepared to see their mother and her lover in bathing suits, arms and legs entwined. William, who had also made it clear to Prince Charles that he was not interested in getting to know Mrs. Parker Bowles, complained to his mother about the photos taken aboard the *Jonikal*. "She hated disappointing William in particular," a confidante said. "But she felt it was her life, and she wanted the world to know she was finally happy."

Over the coming weeks, Dodi and Diana pursued their romance over candlelit dinners in Paris, at his penthouse flat in London's Mayfair district, and aboard Mohamed Al Fayed's sleek, white-hulled yacht. As the *Jonikal* cruised from the French Riviera to Sardinia, William and Harry hiked, fished, and hunted with the rest of the royal family at Balmoral. At one point, Prince Charles, wearing the red-and-gray plaid royal Balmoral tartan kilt and burgundy knee socks, posed with the boys for photographers on the rocky banks of the Dee. Diana was a superb shot who had actually killed several stags as a daughter of Britain's aristocracy—most recently during her honeymoon at Balmoral. Although she now abhorred the ruling class's enduring passion for "killing things," Diana understood that such country pursuits were part of her sons' heritage. It was also an important opportunity for the boys to bond with their grandparents in a decidedly informal atmosphere. "Walks, picnics, dogs—a lot of dogs; there's always dogs—and people coming in and out all the time," their cousin Princess Eugenie said of life at Balmoral. "It's a lovely base for Granny and Grandpa, for us to come and see them up there—where you just have room to breathe and run."

Every day Diana called to inquire about how many fish they had caught and game birds they'd bagged, and they, in turn, listened intently as she gushed about her unfolding romance with the attentive new man in her life. Occasionally, she even asked them to put their father on the line, and those conversations were—it still seemed almost impossible for William and Harry to believe—full of laughter and affection. Diana had even come to accept Tiggy, who, while no longer on the payroll, still spent time with William and Harry. "She is devoted to the children, and they are devoted to her," Diana said to her friend Lady Elsa Bowker. "Because she gives them happiness, I now accept her." As Lady Bowker reflected later, "When you are happy, you can forgive a great deal."

Diana had every reason to be happy. Dodi showered her with expensive gifts as well as attention—a gold Cartier Panthère watch, a diamond bracelet, a Bulgari ring—and she picked up the phone to tell her sons about every one. She knew he intended to give her a $40,000 diamond ring purchased from Monaco's Repossi jewelers, but insisted that, regardless of Dodi's intentions, it was going squarely "on the finger of my right hand. The last thing I need is a new marriage. I need it like a bad rash on my face." Yet she was undeniably smitten with her Egyptian lover. When her friend Rosa Monckton asked her over the phone, "Just tell me: Is it bliss?" Diana replied: "Yes, bliss. Bye-bye."

Marriage or no marriage, Diana was hatching a plan to make a major change in William's and Harry's lives—one that would, at least in Harry's case, turn out to be astoundingly prophetic. One evening at Kensington Palace, the princess excitedly summoned Paul Burrell to her sitting room. Closing the doors behind her, she dropped to her knees and spread out on the floor a map of Southern California along with house plans. Dodi, it seemed, had quietly shelled out $7.4 million for a nine-thousand-square-foot Tuscan villa on five beachfront acres in Malibu that for decades had been the home of actress Julie Andrews and her husband, *The Pink Panther* director Blake Edwards.

Realizing that William's and Harry's status as second and third in line to the throne meant that their principal residence had to be in England, Diana intended for the princes to divide their time between London and California. "This is our new life," she told Burrell. "Just won't it be great? Think of the lifestyle for the boys!" It was a way for William and Harry to escape Britain's unslakable tabloids, not to mention the stultifying influence of the omnipresent Buckingham Palace apparatchiks. "Nobody's judgmental in America," Diana said. "You don't have the class system, you don't have the establishment."

There was bound to be pushback, but Diana believed that ultimately the Queen would permit William and Harry to spend at least part of each year with her in Malibu. "Why couldn't they come and spend a portion of their time in America?" asked Burrell, who worked for the Queen before he worked for Diana. "That would be very stiff and staunchy if the queen would say, 'No, they can't go.'"

"Stiff and staunchy" were the very words that defined the monarchy, however—and no one understood this better than the Princess of Wales. "Diana knew she had her work cut out for her, but she was determined to make the change," said her acupuncturist, therapist, and friend Oonagh Toffolo. Lady Bowker agreed. "She felt she had to escape with William and Harry," she said, "or they would all just be buried alive. She didn't want her sons going through the pressures and the heartache that she went through. There was no love in the royal family, no heart. She didn't want William and Harry to grow up to be unfeeling automatons like the rest of them."

At around ten on the evening of August 31, 1997, William and Harry headed toward the Queen's Drawing Room to say good night to their grandparents. It was impressed upon the boys throughout their lives that the Queen was more than a woman and even more than a figurehead—she was the embodiment of the nation; an iconic and utterly unique historical figure who commanded the respect and even affection of generals, popes, heads of state, cabbies, sheep farmers, and garden club ladies alike. Even with her ubiquitous purse dangling from her left arm, she could be, and often was, intimidating—keenly intelligent, curious, questioning, and aware that, whatever room she was in, she outranked everyone in it.

Yet, as they entered this serene, tartan-splashed, memento-crammed inner sanctum within an inner sanctum, the white-haired, cardigan-clad woman they saw sitting in a slipcovered armchair beside the fireplace was—in this space and at this time—simply Granny. Prince Philip sat in a chair opposite the Queen, and the two brightened when their grandsons materialized in the doorway. Both Queen and consort were, surprisingly, night owls—especially Her Majesty, who never went to bed before midnight. That presented problems for others, since one hard and fast rule was that no one retires for the night before the sovereign. "Nobody felt it was right to go to bed before the Queen did," said her former private secretary Sir William Heseltine. Diana, an early riser, struggled to stay up with her mother-in-law, but often gave up and excused herself.

Fortunately for young William and Harry, they were exempt from this particular rule. They would be allowed to go off to their rooms, but not before telling Granny how the day had gone, where they'd been, and what they'd done on Balmoral's fifty thousand acres of forests, mountains, valleys, pastures, and lochs. They knew already that she had spent her day riding across the moors, then taking the wheel of a Land Rover and driving at breakneck speed along the narrow dirt roads that snake through the estate. There had been the usual midday picnic lunch, with Prince Philip grilling up sausages and the Queen clearing the dirty dishes and then pulling on a pair of rubber gloves to wash the plates in a portable basin. Everywhere, at all times, there were dogs—corgis, dorgis (a dachshund-corgi crossbreed), cocker spaniels, and a wide variety of hunting dogs, including Labradors, pointers, setters, and retrievers.

Before they left, the Queen asked one final question: "Did you speak to your mother today? Is she still in Paris?"

"Yes," William answered, remembering their brief phone chat that afternoon when both he and Harry cut the call short so that they could play with their cousins. "But she's coming home tomorrow, and we can't wait to see her!"

"Lovely," the Queen answered.

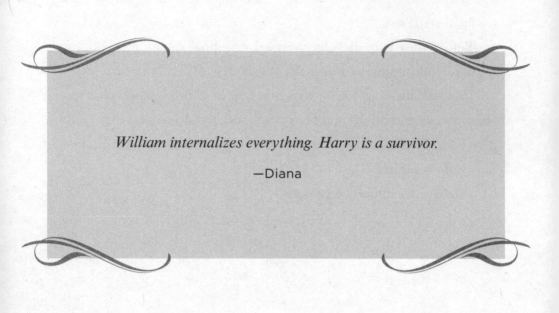

William internalizes everything. Harry is a survivor.

—Diana

THREE

"THE DISTINCT POSSIBILITY THEY MIGHT KILL EACH OTHER"

Highgrove House
Eight Years Later, January 13, 2005

H ARRY LOOKED DOWN at the tabloids spread out on the table for him—a head-spinning swirl of headlines, each more damning than the last. "Harry the Nazi," screamed the *Sun* alongside a full-page photo of the prince with a drink in one hand, a cigarette in the other—and a large swastika band on his left arm. "Come Out and Say Sorry: Worldwide Clamor for Harry to Make Full Apology for Nazi Outrage," chimed in the *Daily Mail*. Even the normally staid *Times* of London decried "Prince Harry's Sorry Mess." "I don't understand," said Harry, who was not at all reluctant to have his photo taken at a costume party at the South Gloucestershire home of three-time Olympic gold medal–winning equestrian Richard Meade. The theme for the evening, in keeping with the notoriously tin ear of Britain's upper classes, was "colonials and natives." Was it "that bad to wear a German uniform?" Harry kept asking. He wanted to know if placing the infamous red-white-and-black swastika armband on the sleeve of his khaki shirt was really "that terrible?"

Oh, yes—particularly coming just days before ceremonies marking the sixty years since the liberation of the Auschwitz Nazi death camp in Poland. Reaction to the princely gaffe was immediate, unanimous, and scorching. "Does This Offend You?" asked the headline in the *Independent*, directly below a close-up of Harry's Nazi armband. Holocaust survivors and their families, the Israeli foreign minister, numerous World War II veterans' organizations—not to mention several members of Parliament—excoriated the Spare.

"Appalling!" declared Lord Michael Levy, Britain's envoy to the Middle East. Harry had "let the country down" and "sent shock waves through the international community. It shows the prince is clueless about the reality of what happened in the Holocaust." A Hitler biographer, Sir Ian Kershaw, condemned Harry for his "grotesquely bad taste," while the Simon Wiesenthal Center's Rabbi Marvin Hier declared the young prince had committed nothing less than a "shameful act." Longtime Buckingham Palace spokesperson Dickie Arbiter was also in a froth. "Once again Prince Charles has been let down by his wayward son," Arbiter said. "It can't go on."

A week earlier, William and Harry had bid farewell to the Queen and the rest of the royal family after celebrating the Christmas holidays at Sandringham. Charles and Camilla, who were about to announce their engagement, dashed off to Balmoral to spend some time alone. Now Harry, who since Diana's death had garnered a reputation as the Windsors' loosest cannon, was once again picking up the phone to call his father and apologize. The Prince of Wales, however, was not in a forgiving mood. "Shouting at the top of his lungs," as one royal protection officer put it, Charles repeatedly demanded to know how he could have done "such a stupid thing." Prince Charles, he went on, was "apoplectic, and by the time he was finished, poor Prince Harry was shaking."

It was a far cry from Harry's previous major scandal just four years earlier, when Charles took a more measured, fatherly approach to his second son's misbehavior. At that time, in mid-July 2001, staff members at Highgrove detected the distinct odor of marijuana following one of the parties Harry often threw when his father and his brother were away. In addition, Charles was informed that Harry had been smoking pot with his friends in a toolshed behind the Rattlebone Inn, a four-hundred-year-old pub just four miles up the road from Highgrove. Worried that Harry was about to follow in the cocaine-dusted footsteps of at least a dozen members of William's inner circle—including Camilla's son, Tom Parker Bowles, and her niece Emma Parker Bowles, and the princes' cousins Nicholas Knatchbull and Lord Frederick Windsor—Charles quietly arranged for Harry to spend a day talking to recovering addicts at the Featherstone Lodge Rehabilitation Centre in South London. Featherstone staffer Wilma Graham said Harry was "quite shocked that you can be using 'soft' drugs and suddenly you're moving toward hard drugs. I think it was quite an eye-opener for Harry."

Somehow, both Harry's pot consumption and the visit to Featherstone were kept under wraps for months—until newspapers got wind of the story in January 2002. "Prince Harry: I Took Drugs," blared the *Daily Mail*, while the *News of the World* trumpeted, "Harry's Drug Shame." The Queen decided it was best to simply own up to what had happened. St. James's Palace issued a statement confirming that Harry had "experimented with the drug on several occasions," but emphasizing that his use of marijuana was "not regular."

In the end, even the most hard-boiled tabloid editors were reluctant to come down too hard on the young prince. The *Sun* cautioned in an editorial that Britons "should be wary of pouring too much vitriol on poor Harry's head," adding that his marijuana use was "an all-too-common rite of passage being lived out in public."

No one seemed particularly rattled at the Rattlebone Inn, where owners hung up over the bar a doctored Harry Potter poster depicting Prince Harry smoking a joint beneath the title "The Rattlebone Inn Presents Harry Pothead and the Philosopher's Stone." The owners' attempt at humor belied the fact that William had spent many hours drinking and carousing at the Rattlebone as well. On one occasion, he ducked into an alleyway behind the pub when local police raided it looking for illegal after-hours drinkers. Harry, who was only fifteen when he first accompanied Will to the pub, often had to be kept in check by his brother. When Harry called the Rattlebone's French-born bar manager Pierre Ortet a "fucking frog," it was William who brought his brother back inside to apologize. "Remember what happened to royalty in France," he told Harry—making a slitting motion across his throat.

On his own, however, Harry reverted to his old, unacceptable ways. "Sometimes Harry would get drunk and say, 'Hey, Froggie, get me a pint,' and 'Come here, Froggie,'" Ortet said. "When he was drinking in the pub, some of our regulars would call him a little brat under their breaths."

Later, when once again William wasn't there to restrain him, Harry—who was still two years under Britain's legal drinking age of eighteen—knocked back several pints of Stella Artois beer before deciding it would be fun to stage a mock barfight with his friends. As part of the act, Harry, whose ever-present protection officers were under strict orders to essentially look the other way, scuffled with his pals while shouting obscenities at the top of his lungs. Within minutes, the prince was unceremoniously tossed into the street with the others.

Not that it mattered. Highgrove itself provided a refuge for the boys in the wake of their mother's death; after Diana's apartments in Kensington Palace were shuttered, the country manse in Gloucestershire was the last place that held memories of what daily life with the late princess was like. Understanding how much this connection meant to his sons, Charles made sure that framed photographs of Diana were scattered throughout the house. At Camilla's insistence, he also made a concerted effort to transform Highgrove into an appealing refuge for two teenage boys. Toward that end, the basement became "Club H," complete with dance floor, jukebox, video games, a state-of-the-art in-wall stereo system, and a fully stocked bar.

Harry made full use of Club H, often approaching one of the young ladies attending the nearby Westonbirt School with a line that few were entitled to deliver: "Would you like to come back to my palace for a drink?"

In the wake of Harry's visit to Featherstone, Charles was widely commended for the way he handled the situation. Tony Blair, whose own son Euan had been arrested for being "drunk and incapable" in London's Leicester Square when he was sixteen, praised the Prince of Wales for "handling this absolutely right—in a very responsible . . . and sensitive way for their child." The situation was difficult, said the prime minister, adding, "I know this myself."

What everyone failed to mention was that twelve days after his "eye-opening" experience at Featherstone, Harry was partying hard in Marbella on Spain's Costa del Sol—downing shots until he passed out on a couch. "The Sponge," as Harry was now called, then picked up where he left off at clubs in London—where he was photographed stumbling out into the night red faced and wasted—and at bars around Highgrove. Harry "would never come in and have one drink," recalled Nick Hooper, a bartender at another of the prince's favorite local hangouts, the Vine Tree. "With him it was binge, binge, binge." At one point, a typically inebriated Harry staggered outside with his friends to get sick in the street, then came back into the Vine Tree, Hooper said, "smeared with vomit."

Pub owners and shopkeepers admitted, however, that, by and large, William and Harry were polite, cordial, and extremely well mannered. Equally important, they always made certain before they exited that they had left enough money to pay the bill, along with a hefty tip. This was not the common practice among members of the British aristocracy, who seldom carried cash and were confident that somebody else would settle the check.

One incident following Harry's visit to Featherstone underscored the sometimes tense relationship between the two young men whose brotherly bond was, as far as the world knew, unbreakable. When Harry downed two bottles of Moët & Chandon champagne at the Beaufort Christmas Ball that year and ambushed twenty-three-year-old model Suzannah Harvey with a deep kiss, William became incensed. "Harry was feeling my bum right in front of the other guests," said Harvey, who said he then pulled her outside. "I almost forgot he was seventeen—he handled me like a grown man. He grabbed me by the waist, he kissed and nuzzled my neck. It was so hot, steam was rising from us into the freezing cold air."

All the while, William tried in vain to get his brother to back off and not cause another drunken scene. "William was glaring at Harry," remembered Harvey, who said the Heir took to the dance floor and then tried to break them up by dancing between them. "It was all quite unnerving. Everywhere I turned, there was William. He had an odd expression on his face. He didn't look happy. It was bizarre."

Several times that evening, William did manage to pull Harry aside, but the younger prince was having none of it. Out of desperation, one of William's older friends intervened—only to have Harry bluntly tell him to shut up. When Harry finally did get Harvey alone, she told him that it wouldn't do to cause a scandal and that they should rejoin the party. She was also concerned that Harry's bodyguards would soon come looking for him. "They don't bother about me," Harry told her. "I'm not the important one. William is."

William had, in fact, already generated more than his share of unflattering press. Like Harry, he had been photographed in the early-morning hours exiting trendy clubs such as Foxtrot Oscar, K Bar, Mimo, and China White in less than pristine condition. Both boys drank too much and smoked too many Marlboro Lights—a vice Diana would never have tolerated, but one that nonsmoker Charles could scarcely object to, given his willingness to overlook Camilla's two-pack-a-day habit.

Harry would later look back and realize that his misbehavior was all symptomatic of one thing: grief. After his mother's death, he observed, "I shut down all of my emotions for the next twenty years. My solution was to stick my head in the sand, refusing to ever think about my mum, because why would that help? It's not going to bring her back." His solution, then, was "just don't have emotions about anything."

THE SEEDS OF WHAT would become a lifelong depression were sown early by relatives who were determined to maintain the proverbial British stiff upper lip. It had been only sixteen days after Diana's death when both sides of the family got together at Highgrove to celebrate Harry's thirteenth birthday. Diana's sister, Lady Sarah McCorquodale, presented Harry with what would turn out to be his most treasured gift that day—the Sony PlayStation Diana had purchased on the eve of her fatal accident. "Happy Birthday, Harry," read the card. It was signed, "Love, Mummy."

That night, Harry cried on the shoulder of the one person who could provide the sort of maternal affection he craved. Tiggy Legge-Bourke had been invited to spend that fateful August with the royal family at Balmoral—a detail Charles had not shared with Diana—and stayed on to comfort William and Harry. Diana's suspicions aside, even the princess's closest friends felt she would have been thankful for Tiggy's role in comforting her anguished sons.

His famously easygoing, boisterous nature notwithstanding, Harry was especially fragile. A chronic thumb sucker until the age of eleven, he had always been the needier of the two boys. "William has always been the strong one—always," a friend noted, adding that Diana "smothered Harry in love." In the weeks after his mother's death, when Harry would suddenly begin sobbing at bedtime, it was Tiggy who held him in her arms and rocked him gently to sleep.

It also helped that Tiggy was an irrepressible tomboy. Following their mother's funeral, Charles brought William and Harry to Highgrove for the sole purpose of exhausting them physically so that they, in the Prince of Wales's words, would have "no time or energy to dwell on things." He was right about one thing: neither boy wanted to talk about the terrible tragedy that had happened. "All William and Harry wanted to do," Papa said, "was kick a soccer ball."

Preparing for his third year at Eton, William had confided in Tiggy that he was "very worried about Harry." Charles had decided that his younger son, who was struggling with his studies at Ludgrove, should be held back an additional year before joining his brother at Eton. William believed this was not the time for the two brothers to be separated, and he told Tiggy and his father that he doubted Harry was emotionally resilient enough to return to Ludgrove alone. "I don't want to go away from him now," William said. "He needs me."

Tiggy reassured William that Harry would continue to be well looked after by the school's headmaster and his wife, and that the Spare, who, as a gifted athlete had no difficulty making friends, was one of Ludgrove's most popular students. Harry was also told he could call William anytime he wished—and vice versa. "The return to routine will be good for them," Charles insisted. "They need to see that life goes on."

Perhaps, but there were times when Harry suddenly became quiet—"lost in thought and sad looking," a fellow student remembered. Prince Harry would say later that he did his best "to act as if everything was fine and normal, because that's the way everyone else around me behaved. But everything wasn't okay. I certainly wasn't okay."

In contrast, William seemed to be adjusting well—so well that teachers and friends were concerned. "You had to put on a brave face and act as if nothing had happened," he said later. "No one was telling us at the time that it was okay for us to grieve." William added that the message he was receiving from Charles and others around him was "very much 'Let's get on with it.' So that's what I did."

Not everyone agreed with the "keep calm and carry on" approach. While the princes' Spencer relatives and Diana's friends were gradually being eased out of the picture, several still spoke out on behalf of getting William and Harry professional grief counseling. "There is no question that both boys need to see a therapist—none whatsoever," Diana's friend Oonagh Toffolo said. "It is simply unconscionable to imagine that they are expected to deal with such a horrible upheaval on their own. I can see it in their eyes; they are children, and they need help."

Palace operatives—specifically, the anonymous, string-pulling Men in Gray who actually ran things behind the scenes—did not agree. At one point shortly after Diana's funeral, the same Prince Charles who had steadfastly resisted hiring a therapist for William and Harry during the nasty breakup of their parents' marriage now approached the Queen about seeking grief counseling for his sons. "The Queen initially agreed that it was a good idea," a St. James's Palace staffer said, "but was talked out of it." There was concern among some of Her Majesty's advisors that it "would simply not look good at the moment" for members of the royal family "to be seen to have mental health issues."

Complicating the matter of whether or not to seek treatment for William and Harry was their mother's decision to go public with her twin battles against bulimia and suicidal depression. Diana had, after all, skillfully weaponized her own psychological problems, publicly accusing Charles of treating her as if she were "a problem, a cracked vessel." In royal circles, according to the Queen's cousin Margaret Rhodes, "all the talk of mental health and therapy may have left a bad taste in some people's mouths." Agreed the *Times* of London's Alan Hamilton: "They're not a very introspective lot. They're not especially sympathetic, either. They think admitting that you have problems is a sign of weakness, and this was not a time for the monarchy to appear weak." (It was no small irony that for a fifteen-year period starting in the late 1970s, Charles was treated first by Jungian psychotherapist Ingaret van der Post and then by Dr. Alan McGlashan—a fact that would not become fully known until 2018.)

Confident that William was handling the situation, Charles turned his attention to Harry. While the Heir remained at Eton, Charles took advantage of Harry's half-term break at Ludgrove to invite him along on his long-planned official tour of South Africa. The Prince of Wales, eager to show the world that he was stepping in to at least try to fill part of the void left by Diana, nonetheless brought Tiggy along to make sure Harry was occupied whenever Papa had to step away for official business.

By the time the tour was over, Harry had gone on safari in Botswana, figured out the intricacies of a Zulu handshake, and managed not to giggle when he and his father were greeted at the gates of remote Duku by bare-breasted tribal women. Perhaps the high point of the trip was attending a Spice Girls concert in Johannesburg, then going backstage to be greeted by each member of the group with a kiss. "My brother will be very jealous," Harry said, "when he sees this."

PHOTOS OF HARRY GRINNING from ear to ear alongside his father as they traveled abroad went a long way toward reassuring a wary public that the tousle-haired thirteen-year-old was "going to be okay," said veteran royal correspondent Peter Archer of the *Press Association* news agency. "Everyone already knew that William had tremendous poise and could handle the press like a pro. But it was the first time people got a good look at Harry's star power. He was charming, relaxed, unaffected—a natural at connecting with people, like his mother."

Fleet Street, aware that a sizable chunk of the British public blamed reporters for hounding Diana to her death, had already agreed to give William and Harry some space until they turned eighteen. In exchange, the Palace agreed to arrange the occasional photo op. But Charles was not above using his telegenic sons as pawns in the game to boost his own approval ratings. In their first international outing as a Diana-less family, all three Windsor men invaded Vancouver in March 1998. William, in particular, was initially rattled by the pure pandemonium that broke out wherever they went. Harry, on the other hand, delighted in the madness. When thousands of schoolgirls screamed and wept at the mere sight of his heartthrob brother, Harry could scarcely contain himself. "It's so funny, isn't it, the way they keep chanting, 'William, William, William'?" he asked his father. "Just ridiculous."

Taking his cue from Diana, the Heir reached out into the crowd to accept flowers, shake hands, and—this was an important part of the job, his mother always said—look directly into people's eyes. Soon he was playing to the crowd, waving and smiling and, when presented with jackets worn by Canada's Olympic team, striking a pose. Harry, meanwhile, seemed equally comfortable cast as the adorably impish little brother.

The Heir and the Spare were rewarded for their efforts with four uninterrupted days of skiing at British Columbia's Whistler Mountain Resort. Here is where Harry, content to play second fiddle during official engagements, liked to upstage his brother. "Hey, dudes, who's the best skier?" one reporter called out from the sidelines. "I hear it's Harry!" William stopped in his tracks. "I don't know about that!" he shot back, and the two raced off downhill. Not for long, though, as both of them lost control and tumbled face-first into a snowbank.

Tiggy was never far away and continued to play the role of big sister until the preternaturally territorial Camilla gradually edged her out of the picture. Charles's mistress, who alternately referred to the generously proportioned Legge-Bourke as "Big Ass" and "the Help," delivered the coup de grace in the summer of 1998, when photos were published of the princes rappeling down the face of a dam in Wales without safety equipment. Tiggy, Camilla hastened to point out to Charles, was in charge at the time and clearly visible cheering them on in the photos.

Legge-Bourke was no longer the "surrogate mother" Diana once railed against, courtesy of Mrs. Parker Bowles. But Tiggy continued to be a presence in the princes' lives. "We speak all the time—constantly," she said years later. "You know, the way people who care deeply for each other do."

At Tiggy's wedding to former army officer Charles Pettifer in late 1999, Harry allegedly entertained guests by reaching into a fish tank, pulling out a goldfish, and swallowing it. Twenty months later, he visited the Pettifers and their infant son, Freddie—Prince Harry's godson—at their home in South London. "Finding that he was no longer Tiggy's number one little boy may have affected him deeply," observed author Penny Junor, who lived not far from Highgrove. There was "no doubt," Junor went on, that Harry "missed a mother figure in his life."

Tragically, it would be years before William and Harry would start to grapple seriously with the impact that Diana's sudden and senseless death had on their lives—and the lives of those around them. In the interim, they would be buffeted by a series of conflicts, controversies, and outright scandals. William took it upon himself to defuse an old one on June 12, 1998—just nine days before his sixteenth birthday—when he popped into York House at the last minute on his way to the movies and introduced himself to Camilla for the first time.

Proving himself to be a master at the art of "getting on with it," William preferred to treat Mrs. Parker Bowles as the woman who made his father happy, rather than the woman who destroyed his parents' marriage. After Charles excused himself so that they could get to know each other, William broke the ice by talking to Camilla about their shared love of foxhunting and polo—time-honored country pursuits that nonetheless had gotten them both into hot water with animal rights groups—as well as how excited he was that Harry would soon be joining him at Eton. Camilla, having now overcome one of the major hurdles to her acceptance as the wife of a future king, told Charles his elder son was "lovely," but allowed that the encounter had left her a "nervous wreck." Her hands trembling, Camilla turned to Charles and asked him to ring for the butler. "Darling," she said, "I *really* need a vodka and tonic."

Several weeks later, Charles arranged for a similar meeting between Harry and Camilla, this time at Balmoral. Harry, who had already been briefed by William about Camilla's throaty laugh, smoker's cough, and casual nature, was no less intent on seeing that the woman his father loved felt at ease. "I like her too," Harry reported to William. "But she's nothing at all like Mummy."

It was precisely because the two women had so little in common—aside from the Prince of Wales—that Camilla seemed such a benign presence as far as the boys were concerned. As drab and earthy as Diana

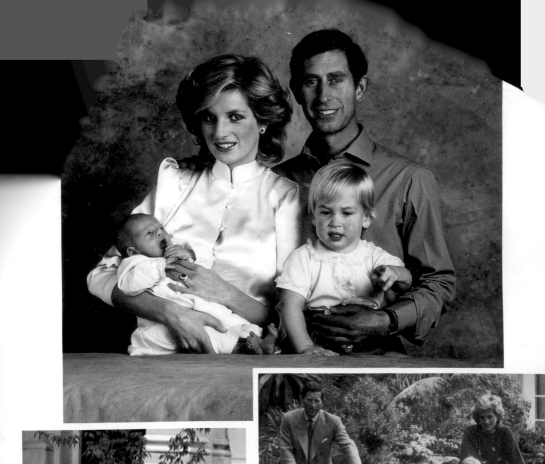

The royal marriage had already been in turmoil for years, but the public was completely unaware of it when the Prince and Princess of Wales posed for Lord Snowdon with their two sons shortly after Harry's birth in 1984. Three years later, Harry arrives for his first day of nursery school and extends his hand—only to have the teacher reach over his head to greet Prince Charles and William. The Waleses struck a happy family pose on bikes during a vacation on England's Scilly Isles in 1989.

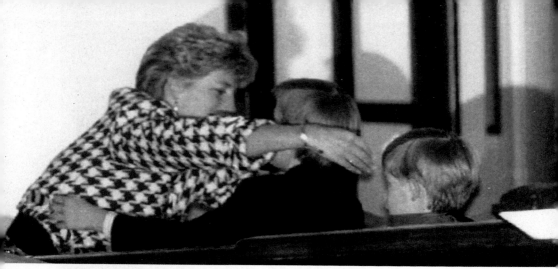

Diana greets William and Harry when they join their parents in Toronto aboard the royal yacht *Britannia* during a royal tour of Canada in 1991. "She would just engulf you and squeeze you as tight as possible," Harry said. "I can still feel the hugs that she used to give us, and I miss that." Diana got soaked with her sons on an amusement park flume ride in 1993, and Harry took the plunge while William waited his turn during their 1994 holiday on the Spanish island of Mallorca.

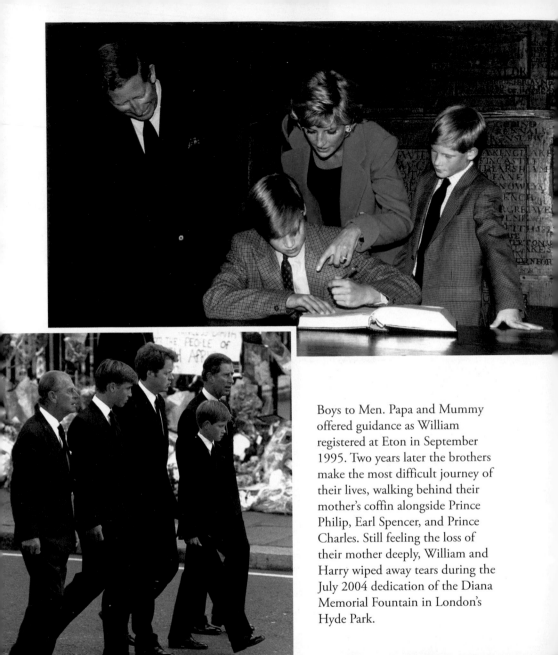

Boys to Men. Papa and Mummy offered guidance as William registered at Eton in September 1995. Two years later the brothers make the most difficult journey of their lives, walking behind their mother's coffin alongside Prince Philip, Earl Spencer, and Prince Charles. Still feeling the loss of their mother deeply, William and Harry wiped away tears during the July 2004 dedication of the Diana Memorial Fountain in London's Hyde Park.

Even though his brother helped him pick it out, Harry was widely condemned for wearing a Nazi uniform complete with swastika armband to a costume party in January 2005.

Three months later, it was the brothers' turn to keep Papa out of trouble when Charles began bad-mouthing reporters over a hot mike during his annual ski trip to Klosters, Switzerland.

Harry, William, the Queen, and Prince Philip were right behind the happy couple as newlyweds Charles and Camilla left St. George's Chapel on April 9, 2005.

Harry having a little fun in Lesotho, where in April 2006 he launched Sentebale, his new charity to benefit children orphaned by AIDS. The Queen demonstrated her playful side in 2006, when she stopped to trade glances with graduating cadet Harry Wales at Sandhurst, and again later that same year when Prince William graduated from the royal military academy.

Even as he prepared to embark on a military career, Harry caroused at London clubs like Boujis, where in March 2007 the inebriated prince stumbled while leaving in the early morning hours. Later that year, he was secretly deployed to Afghanistan, where he called in air strikes against the Taliban. Then-girlfriend Chelsy Davy was on hand when, in 2010, Harry earned his wings to fly Apache attack helicopters.

During their five-day visit to Africa in June 2010—their first official joint royal tour—William and Harry were introduced to a fifteen-foot-long python before showing off their soccer skills.

First up as best man, Harry wore the black uniform of a captain in the Blues and Royals regiment while the groom dressed in the scarlet uniform of a colonel in the Irish Guards during William's wedding to Kate Middleton at Westminster Abbey on April 29, 2011. Harry brought tears to everyone's eyes when, as part of his best man's toast, he told his brother, "Our mother would be so proud of you."

Immediately after his wedding, William returned to his job as an RAF search and rescue pilot in Wales.

On the Buckingham Palace balcony during Trooping the Color ceremonies in 2014, aviator Harry discussed the aircraft passing overhead with his navy-veteran grandfather, Prince Philip.

During the launch of his Invictus Games for wounded warriors later that year, Harry joined in a game of sitting volleyball.

"This beautiful woman just sort of tripped and fell into my life—I fell into her life," said Harry when he and Meghan Markle announced their engagement in November 2017.

Even before their marriage, Meghan was being hailed as one of British royalty's "Fab Four"—here launching their mental health initiative in February 2018.

Mother of the bride Doria Ragland arrived with Meghan at Windsor Castle, but it was Prince Charles who would step in for the bride's absent father and walk her down the aisle. As evidenced by the official wedding photograph, the Duke and Duchess of Sussex would change the look and the substance of Britain's Royal Family forever.

The Queen was delighted with her new granddaughter-in-law on their first official outing together in June 2018. Meghan continued to charm members of the Firm the following month, when senior royals appeared on the Buckingham Palace balcony to join in celebrating the RAF's centennial.

During their October 2018 tour of the South Pacific, Meghan was moved when an Australian schoolboy threw his arms around her. The hugely successful tour stirred up rivalries inside the Palace, and marked a turning point for the Sussexes.

Only hours before attending an event at London's Royal Albert Hall, a desperately unhappy Meghan told Harry she was contemplating suicide. They went anyway, and clenched hands so tightly, said Meghan "you can see the whites of our knuckles." At Commonwealth Day observances in March 2019, protocol dictates that Kate, as wife of the Heir, comes first. Two months later the proud parents show off newborn son Archie, while behind the scenes trouble is brewing.

This time during the Royal Family's annual Trooping the Color balcony outing, the Cambridges—including George, Charlotte, and Louis—are front and center while Harry and Meghan are pushed to the rear.

The brothers battle ferociously on the polo field during a charity match in July 2019.

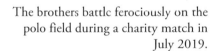

The Sussexes reclaimed the spotlight when they took Archie along on their ten-day royal tour of South Africa that September.

The final straw. Harry and Meghan were included in photos displayed on her desk during the Queen's 2018 Christmas Address (top). The following year, with Megxit underway, the Sussexes have been erased from the family display. In March 2020, the Cambridges chat with Prince Edward and his wife, Sophie, while Harry and Meghan—ignored since throwing the family in turmoil—fume.

In September 2020, the Cambridges helped out in the kitchen at East London's Beigel Bake Brick Land Bakery, one of the local businesses hit hard by the coronavirus pandemic.

While the Sussexes spent the holidays in California, William, Kate, George, Charlotte, and Louis posed for their 2020 Christmas card surrounded by firewood and bales of hay on the grounds of Anmer Hall.

The feuding brothers were intentionally separated by their cousin Peter Phillips as they walked behind Prince Philip's coffin at Windsor in April 2021.

had been dazzlingly chic, Camilla was most content riding to the hounds or digging in the gardens at Highgrove and Ray Mill House, her own home just twenty-five minutes from Highgrove. The fact that William and Harry had been maneuvered into accepting her presence in their lives did not sit well with Diana's friends, one of whom told journalist Richard Kay that the meeting was "astonishingly insensitive." The princess had clearly come to accept that the love between Charles and Camilla was genuine, but, suggested Elsa Bowker, that hardly meant that she wanted Camilla to be a "stepmother figure to her boys. Not at all."

Yet Charles pressed on with a campaign to sell the once detested homewrecker to the British public—a secret campaign masterminded by public relations wizard Mark Bolland and known inside the walls of St. James's Palace as Operation PB (Operation Parker Bowles). The head-to-toe makeover of Charles's mistress involved the deployment of a small army of hairdressers, plastic surgeons, dentists, cosmetologists, fitness experts, and fashion designers—all to be followed by a full-on media blitz. "They had to repackage Camilla," said Harold Brooks-Baker, former *Debrett's Peerage & Baronetage* owner and longtime publishing director of *Burke's Peerage*, the almost two-hundred-year-old genealogy guide, "if they had any hope of selling her as Charles's wife, much less as the next queen. The boys were always part of the deal."

Charles sought to soften his own image as well. Diana's devotion to William and Harry was undisputed, and, for years, Charles had battled efforts to portray him as a cold and distant dad. In the summer of 1998, the Prince of Wales took his sons on an Aegean cruise aboard the *Alexander*, the same luxury yacht on which he had embarked on an ill-fated "second honeymoon" with Diana seven years earlier. But first, since Harry and Charles would be flying to Athens

in one plane and William in another—as a safety precaution, the first and second in line to the throne were mandated to travel separately—the Prince of Wales invited the press to be there to snap photos when he strolled out onto the tarmac at Heathrow and kissed his towering elder son good-bye.

Displays of filial intimacy between Charles and William were comparatively few and far between. The opposite was true when it came to the more openly affectionate Harry, who had no qualms about hugging his father or holding his hand. A favorite Harry pastime: covering Papa's face with kisses until the Prince of Wales playfully waved him off.

Perhaps most significantly, the intense bonds the boys had formed with each other and with their father were being reinforced without the civilizing influence of their mother at Highgrove, Sandringham, and Balmoral. At these and other royal venues, the princes were "pushed into the traditional 'maleness' of the royal family—the foxhunts, the shooting parties, and the polo," Richard Greene said, "and away from the emotional, raw, open, honest side of their psyches that Diana was reinforcing."

That September of 1998, when Harry joined William at Eton, the brothers were arguably closer than they had ever been—or perhaps would ever be. Charles, once again looking over his younger son's shoulder as he registered for classes, wryly cautioned him to "be sure and sign in the right place." Harry shook his head in mock exasperation and shot back, "Oh, shut up!"

With William there to help, Harry made what appeared to be a seamless transition to life among the F-Tits. Yet despite the fact that $1.5 million was spent each year to protect them during their time at Eton, the princes couldn't be protected from themselves. Each was so

determined to outdo the other as an athlete that, in the first sixty days of the term, they both wound up in the hospital with multiple injuries: numerous small fractures and sprains, in Harry's case; and for William, a badly broken arm. As the father of "two rapidly growing offspring who continuously injure themselves," Charles thanked the local doctors for "taking care of these sort of things."

The game of polo, which the brothers now pursued in earnest, presented special challenges for William. The Heir's injuries seemed inevitable, since he was one of those rare players who was left-handed; for safety considerations, the rules of the game stipulate that players "meet" right hand to right hand, so, in order to compete, William spent months training himself to essentially *become* right-handed.

If the brothers seemed a little too willing to take chances on the playing field, they learned from the master. The Prince of Wales had suffered countless injuries on the polo field, and on those occasions when the three men competed on opposing teams, there was always, said a member of the Beaufort Polo Club, "the distinct possibility they might kill each other. They are all ferocious competitors."

This was no less true when it came to foxhunting, a royal pastime that did not sit well with the vast majority of Britons who considered it to be, in a word, barbaric. Ever since he turned sixteen, William had been riding to the hounds at Sandringham, Balmoral, and the Beaufort Hunt Club near Highgrove. Harry was hot on his brother's heels, but when the jodhpur-clad Heir was photographed skimming over hedges not far behind a pack of barking hunting dogs, public reaction was swift. Charles and his sons, said animal rights activist John Cooper, were "engaging in the practice of setting a pack of hounds on a wild animal for fun—animal abuse in the name of tradition. . . . It is cruel and has no place in the twenty-first century."

Not that it mattered to the brothers—or the rest of the royal family. After William was denounced on the floor of Parliament for his "upper-class arrogance," both he and Harry simply shrugged off the criticism. "Those people," Charles reassured his children, "have no idea what they are talking about. Imagine trying to tell *us* what we can and cannot do."

THERE WERE MANY PHYSICAL close calls built into their lives as royals, but at least they served a purpose—and Charles and the Queen were determined to do all they could to distract the boys from the first anniversary of Diana's death. The Prince of Wales made certain that this time UK flags around the world were lowered to half-staff in honor of the princess, and, unlike the Sunday-morning service that was held on the very day of her death, this time congregants at Crathie Church mentioned Diana's name in their prayers. But beyond these brief nods to the late princess's memory, Charles and the Queen focused on keeping the boys occupied hunting, riding, fishing, and hiking with Granny and the rest of the royal family at Balmoral.

Before fleeing to the Scottish Highlands, William and Harry distracted themselves with a project of their own. For weeks, they planned a surprise fiftieth birthday party for the Prince of Wales at Highgrove, and to throw everyone off the scent set the date for July 31—more than three months before their father's actual November 14 birth date. Even though the *Sunday Mirror* let the cat out of the bag ten days early—prompting Charles to issue a statement scolding the media for upsetting his sons—William and Harry worked hand in glove to pull off the big event with the help of actors Stephen Fry, Rowan (Mr. Bean) Atkinson, and Oscar-winning actress and screenwriter Emma Thompson. To offset the cost of the affair, which included a spoof of Atkinson's British TV comedy series *Blackadder*, William and Harry charged each of the guests $40.

Months later, they showed up at yet another fiftieth birthday party hosted by Camilla, this one also held at Highgrove. Arriving late in battle fatigues, William explained to surprised guests that he was a member of Eton's combined cadet force and had rushed straight from field exercises. Given their lifelong affection for all things military, it came as no surprise that William and Harry excelled as cadets, although, as was the case in so many things in life, William was awarded the coveted Sword of Honor while Harry had to settle for runner-up.

Still, as William quickly changed into his tuxedo at their father's party, Harry could not resist poking fun at the Heir. "Yeah, 'field exercises'—a likely story," he joked. "My brother is always trying to upstage me. Just has to be the center of attention." Later, as the party stretched into the early-morning hours, the princes stole the show by performing an impromptu *Full Monty*–style striptease to Hot Chocolate's 1975 hit "You Sexy Thing"—ripping off their shirts and unbuckling their trousers before dissolving in hysterics.

It had been scarcely fifteen months since they were deprived of their mother's sound counsel, and already it looked as if the boys might easily get themselves in serious trouble—even under the watchful eye of the Boss. Shortly before Christmas 1998, William and Harry invited fourteen of their Eton pals to join them for dinner with the Queen at Windsor Castle. After drinks with Her Majesty and Prince Philip in the Green Drawing Room, everyone repaired to the cavernous private dining room for dinner and more alcohol—white wine with the Dover sole, red wine with the pheasant, followed by tawny port with the Stilton cheese. Once the Queen excused herself, they were free to raid the castle's unparalleled supply of top-shelf liquor.

After a midnight run down the grassy slopes of Castle Hill on silver serving trays purloined from the pantry, the hungover princes and their equally indisposed buddies awoke before dawn, grabbed their assigned shotguns, and went off rabbit hunting in Windsor Great Park. At one point, one of the guns went off accidentally, sending buckshot whizzing past William's ear. Once the royal protection officers on the scene were convinced it had all been a simple mishap and that no one had been injured, the bloodshot-eyed teens were allowed to pick up where they left off. "Remember, when we say 'Fire at will,'" Harry cracked to his chagrined friends, "we don't actually mean 'Fire at Will!'"

Such potentially deadly hijinks notwithstanding, Charles understood his sons' desire to take risks and experience new things away from clamoring crowds and whirring press cameras. After listening to William beg for months to have an African adventure of his own, Prince Charles enlisted the help of their former nanny Tiggy to plan a secret visit to the Moremi Game Reserve in northern Botswana's Okavango Delta. Desperate for a little solitude—"I want to be cut off from the outside world"—William insisted that the princes' security officers bring a single satellite phone.

"I fell in love with Africa on that first trip," said William, who along with Harry spied cheetahs, elephants, and wildebeests when they weren't paddling dugout canoes in search of hippos and crocodiles. "It was thrilling," he told an Eton chum later, "but also there was a feeling of peace I never experienced before—a sense that this is where I belonged."

That sense of peace was short lived. No sooner had William set foot back on English soil than Camilla's son, Tom—who had become one of the princes' closest, nightclub-hopping chums—admitted to using cocaine. To make matters worse, papers ran graphic photos from the night Tom attended a "Fetish Party" dressed as a whip-cracking dominatrix in fishnet stockings and stiletto heels. Not long after, another Parker Bowles—Camilla's niece Emma—admitted to having been treated for alcohol and drug dependency at a clinic in Arizona.

The Queen, upset that her family was being tainted by yet another Parker Bowles scandal, promptly reacted by banning Camilla from the June 19, 1999, wedding of Charles's youngest brother, Prince Edward, and Sophie Rhys-Jones. Tom and Emma would eventually work their way back into the young princes' lives, but not before the tabloids had another field day with William—this time revealing that he had invited three stunning young ladies—Davina Duckworth-Chad, Emilia d'Erlanger, and Mary Forestier-Walker—along on the Waleses' annual midsummer cruise aboard the *Alexander*. In the considerable wake of William's "Royal Love Boat" cruise, speculation concerning the Heir's love life reached a fever pitch when it was discovered that he and pop idol Britney Spears were planning a Valentine's Day summit. (Spears was one of William's favorite pinups; Harry preferred to decorate his room at Eton with posters of actress Halle Berry.)

Once the press got wind of it, the rendezvous with Britney never materialized. Nor did another planned assignation that began with what a friend called "sexy, very intimate" cyber correspondence—this one with model Lauren Bush, niece of US president George W. Bush and granddaughter of former president George Herbert Walker Bush.

As the new century approached, the Heir considered Highgrove as the site of his much-ballyhooed "Willennium" celebration but opted instead to ring in the year 2000 away from his royal relatives. Instead

William whooped it up with Eton friends at a tin-roofed village hall near Sandringham, getting, in his words, "very seriously, seriously drunk" in the process—so drunk, the prince later admitted, his hang-over lasted forty-eight hours.

Harry, meanwhile, was cutting loose at Broadlands, the Mount-battens' Palladian-style mansion in Hampshire where the Queen and Prince Philip spent their honeymoon in 1947. Lord Mountbatten of Burma was a towering figure in modern British history: among other things, a World War II naval hero, the last Viceroy of India, and mentor to both his nephew Prince Philip and his grand-nephew Prince Charles. In 1979, the Irish Republican Army blew up Lord Mountbatten's fish-ing boat, killing him and three others, including his fourteen-year-old grandson, Nicholas.

History was apparently not on the mind of Lord Mountbatten's great-grandson, the Spare's cousin Nicholas Knatchbull, when Nicholas reportedly passed what one onlooker called a "huge" joint to the young prince. Harry, according to Knatchbull's girlfriend Jessica Hay, took a puff and instantly turned crimson. "His reaction was kind of startling to all of us," she said. "He obviously wasn't ready for it."

William, meanwhile, had his own hands full coping with the kind of attention usually lavished on pop singers and movie stars; as he ap-proached his eighteenth birthday—the age of majority in Britain—the Heir found himself the subject of countless magazine covers and TV specials. "I've been given my marching orders—*again*," he complained to classmates as he posed for photos strolling through Eton's chapel cloisters, playing soccer and water polo, and showing off his modest cu-linary skills in the kitchen. These, along with William's evasive answers to a series of questions submitted in writing by the Press Association, were designed to appease newspaper editors who had abided by the hands-off rule but were now champing at the bit for the press ban to be lifted. "No one wanted to cause Prince William and Prince Harry any unnecessary pain after all they went through with their mother's death," one journalist observed. "We all know how they feel about the press, but they are public figures. We've waited long enough."

Harry still had at least two years to go before he turned eighteen, although he seriously doubted that withdrawing the moratorium would make much of a difference in his case. With each passing year, it became more and more clear to Harry that he would likely never emerge from his brother's looming shadow, such was the public appetite for all things William. When Harry was confirmed in the Anglican faith at Eton, the event was billed by Palace-watchers as his "rare day in the limelight." Instead, he was virtually ignored by photographers, who scrambled to get a shot of William. "You can see it in Harry's face," said one of the paparazzi. "He puts on a good show, always smiling. But every once in a while, you get a glimpse of him giving Will that look. He's got to be wondering, 'When will it be *my* turn?'"

Not that William was enjoying all the attention, or the seemingly never-ending insistence that he toe the Palace line. To assert himself, William led Harry in committing small acts of rebellion. In defiance of orders essentially banishing the disgraced Duchess of York, Sarah Ferguson, from the annual yuletide celebration at Sandringham, William and Harry boycotted the festivities. Then they paid their own separate Christmas Eve visit to Fergie and their cousins Beatrice and Eugenie, who had been exiled to a cottage in a remote corner of the estate. "Mummy loved her," he explained, choosing to overlook the rift in the women's relationship right before Diana's death. "She would have hated to see Aunt Sarah being treated in this way."

William risked offending not only his father and grandmother but also half the royal family when he decided not to show up at his own eighteenth birthday party at Windsor Castle—a multigenerational, once-in-a-lifetime event that used William's birth date to celebrate four more benchmarks occurring in 2000: Prince Andrew's fortieth birthday, Princess Anne's fiftieth, Princess Margaret's seventieth, and the Queen Mother's one hundredth. Charles, the Queen, and Prince Philip were all there, and even the Duchess of York was permitted to attend.

The stubborn birthday boy, however, was a glaringly obvious no-show. William's excuse: he was busy poring over his books at Eton, lost in preparation for the next morning's final exam in art history. The fact remained, however, that the party was a seven-minute stroll from his rooms at Eton, and everyone knew it—the argument Harry had used when he tried to convince his brother to at the very least make a brief appearance. William stood his ground "strictly to prove that he could," an Eton classmate said, leaving Harry to attend the birthday gala solo. "I'm going because it would hurt everyone's feelings," the Spare explained to one of his royal protection officers. "But he's the one they really want."

For all intents and purposes, it looked as if William joined Harry and all his Windsor relatives just ten days later in ignoring another invitation, this time for the dedication of the Diana, Princess of Wales Memorial Playground in Kensington Gardens. Located just steps from the palace, the playground was the first official London memorial in her honor. One of the organizers complained that "everyone involved was so saddened when no one from the royal family showed up." He went on to say that the princess "would have been shattered that her own boys didn't think it was important to be there."

In truth, no one had bothered to inform the princes about the dedication. "They were both furious when they found out—particularly William," a former deputy private secretary at St. James's Palace stated. "His father claimed to be in the dark about it as well," Harold Brooks-Baker said, "but that wasn't true. He wanted the focus off the princess and on Camilla once and for all. Every time the public was reminded about the love Diana had for her boys, Charles and Camilla both took a dive in the polls."

William did not press the issue with his father, but he did make it known to his St. James's Palace handlers that in the future he wanted to be informed about any similar invitations. "We cannot allow people to feel as if we're ignoring them," he said at a meeting that included Prince Charles and senior staff. "It's simply cruel, and it makes Harry and I both look like asses."

There were other ways that the older brother had decided to start asserting himself. Resisting pressure to either enroll at Cambridge University (Charles's alma mater) or follow in the footsteps of the male Spencers at Oxford, William vowed "not to do what everyone expects me to do." Rather, the Heir made it clear that he would "decide what's best for *me*."

Imbued by both his father and grandmother with a deep love of Scotland, William listened carefully when Her Majesty spoke of her desire to keep hers a truly United Kingdom. With Scottish nationalism on the rise, there now existed the real possibility that the country would assert its independence and break away. While neither William nor Harry had yet gone so far as to embrace Papa's fondness for kilts ("I find it a bit drafty," cracked the Heir), the concept of one day ruling over a kingdom that did not include Scotland struck William as, in his words to the sovereign, "unthinkable."

Since no one—not Prince Charles, Earl Spencer, or Buckingham

Palace—had actively lobbied for him to select a Scottish university, the notion of choosing one over an English school had a special appeal. It was also hard to think of a better way to send a message of unity than to have a future monarch earn his college degree in Scotland. With perhaps a little added prodding from his housemaster and mentor at Eton, Andrew Gailey, William decided on Gailey's alma mater, the University of St. Andrews—the oldest in Scotland, third-oldest in the English-speaking world (behind Oxford and Cambridge), and most famously, the birthplace of golf in the 1440s.

As soon as William announced his intention to enroll at St. Andrews—a chilly, fog-shrouded outpost jutting into the North Sea some seventy-five miles north of Edinburgh—applications shot up 44 percent over the previous year. The increase, as might easily have been expected, was accounted for almost entirely by women. Ironically, the one woman who would ultimately win William's heart was actively resisting pressure from her own socially ambitious mother to join the crowd—at least for now.

Prince Charles would have liked William to become a Cambridge man, but he put considerable stock in Gailey's opinion and believed that William might benefit from being educated away from London and somewhat outside Fleet Street's normal orbit. The Prince of Wales was also savvy enough to know that he stood to inherit a fractured kingdom if something wasn't done to tamp down Scottish nationalism. William was once again proving useful not only in promoting the monarchy but also in actually holding the country together. "Princess Diana understood how important it is to take the initiative and reach out to people," one member of the Scottish Parliament said, "and as gestures go, the impact in Scotland was impossible to overstate."

Before starting college, however, William would be testing his own mental and physical limits during the traditional gap year of self-exploration. He started off by secretly training with a unit of the Welsh Guards in the torrid Central American jungles of Belize. While there, he received his Eton final-exam grades via email from Prince Charles (an A in geography, a B in art history, a C in biology). William followed up his Belize experience by signing on with the Royal Geographical Society's marine observation program on equally steamy Rodrigues Island in the Indian Ocean.

Although Harry was already binge drinking and smoking pot, much was made of his first official trip to a pub upon turning sixteen. Hoisting a pint at the Ifield, a historic tavern frequented by the likes of Brad Pitt and Madonna, Harry thanked owner Ed Baines for putting up with the crush of reporters and promised, "I'll tell my grandmother to pop in!" (The Queen's first-ever visit to a pub, two years earlier, was designed to soften her image following the public outcry over Princess Diana's death. Around the same time, she also rode in a London taxi for the first time and stopped in at a McDonald's—her first visit to a fast-food restaurant of any kind.)

Now that he had left the cosseted environs of Eton, William was determined to stand up and make his own voice heard—literally. When one of Diana's closest aides published a tell-all memoir that painted a devastating portrait of the princess, William phoned his brother at Eton and told him he intended to do something about it. As far as the Heir was concerned, Diana's longtime private secretary Patrick Jephson—who, at one point, she trusted to be coexecutor of her will—had committed an unforgivable act of betrayal. In the pages of *Shadows of a Princess: An Intimate Account by Her Private Secretary*, Jephson depicted his former employer as, among other things, neurotic, scheming, manipulative, spoiled, and just plain mean. He claimed she was "several people in one" and marveled at her "style of aggression, which, with sinuous dexterity, combined a radiant smile with a knife between the shoulder blades."

With Granny glued to the television set in her Buckingham Palace study and Harry watching at Eton, William stepped before cameras with Prince Charles at his side to denounce the book.

"Of course Harry and I are both quite upset that our mother's trust has been betrayed," he said, "and that even now she is still being exploited." Once he'd made his case, the Heir, who at six foot three struck an imposing figure in a Burberry sweater and jeans (he will be the tallest monarch since Henry VIII), graciously thanked the press for keeping their distance during his last two years at Eton. "You all left me alone, and it really has been brilliant," he said. "It made a big difference with everyone not trying to snap a picture every time I was walking down the street, and I hope that goes for Harry, too, while he is there."

Days later, William arrived in a remote corner of Patagonia in southern Chile. He had wanted to play polo in Argentina, but Charles vetoed the idea as "too elitist." Instead, he spent ten weeks with 110 other young volunteers—many of them juvenile offenders and at-risk urban teens—scouring toilets, painting houses, chopping wood, and tutoring children in the coastal village of Tortel.

It was not all hard work. There was kayaking along the rugged Patagonian coastline and days spent searching for rare and exotic Huemul deer in the Tamango National Reserve. Much of the time, however, William huddled in his tent while "the wind whipped up into a storm. The tents were flapping so violently that we thought we were going to blow away. I had never seen rain like it," he recalled. "It was so heavy, and it just did not stop. . . . It was so demoralizing. I don't think I have ever been as low as that."

Not so low, though, that he couldn't find some consolation from several attractive young women whose tents were also being buffeted by gale-force winds. Pointing out that he and his father both benefited from weekly deep-tissue treatments administered by the royal family's on-call team of Swedish masseurs, William started giving massages to any female member of the team who was interested. Not surprisingly, many were. In the end, William connected with several ladies during his stint in South America—in one case, reportedly spending the night with two women, "one blonde, one brunette," according to a fellow volunteer who described the prince as a "one-man wrecking crew among the girls. There's been a lot of bed-hopping going on."

On their final night in Tortel, William was determined to make an impression at the group's farewell party. After knocking back several drinks, he started "dirty dancing with a lot of girls and making a spectacle of himself," said Kevin Mullen, a recovering heroin addict. "The girls didn't seem to mind."

There were moments of serious reflection as well. At one point at the end of the trip, everyone sat shivering around a campfire and shared his or her plans for the future. Once they got home, some would be enrolling in college, others would be starting work, and a few even discussed marriage plans. "You're all so lucky," William said. "I don't have much choice about my future. One day I will be king, and, to be honest, I'm not much interested in that at all at the moment."

Within days of arriving home, William was reminded yet again why he wasn't "much interested" in being king. The Brothers Royal were served up another major betrayal—or so they were led to believe—when Diana's trusted butler Paul Burrell was arrested on January 1, 2001, for stealing items worth an estimated $7.7 million from the princess's Kensington Palace apartments. Burrell was the man Diana called "my rock," the man who dressed her body for burial and who held the brothers by the hand as they walked from room to room picking out mementos from their mother—most significantly, Diana's sapphire-and-diamond engagement ring for Harry, and, for William, the Cartier Tank watch that had been given to the princess by her father. Diana had left Paul $80,000 in her will. Understandably, then, according to one of the boys' godfathers William and Harry were in a "complete state of disbelief."

The two of them asked repeatedly to intervene on Burrell's behalf but were told each time that it was impossible: Scotland Yard insisted it had an airtight case, and the Palace felt it was inappropriate for the Crown to involve itself in a matter before the courts. More to the point, Charles was adamant that his sons not be called to testify on Burrell's behalf. "I will not have William and Harry questioned in open court about their mother and Paul," he told a senior aide. "It would be too painful for the boys."

Unfortunately for Burrell, no one from the royal family spoke up to defend him. "The silence was deafening," Diana's rock said. "I thought I was being fed to the lions."

In essence, he was. Charles had, in his view, far more pressing matters on his mind—namely, extending the gentleman's agreement restricting press coverage of William to include his time at St. Andrews, and selling the British public on Camilla. On February 7, 2001, Harry stayed out of the line of fire studying for exams at Eton while William made his first official public engagement: an appearance at the tenth anniversary of the Press Complaints Commission (PCC), then the voluntary regulatory body for newspapers and magazines in Great Britain.

(The Independent Press Standards Organization replaced the PCC in 2014.)

Ostensibly a way for William and Harry to thank reporters for showing restraint since Princess Diana's death, it also provided an opportunity for Mrs. PB to be seen at the same event (more or less) with Charles and William. This was a risky undertaking, given the fact that Her Majesty was not yet willing to have Camilla and her grandsons photographed together.

Already a master of cocktail party banter, the nineteen-year-old prince exuded poise and confidence as he moved, drink in hand, from one group of journalists to the next. Not far away, his father did the same, occasionally looking over heads to see if he could spot Camilla. By design, he couldn't: she planted herself at the farthest end of the building, just so that her bumping into William wouldn't provide a field day for photographers. After two hours, the princes left together. Once given the all-clear, Camilla made her departure—again, from the far side of London's stately Somerset House, the sprawling complex of neoclassical buildings built where Lord Somerset's sixteenth-century Renaissance palace once stood on the banks of the Thames.

The ploy worked. They may have not been photographed together, but the fact remained that Camilla had attended an event where Charles and William were both present. "The evening was unquestionably a triumph for Camilla," journalist James Whitaker said. "William's mere presence sent a message that the royal family was accepting her."

FOR HIS STELLAR PERFORMANCE at the Press Complaints Commission gala, William was rewarded with yet another gap-year adventure. He spent the next four months digging trenches, repairing fences, and tracking wildlife at the Lewa Wildlife Conservancy, a fifty-three-thousand-acre wildlife preserve in Kenya. Despite the hardships—coping with poisonous snakes, hyenas, and a lack of indoor plumbing—he managed to squeeze in a brief workplace romance with Jessica "Jecca" Craig, the stunning, ash-blond daughter of the game preserve's owner. At one point, they even staged a mock engagement at the foot of Mount Kenya—near the very spot where, ten years later, William would pop the question in earnest to a different young woman.

When William returned, the Burrell affair was still dominating the news. Incredibly, it would drag on for two years, nearly bankrupting the onetime royal butler and prompting him to consider suicide. Finally, the case collapsed after Charles forced a public admission from the Queen—who apparently had been reluctant to get involved—that she had met with Burrell at Buckingham Palace shortly after Diana's death, and that he told her he was holding on to various items for safe-keeping. "It's the Queen," Burrell said after the charges were dropped. "It's all thanks to the Queen."

William and Harry were delighted that the butler had been cleared, and issued a statement saying so. Even after Burrell spilled secrets about Diana—including steamy details of her assignations with Hasnat Khan—to the *Daily Mirror* for $468,000, William strongly denied that he and Harry had branded the butler "Paul the Betrayer." Not even the Queen was angry with Burrell, who revealed in the newspaper that Her Majesty had once cautioned him to "beware, Paul. There are powers at work in this country about which we have no knowledge." The Queen's ominous words of warning resonated with Diana's sons, who had on countless occasions heard the princess complain about the Men in Gray who "move people around like pieces on a chessboard." For William in particular, observed one former deputy private secretary at St. James's Palace, "it must have been sobering to hear that the Queen was also intimidated by them."

The princes were anything but pleased a year later, however, when Burrell aired more tawdry royal family tales in his book *A Royal Duty*. Among other things, the butler revealed that Diana believed she would be murdered in a staged car crash. "We cannot believe that Paul, who was entrusted with so much, could abuse his position in such a cold and overt betrayal," the princes said in a rare joint statement. The book's contents were "deeply painful for the two of us," the statement continued, "and it would mortify our mother if she were alive today. We ask Paul please to bring these revelations to an end."

Before it concluded officially, the Burrell affair uncorked a number of scandals that had the Windsor dynasty reeling. The most sensational of these involved the revelation that all along Scotland Yard had been in hot pursuit of Diana's "box of secrets," which, among other things, supposedly contained a taped 1996 conversation she had with former Buckingham Palace footman and valet George Smith. A heavy drinker who suffered debilitating bouts of depression, Smith claimed that he had been raped not once but twice by one of Prince Charles's manservants. Smith also insisted that he saw the same manservant engaged in a sexual act with a senior member of the royal family.

It was impossible for the princes to ignore the screaming headlines, although they were not entirely sure what to make of them. Prince Charles had, in fact, paid the accused manservant's legal fees to the tune of $200,000 and settled $59,000 on George Smith to make the allegations go away. St. James's Palace staff certainly wasn't going to spell out the details. "William and Harry were surrounded by people who kept telling them everything in the press was a lie," one courtier said. "So they became very accustomed to just tuning out all the noise."

That summer of 2001, William had plenty to distract him after meeting chestnut-maned Arabella Musgrave on the Beaufort Polo Grounds near Highgrove. The daughter of Major Nicholas Musgrave, who managed the competing Cirencester Park Polo Club, "Bella" Musgrave was a member of the so-called Glosse Posse—the well-heeled offspring of Gloucestershire's well-to-do gentry class. Soon rightly convinced that William had a "roving eye," Bella ended their affair abruptly before the prince headed off to St. Andrews. "He was taken by complete surprise," a friend of the Musgrave family said, "and took the breakup quite hard."

Even after he and Harry joined their Windsor relatives for their usual late-summer vacation at Balmoral, William pleaded over the phone with Bella to reconsider. It was shortly after one of these conversations that the Queen's private secretary, Robin Janvrin, called on September 11, 2001, to inform her that airliners had been flown into the US Pentagon, both towers of Manhattan's World Trade Center, and a field in Pennsylvania, killing thousands.

For the next several hours, William and Harry sat with the Queen, Prince Philip, Prince Charles, and the Queen Mother watching the horrific events unfold live on BBC Television—all riveted by the incredible images of crumbling skyscrapers, smoldering rubble, panic in the streets, and smoke-filled skies. The next morning, Her Majesty disclosed that she was "watching developments in growing disbelief and total shock."

The brothers were hit particularly hard by the events of 9/11. They shared Princess Diana's fondness for America and Americans, and treasured memories of their time with her there. They also remembered how excited they had all been about Diana's plans to spend at least several months a year with them at their new house in Malibu.

There would be official declarations of support, tributes, and services—all orchestrated by the Palace apparatchiks in the name of the monarch. But it was clear to the brothers that their grandmother, who so seldom displayed emotion in public, was genuinely and deeply shaken by what had happened across the Atlantic. At a memorial service for the thousands who perished in the terrorist attacks that was held inside London's St. Paul's Cathedral, the Queen wiped away a tear and then did something she had never done before: she stood up to sing "The Star-Spangled Banner." Not only was it the first time a British monarch sang the US national anthem, but also it was the first time the Queen ever sang *any* national anthem—including Great Britain's. "Her mouth," Richard Kay said, "never opens when they are played."

Harry, in particular, was moved to see tears roll down his grandmother's cheeks when the choir launched into a thunderous rendition of "The Battle Hymn of the Republic." There were more than six hundred relatives of 9/11 victims in attendance at the service, and when it was over, Harry, who knew something about grief, went to console as many people as he could. "Prince Harry was so kind and gracious," said the British parent of a World Trade Center victim. "He connects with people—I think both William and Harry do. They obviously got that from their mother."

Expressions of compassion and solidarity from the royal family were important, but equally important was the very real concern that the United Kingdom might be next. Along with the Queen and Prince Charles, William and Harry were now regarded as potential terrorist targets. New measures were taken to harden all the royal palaces: the installation of steel-walled panic rooms at Buckingham Palace and Windsor Castle, for example, and beefed-up security within the gated confines of Eton.

Yet one royal was headed for perhaps the most sybaritic campus in the entire realm. Narrow streets and alleys with names like Mercat Gate and Butts Wynd wound past the town's twenty-two pubs—more per square mile than any other town in hard-drinking Scotland. Binge drinking was common on any university campus, but by all accounts St. Andrews had taken the practice to a whole new level. The so-called Student Run, for example, was a marathon pub crawl during which students paused between each stop to urinate in the mail slots of private homes.

From a security standpoint, however, St. Andrews was not the worst choice for William. The Royalty Protection Group (also known as SO14) of Scotland Yard informed the Queen that the Heir could be better protected at St. Andrews than, say, at the University of Edinburgh, which is situated in the teeming center of the Scottish capital. As one Scotland Yard official explained, St. Andrews was "easier for us because no one is going to get lost in the crowd without being spotted, like they would in a big city. It's impossible to hide. It's in the middle of bloody nowhere!"

Perhaps, but that didn't seem to matter to the frenzied throng that greeted the racing-green Vauxhall estate car that drove slowly through the narrow archway beneath St. Andrews's medieval clock tower. Once Charles and William emerged, smiling wanly, an earsplitting roar went up from the crowd. "I feel kind of sorry for the dude," said Allie Gidding, an American student at the university who watched as four thousand screaming fans jostled to catch a glimpse of the prince. William worked the police barricades with ease and grace, much as his mother had, shaking hands and smiling broadly as he chatted with students and locals alike.

Despite Prince Charles's immediate concerns about what he called the "mob" of reporters, their presence was only temporary; under terms of a new agreement, the press was allowed free access to William upon his arrival at the university—but for only twenty-four hours, after which they agreed to vanish.

Uncle Edward, however, didn't believe the rules applied to him. Charles's youngest brother had signed a deal to produce documentaries for American television and toward that end had hired a production crew to record his nephew moving into his residence hall, St. Salvator's ("Sallies" to faculty and students), then follow him around campus for an entire week. When the Prince of Wales was told they refused to leave with the rest of the working press, he turned "incandescent with rage," said Mark Bolland. After being at the receiving end of a blistering, expletive-laden phone call from Charles, a chastened Prince Edward backed down.

It might actually have helped if the press had stayed, since within weeks William was calling home with complaints that St. Andrews was "too cut off from everything" that mattered to him. Nevertheless, from the first day he had made friends with the other students housed at Sallies—most notably, it would turn out, with a young woman from the West Berkshire town of Bucklebury whose mother had made a sizable fortune selling children's party favors online. As Kate would recall later about their first encounter, she "turned bright red and sort of scuttled off, feeling very shy about meeting him."

Middleton's friend Carly Massy-Birch was not so shy, apparently. Carly and William dated for two months before Massy-Birch decided that, despite the best efforts of the royal bodyguards to remain out of sight, it was "simply too nerve-wracking" having them "lurking in the shadows wherever we'd go. Constantly being chased by the wretched paparazzi, the constant attention—it's all William has ever known, but it's too much for me."

To be sure, the cloak-and-dagger routine required for simply going on a date wasn't for everyone. On several occasions, she would be picked up by one of William's protection officers, driven to a pub, then escorted out the back door to a car waiting to take her to another restaurant where the prince would be waiting at a back table. Carly "found it all very hard to handle," said her mother, Mimi Massy-Birch. "It wasn't the kind of life she wanted."

What Carly didn't know was that William was also desperately trying to rekindle his earlier affair with his old Glosse Posse girlfriend Bella Musgrave. As it turned out, most of William's love life during this period revolved around his weekend trips to Highgrove. In addition to Bella, there was Beaufort Polo Club staffer Amanda Bush (called "Tigger" because of her bouncy personality), and, perhaps most significantly, Rose Farquhar. William and Rose, whose father was the master of the Beaufort Hunt, had known each other since childhood, and now he was using the word "serious" to describe their relationship. Rose, in turn, would later describe William as the first true love of her life, and laugh as she recalled the time she and the future king were caught by a farmer while making love in a field.

Such distractions notwithstanding, by Christmas William was begging his father to at least let him transfer to Edinburgh University, where he had friends from Eton and where there was "real civilization." At the same time, Kate Middleton, also feeling homesick and "desperately lonely," was imploring her parents to let her transfer to Edinburgh.

"Nothing more than a wobble—a touch of homesickness," Mark Bolland assured his boss, the Prince of Wales. "Entirely normal." William's pleas had become increasingly desperate, but the Men in Gray had no intention of permitting him to leave St. Andrews—an act that would have made him appear weak, indecisive—"a complainer and a quitter," as one courtier put it, "and very soft, which is something a future monarch simply cannot be."

"He got the blues, which happens," said St. Andrews Rector Andrew Neal. Determined to hold on to the prince, Neal made sure he received counseling. Papa did what he could, offering William a $32,000 gold-inlaid hunting rifle. But Kate was the real reason William decided to stick it out. She agreed to remain for at least another year if he would stay as well. "If we feel then like we do now," she promised him, "I'm leaving with you!"

Around the same time, the world first learned of Harry's pot smoking at Rattlebone Inn and his daylong visit to the Featherstone Lodge Rehabilitation Centre. While Prince Charles emerged not only unscathed but garlanded with praise for being such a savvy, hands-on dad, his younger son was stung by the brutally demeaning "Harry's Drug Shame" headlines. As for William, the Heir was depicted as the more mature and dependable brother of the two—a loving young man whose sole transgression was going off to help impoverished villagers in South America during his gap year, leaving his heedless younger brother to his own devices.

Harry's first genuine scandal also marked the first serious rift between the brothers in the years since their mother's death. William had begun frequenting the Rattlebone Inn long before Harry, had gotten drunk there, and narrowly escaped being arrested there during a police raid. It was William, in fact, who brought his underage brother to the inn in the first place. Moreover, William's own reputation as a nightclub-hopping party animal was well documented, as were his close ties to a number of young aristocrats arrested on a wide range of drug offenses. Yet, in stark contrast to the withering criticism leveled at the Spare, the Heir's reputation remained, in the Queen's words to her private secretary, "unsullied, thank goodness."

Harry conceded that he was "upset and embarrassed" at the "shame" he had brought on himself and the royal family. But he also rankled at the blatantly obvious double standard that allowed his brother to sail above the fray. "Why does William get away with everything?" Harry complained. "It's completely unfair, but there's nothing I can do about it." According to one of his closest friends at Eton, Harry was "very angry with William—*very* angry. But," he continued, "Harry was almost as angry at Prince Charles and the Palace for letting it happen."

The media uproar over Harry's pot smoking was soon overshadowed by fast-moving events inside the House of Windsor. On February 9, 2002, Princess Margaret died at age seventy-one after suffering the final in a series of strokes. The Queen's younger sister and only sibling had once been the most flamboyantly glamorous member of the family, and decades of carousing had taken their inevitable toll.

Only six weeks later, on the afternoon of March 30, Charles and the boys were vacationing at the Klosters ski resort when they learned the Queen Mother had died at Royal Lodge, her Windsor Great Park home, with the Queen at her bedside. All three men broke down. "Shattered, absolutely destroyed," were the words William used to describe his father. Harry "just couldn't take" watching his normally stoic father weep openly.

The Queen Mother, who had indisputably been the most beloved member of the royal family ever since she and her husband, King George VI, bravely stood up to the Nazis, was 101. To those who worked at the Palace, she was referred to as "the Old Queen," as distinguished from "the Young Queen"—by comparison, at any rate—who currently sat on the throne. To Harry and William, the Queen Mother was simply "Great Gran," the twinkle-eyed embodiment of grand-motherly perfection who drank throughout the day (her favorite cock-tail: gin and Dubonnet), spent millions on horses and clothes, and loved the long-running American TV sitcom *The Golden Girls* so much that she asked for—and in 1988 got—a live command performance of a scene from the show by Betty White, Bea Arthur, Rue McClanahan, and Estelle Getty. When during a visit to Balmoral, the Queen Mother's favorite place in the world, William confided that he had decided to attend St. Andrews, she replied without missing a beat, "If there are any good parties, invite me down!"

No one, though, was closer to the Queen Mother than Charles. She supplied the warmth and nurturing that, for some reason, his parents seemed either unwilling or incapable of giving. Well into his fifties, Charles was still calling his "Gran" to chat several times a week; just two days earlier, he had dropped in to see her at Windsor Great Park. "Somehow, I never thought her death would come," Charles said in an emotional televised tribute. "She seemed gloriously unstoppable, and ever since I was a child, I adored her."

So did the more than one million people lining the funeral route from St. James's Palace to Westminster Abbey. William and Harry were among the 2,200 crowned heads, titled aristocrats, heads of state, and assorted world leaders who had come to pay their respects. For much of the service, William and Harry flanked their father, who, along with Prince Philip, wore the full-dress uniform of a rear admiral.

Military regalia went hand in hand with such ceremonial events—the Prince of Wales, for example, was the honorary colonel in chief of no fewer than seventeen military regiments—but there was also a long tradition of royals serving in the armed forces that both William and

Harry, fascinated since early childhood with all things military, fully intended to pursue. In addition to his rear admiral rank, Charles achieved
the rank of air vice marshal by the time he retired in 1976 after seven
years of active duty.

For now, however, the young Windsor princes would have to con-
centrate on their studies. On his return to Eton, Harry discovered
there would be immediate consequences for his highly publicized encounter with cannabis at the Rattlebone Inn. At Eton, William had
been chosen as one of the twelve members of the elite student leadership society known as POP. "Poppers" were in a position to police the
behavior of other students, write them up for campus rule violations,
and essentially order them around at will. They were identified by dis-
tinctive vests of their own design: in William's case, one with polka
dots; another emblazoned with the slogan "Ban the Bomb"; and a
third bearing a Union Jack design and the phrase made famous by
American comedian Mike Myers in his popular series of Austin Powers
movies—"Groovy, baby."

Harry expected to follow in his brother's footsteps and become a
popper by virtue of his athletic achievements, his performance as a
cadet, and his overwhelming popularity with the other students. None
of that mattered now. Instead, he was passed over on the grounds that
it would be "hypocritical" for Harry to tell underclassmen what to
do—particularly when it came to substance abuse.

Then there was the matter of Harry's dismal academic performance.
No match for his brother scholastically, Harry struggled with all his
courses, failing two out of three. His D in geography was actually the
lowest grade in his class. These failures, coupled with still-unaddressed
feelings of grief and a newfound sense of shame, led Harry to believe he
simply "didn't measure up. I didn't like school at all," admitted Harry,

who began to embrace the role in which Fleet Street had cast him. "I wanted to be the bad boy."

The Spare had always been able to channel these feelings of doubt, frustration, and rage into his performance on the playing field. Only now that his brother was away at St. Andrews, he realized that he suddenly had a target on his back. Given his reputation as a spoiled-rotten hell-raiser, Harry said that "people actually put in bigger tackles because it was me. They would see me on the rugby field as an opportunity to smash me up."

While Harry was coping with life as the lone royal at Eton, William was still having a difficult time adjusting to his new life of comparative quiet and isolation at St. Andrews. Wary of getting into trouble like his brother, the Heir kept to himself, eschewing events for first-year students such as Raisin Weekend, which featured a costume party, a liquored-up shaving cream fight, and the requisite drink-until-you're-blind pub crawl. Instead, he'd order Chinese takeout from Ruby's or duck into P.M.'s diner for its famous southern fried chicken—all the while knowing that his protection officers were never far away. To maintain his anonymity around town, he would often forsake his white Volkswagen Golf for the 125 cc Kawasaki motorcycle his father had given him, tailed by his bodyguards in a Land Rover. There was an added benefit to riding his motorcycle: the prince could effectively hide inside his helmet. "I look right at them," he told his friend Hamish Barne, "and they can't see my face!"

For the most part, during the week William buckled down to his studies. Up at five thirty in the morning so that he could run through St. Andrews's back alleys under cover of darkness, he then returned to his fifteen-foot-by-fifteen-foot dormitory room, showered, dressed, and headed off for class on his motorcycle. At the Buchanan Building, a concrete abomination in the center of town, William went straight to the auditorium balcony and settled behind a pull-down wooden desk presumably intended for grade-schoolers. Graffiti covered every square inch of each desk, and while the Heir initially blushed at reading "Prince William Is a Sex God," he soon realized that on several other desks, even more graphic praise had been bestowed on one of his instructors.

Despite making a few friends and carving out a tolerable life for himself, William grew restless when classes weren't in session. "Weekends at St. Andrews," he explained to journalist Peter Archer, "aren't exactly vibrant"—which explained why he wound up spending only seven weekends there during his first year. In addition to trips to Highgrove and London, William often drove down to Edinburgh to party with friends at hotspots including the Bongo Club and Opal, or took the five-hour train ride to spend time with Charles and his grandparents at Balmoral. "It's easy to feel cut off," said Eton classmate David Walston, "if you're not around the few people you can really count on."

Everything changed in March 2002, when William coughed up £200 for a front-row seat at the university's annual Don't Walk charity fashion show sponsored by Yves Saint Laurent. When his (until now) totally platonic friend Kate Middleton slunk down the catwalk wearing a bandeau bra and black bikini bottoms beneath a transparent lace sheath, William led the applause. When she returned to the runway in a white lace bra and panties, the prince leapt to his feet as the crowd roared its approval. "We were all wowed," their friend Jules Knight said of Kate's transformation from "reserved girl" to "smoldering temptress. It was a side to her we didn't know existed, and it was a turning point in people's perception of her. Everyone took note, including Will."

There was someone else in the audience that day: a darkly handsome, six-foot-two-inch-tall senior whom Kate had been dating for months. Rupert Finch was a star cricketeer at St. Andrews and had been selected to captain the team on its upcoming tour of South Africa. Kate was smitten with Finch, but the fact remained that he was getting ready to graduate and had even scored an internship at a prestigious London law firm.

Not wanting to be the cause of a breakup, Will checked with their mutual friend Fergus Boyd before making his first move on Kate— asking if she was interested in sharing off-campus accommodations with him and Boyd. Once she gave the green light, the Heir snagged a four-bedroom flat on the ground floor of a Georgian-style town house. Each was to pitch in $165 a month for his or her own room, with the Crown picking up the balance to house William's security detail.

As soon as word of the new living arrangements leaked, Fleet Street had a field day. "William Shacks Up with Stunning Undies Model" was the *Sun's* less than gracious contribution, although the *Mail on Sunday* ("William and His Undie-Graduate Friend Kate to Share a Student Flat") wasn't much better.

Before they could start living under the same roof, William and Kate spent the summer apart. While she earned $8 an hour as a barmaid for a catering company called Snatch, William joined Harry and the rest of the Windsors in celebrating their grandmother's half century as Queen. A classical concert preceded the much-ballyhooed Party at the Palace pop concert featuring the acclaimed likes of Paul McCartney, Tom Jones, Tony Bennett, Eric Clapton, Ozzy Osbourne, Annie Lennox, Ricky Martin, and Queen performing inside the Buckingham Palace Garden walls.

Kate watched it all on television, and Will—as he now insisted on being called—phoned her daily to fill her in on all the behind-the-scenes details. It was only logical that the new woman in the Heir's life would find the whole situation "beyond surreal."

In stark contrast to William's mother, Kate had never come close to moving in aristocratic circles, much less royal ones. She was an untitled commoner, a descendant of coal miners and factory workers. Kate's mother, Carole, grew up partly in public housing and was working as a British Airways flight attendant when she met and married fellow airline employee Michael Middleton.

Always with an eye on moving up the ladder of social success—she only invited two people from her decidedly working-class side of the family to her own wedding—Carole could not have remotely imagined just how far up she'd climb when Catherine Elizabeth Middleton arrived on January 9, 1982. Twenty months later, Catherine's sister, Philippa ("Pippa"), was born, followed by brother James in 1987—the same year Carole and Michael decided to turn Carole's knack for making birthday favors into Party Pieces, a mail-order enterprise specializing in children's party supplies. As a little girl, Kate modeled the company's sparkly princess dresses and rhinestone tiaras online. By the time she was ten, Party Pieces was grossing in excess of $3 million a year, and the Middletons moved from their small brick house to Oak Acre, a baronial Tudor-style estate in the West Berkshire village of Bucklebury.

Quietly shy and a head taller than most of her classmates, Catherine—she was sixteen before people began calling her Kate—nonetheless was a star athlete and starred in several student productions at St. Andrew's (not affiliated with the University of St. Andrews in Scotland), the $20,000-a-year private prep school she attended in nearby Pangbourne. At the age of thirteen, just as William was entering Eton, Kate enrolled at Downe House, an exclusive all-girls boarding school in the unfortunately named West Berkshire village of Cold Ash. Bullied mercilessly by one particularly toxic band of mean girls because of her working-class background, Kate transferred the next year to a coed school, Marlborough College.

Unfortunately, it would be a full two years before awkward, self-effacing Kate, who made few friends and spent most of her free time hidden away in her tiny dorm room, finally blossomed. "It happened quite suddenly," Kate's friend and classmate Gemma Williamson said of Middleton's return to school in the fall of 1998. Nor did the onetime wallflower have to make much of an effort. Kate never "wore particularly fashionable or revealing clothes," Williamson said. "Everything looked good on her because she had such a perfect body."

And Kate knew it. Although she avoided romantic entanglements and refrained from the drinking and pot smoking that were an inevitable part of boarding school life, Kate had a mischievous streak. She exposed her backside from the window of her residence hall so often that Kate became known as "Middlebum."

As she packed for her return to St. Andrews University, Kate prayed devoutly that such cringeworthy details from her teenage years would not become fodder for the tabloids. In the meantime, her new roommate and his younger brother were buffeted by a new storm of revelations aimed at tarnishing their mother's memory. In September 2002 Ken Wharfe published *Diana: Closely Guarded Secret*. Among other things, Diana's longtime bodyguard revealed that Diana kept a vibrator in her handbag (she called it "le gadget"), that she often greeted him in the nude, and that she once bought her lover James Hewitt a $30,000 TVR sports car.

"The Queen is very perturbed," said Her Majesty's private secretary, Robin Janvrin. "She is extremely worried about the effect all this will have on her grandsons." She was right to be concerned. Harry called William in tears. Both princes had thought of the ruddy-faced amateur opera singer as a sort of surrogate dad; it was Wharfe who ran in the fathers' race at Wetherby preschool in place of Prince Charles, who thought it undignified. "How could Ken do this?" Harry asked. "How could he write these things?"

William was distraught—in large part because of the impact the book was having on his emotionally fragile brother. "Harry is really upset," he told their friend Guy Pelly. "It's just total treachery, that's all." Their father agreed. Prince Charles publicly accused Wharfe of a "disgusting betrayal" and angrily demanded that Scotland Yard chief Sir John Stevens take some sort of action against the retired royal protection officer. There was nothing anyone could do, however, since Wharfe had never been required to sign a confidentiality agreement.

William and Harry had scarcely caught their breath before James Hewitt emerged from the shadows to take center stage. It turned out that Diana's financially strapped former paramour was hawking sixty-four steamy love letters she had written him while he was commanding a tank squadron in the Persian Gulf War. In some, she refers to Hewitt's penis as "my friend." In others, she refers coyly to his other conquests, calls him "a beastly beast who drives a girl to weep tears of anger" and asks if he enjoyed the pornography she sent him. The letters were all signed either "Julia" or "D," and during a secret meeting with potential buyers at Claridge's Hotel in London, Hewitt demanded $16.5 million for the entire batch.

Now that Harry was turning eighteen, Britain's broadsheets had a field day running photographs comparing the Spare to the notorious "Love Rat" Hewitt. The fact that Harry looked nothing like his Windsor relatives and more like Hewitt—from the shape of his forehead, eyes, ears, and chin right down to his distinctly upturned nose—was as inescapable as it was humiliating.

There was, of course, a way to put an end to the rumors once and for all. Beginning in 1998 a blood sample containing Prince Philip's DNA was used to identify the recently discovered remains of Czar Nicholas II, his wife, Czarina Alexandra, and their five children (Philip was related to Alexandra through his mother and his father)—eighty years after Russia's ruling family was executed by Bolshevik soldiers, putting an end to the Romanovs' imperial dynasty after three centuries. In much the same way, Harry could simply take the DNA—were it not for the Queen. It was undignified, she argued, for any Windsor to be forced into a corner in such a manner to prove legitimacy. It would also not be wise, the Men in Gray suggested, to appear to acknowledge anything the rumor mills churned out about the royal family. In the past, Her Majesty had simply ignored idle chatter of this sort; most notably, a similar rumor regarding Prince Andrew's paternity that had persisted for decades.

But what if the rumors about the Spare were true? Palace officials were aware of the shifting timeline surrounding Diana's affair with Hewitt and the possibility that it had begun as early as 1981—three years before Harry was born. If a DNA test proved that he was not Charles's son, thereby removing him from his place in the line of succession, it would be, as one courtier put it, "like kicking a cane out from under an elderly gent. The monarchy might remain standing, it might not. Pretty wobbly as it is."

Unable to speak up or fight back against the rumors, Harry returned increasingly to his old habits. "Those terrible doubts about who his real dad is have Harry looking for solace at the end of a joint and the bottom of a shot glass," Harold Brooks-Baker said. "Sadly, he fears he might not be who the world thinks he is."

During the Christmas holidays that year, Harry was dealt yet another blow when word came that one of his closest friends at Ludgrove, Henry van Straubenzee, had been killed instantly when the driver of the Ford Fiesta in which he was a passenger lost control of the car in the winter fog and plowed into a tree. Van Straubenzee had been partying with other students on school grounds when the CD player they were using broke, and he went with a friend to fetch a new one. Both he and the driver had been drinking heavily, and neither wore a seat belt.

Both princes were close to all three Van Straubenzee brothers: Thomas, Charlie, and Henry. They had gotten to know each as youngsters at Highgrove, and all of them attended Ludgrove together. But the connection between Harry and Henry ran particularly deep. They shared a love of Africa and of the military; Henry was about to spend his gap year volunteering at a school in Uganda, and he and Harry planned to attend the Royal Military Academy Sandhurst together. Those hopes were destroyed in one reckless instant—just as Diana's had been. It seemed incomprehensible that, at the age of eighteen, Harry would have lost two people so close to him in separate drunk driving accidents.

Determined that their son's body not lie in a morgue over Christmas, Henry's parents hastily arranged a funeral at their local church in Hertfordshire. At the service, William put his arm on Harry's shoulder and attempted to comfort him as he wept. "I haven't seen Harry like that since Mummy died," he told Kate. "It shocked me, but it crushed him." After falling into an understandably steep depression, Henry's parents established the Henry van Straubenzee Memorial Fund to raise money for classrooms in Uganda. William and Harry signed on as co-patrons of the charity—the only one on which they serve jointly.

Refusing to wallow in bitterness, the Van Straubenzees also declined to take their anger out on the driver of the car, who was seriously injured but survived. Claire and Alex van Straubenzee made a formal appeal to the police asking that charges not be pressed against their dead son's friend. "Both of them were drunk," said Henry's mother. "Either of them could have been driving. It doesn't matter."

It did matter, of course. But not even a senseless, alcohol-fueled tragedy like the one that took the life of Harry's closest friend was enough to make either brother change his ways. "It was right before Christmas," said another Ludgrove alumnus who attended the funeral. "So we all went right back to going out to pubs and clubs and getting lashed. When you're that age, it doesn't really sink in that that body in the casket could be you, does it?"

BACK AT ST. ANDREWS, William leaned heavily on his comely new roommate for emotional support. He was more worried than ever that the cavalcade of scandals coupled with losing his friend would push Harry over the edge. Kate offered a sympathetic ear, and William was impressed that, unlike so many of the highborn young ladies in his orbit, she seemed to genuinely care. "There is a serenity about her," one member of their inner circle observed, "a kind of calm. So many of these other beautiful girls don't know when to shut up and listen, and she did." Jules Knight agreed that before Kate was ever Prince William's girlfriend, she was his friend and confidante. "She is very compassionate," he said, "very kind."

Within weeks, William and Kate were lovers. Boyd described the couple's new life with their close circle of friends: shopping at Safeway and Tesco, playing chess, and dropping into local hangouts at Ma Bells, the Keys Bar, and Broons. (William was such a regular at the West Port Bar that he played for its rugby team against the rival Gin House.) Kate and William "could go for a drink and hold hands, and no one batted an eyelid," Knight recalled. "We were all in a safe bubble. . . . It was quite a cozy setup . . . like one big private house party." They soon had pet names for each other: "Babykins" for her, and the even more eyebrow-raising "Big Willy" for him.

Even when he stuck close to home, however, William was hardly abstemious. Usually knocking back as many as nine or ten drinks while Kate nursed a single glass of wine, the Heir frequently bought a round for the house before leaving. At the after-parties that followed closing time, students hoped that William, bottle of Jack Daniel's in hand, and Kate would make an appearance to lend a little star power to the festivities—and they often did, joining in the drinking games that are a part of college life.

Even in their protected bubble, there were moments when William's boozy escapades put him in harm's way. While he relied on a driver to ferry him home if he'd had too much to drink, the prince often chose to walk while his protectors trailed him at a discreet distance in their SUV. On one such occasion, while they were stumbling home from a bar at three in the morning, William spotted a bulge in Jules Knight's jacket, reached into Knight's pocket, and pulled out a harmless pellet gun. Within seconds, royal bodyguards materialized with Glock handguns drawn and aimed directly at Knight. "It was," Jules recalled of the moment, "a very close call."

Not long after, William and Harry, both dressed as characters from the traditional British card game Happy Families, both showed up for a rowdy costume party at the Duke of Beaufort's historic fifty-two-thousand-acre estate, Badminton House. A thoroughly soused Harry, who had already shocked guests at an elegant party thrown at the home of the Duke of Westminster by throwing up under the banquet table, again made something of a spectacle of himself by bouncing on and off the meticulously manicured hedgerows and topiary. His equally blotto brother stripped down to his shorts and went swimming in one of the estate's immense fountains. It was not until William climbed up a statue in the middle of the fountain and then dove off that Jules Knight realized "what a bizarre and decadent atmosphere it really was."

Unlike Harry, William's lapses in judgment and displays of temper were either ignored or downplayed. On one occasion, he was on horseback returning from a foxhunt when he spotted photographer Clive Postlethwaite and rode straight at him, forcing the terrified paparazzo into a ditch. William screamed, "Fucking piss off!" and, according to Postlethwaite, "just went mad. He rode toward me with his eyes wide and his teeth showing." On another occasion, William, driving his VW Golf at twice the legal speed limit, nearly ran the Land Rover driven by septuagenarian Lord Bathurst, a Gloucestershire friend and neighbor of Prince Charles's, off the road.

Neither episode caused much of a stir. However, when William threw an *Out of Africa*–themed twenty-first birthday celebration at Windsor Castle in 2003, a furor did erupt over security lapses after a cross-dressing Osama bin Laden impersonator crashed the party. At one point, self-styled "comedy terrorist" Aaron Barschak, attired in pink satin gown, high heels, fake beard, and a turban, grabbed the microphone out of William's hand as he thanked his guests for coming.

Incredibly, no one criticized how condescending and racially insensitive such a theme might be. The future king's coming-of-age party was definitely born out of the brothers' shared love for Africa and its culture. And in fairness, the Queen had approved the concept only with the understanding that the three hundred guests choose costumes that made no overt reference to race or British colonialism.

Instead, partygoers were led on elephant and camel rides, scores of monkeys swung on vines suspended overhead, and tribal dancers gyrated to the beat of the Botswanan band Shakarimba. As for obeying the dress code, the overwhelmingly Anglo-Saxon attendees came as everything from witch doctors, French Legionnaires, and pharaohs, to Timon and Pumbaa from *The Lion King*. William wore only a loincloth, and Kate—presumably playing Jane to his Tarzan—donned a skimpy, tattered, yellow-and-black animal print dress. Most of the Windsor men—including Harry, Prince Philip, and Prince Andrew— went for a Great White Hunter look, while the Prince of Wales made his entrance wearing the same striped caftan he wore when meditating alone in his Sanctuary garden at Highgrove. A number of titled women, including one lady-in-waiting, sported grass skirts, and heads turned when Camilla arrived wearing a red-and-blue tribal print with a striking red-feathered headdress. Hardly sticking to the rules herself, Elizabeth II of England came as the queen of Swaziland in all white— white sheath, white fur cape, and a white-feathered headdress that, fittingly, resembled a crown.

The royal family would eventually come in for some heavy criticism for its tone deafness on issues of race. But for the moment, speed-loving William was busy "dropping many hints to my father" about his desire for a new, more powerful Triumph 600 cc Daytona to ride instead of the Yamaha motorcycle that had replaced his Kawasaki. Instead, William had to settle for a $165,000 Argentine polo pony as his birthday gift from Dad.

The gift to William did not sit particularly well with Harry. "He was jealous," a fellow player at the Beaufort Polo Club revealed. "Prince

Charles had already bought William two motorcycles and a couple of cars. Besides, William was a good player, but Harry was much better and everyone knew it. If anyone could have really ridden that pony to a championship, it was Harry."

The Spare also chafed at the still-growing perception that William "is the responsible one while Harry is wild, a spoiled-rotten brat, the family rebel. Harry was used to being in Will's shadow," an Eton classmate said. "He could handle that. But he didn't want to be an embarrassment to his father, and especially not to the Queen. He didn't want to let the family down."

Yet when it came to Harry's carousing, William could scarcely be called a steadying influence. In the autumn of 2003 he introduced Harry to Purple, one of Chelsea's most infamously sybaritic clubs. At a wild twenty-fifth birthday party thrown there for well-known British sports broadcaster Natalie Pinkham, she nestled in Harry's lap while he cupped her breast in his hand. "Dirty Harry: Playboy Prince Cops a Feel" read the accompanying headline in the *Sun*. Slumped next to them was a crimson-faced William, occupied with two other women. Three years later, photos taken that evening would wind up on the front page of the *Sun*, but once again William, who was clearly visible in the photos, was more or less let off the hook.

Even after Harry left to spend three months of his gap year working on an Australian cattle ranch, William frequented Purple, drinking for hours on end with friends in the cordoned-off VIP section and taking to the dance floor. The prince would "go flat out for about an hour, dancing like a lunatic with his arms flailing," said one clubgoer, "doing his moves and sweating so much his light-blue shirt was dark." Eventually he would be "so wiped out that he literally had to be carried off."

During these boozy nights out, William flew beneath the radar, largely shielded from the sort of unremittingly harsh criticism that had been heaped on Harry. Enough did leak out, however, for Kate to become concerned—not about William's drinking so much as his openly and often outrageously flirting with other women. Since the Middletons had now taken a flat nearer the action in Chelsea, Kate made the very strategic decision to spend as much time there as possible. Now, whenever William ventured out for a night on the town, Kate made sure the girl he was nuzzling in the VIP section was her.

By this time, Kate had good reason to feel territorial. She had thoroughly charmed Prince Charles, joined several shooting parties at Sandringham ("She's a great shot!" proclaimed early fan Prince Philip), and spent languid summer weekends with William at Tam-na-Ghar, the three-bedroom cottage at Balmoral given to him by the Queen Mother.

Kate had also easily won over Harry. The first time they were introduced was at Highgrove in 2003. When Will's girl looked away for a moment, Harry dropped his jaw and mouthed the words "Oh my God, she is *gorgeous*!"—not realizing that she had caught his reflection in the window.

Often at Kate's insistence, Harry was invited up to St. Andrews to spend weekends inside their comfy bubble. In much the same way that Carole Middleton had urged her daughter to attend St. Andrews once William announced he was going there, she also pointed out to Kate that befriending Harry might well be key to any lasting relationship with the future king. Kate took her mother's advice seriously, but at the same time she, like millions of others her age, had nursed a tender affection from afar for the motherless younger prince. "Everybody had William's picture on their wall," a Marlborough classmate said, "but when Diana died, it was Harry we all felt especially sorry for because he was still just a skinny little child. Very vulnerable." She remembered Kate saying, " 'Poor Harry, poor Harry,' when we watched him walking behind his mum's coffin. He was the one your heart went out to, even more than William."

From the very beginning, said Jules Knight, Kate and Harry "got on like they'd known each other forever." In contrast to William's serious, sometimes sullen moods, Harry and Kate shared a mischievous streak. "They were always full of fun when they were together. They were joking around all the time—always trying to find ways to make each other laugh." When Harry learned about Kate's "Middlebum" nickname and how she earned it, that sealed the deal. Although he had never been caught, Harry, according to fellow classmates at Ludgrove, often joined in mooning other students and occasionally players from visiting school teams. The prankster side of Harry was, in fact, one of the things about him that most appealed to the Queen. A lover of practical jokes—as far back as the 1960s she decreed that only gag gifts of the whoopie cushion variety be exchanged during Christmas at Sandringham—Her Majesty usually assumed that Harry was behind every embarrassing noise, or shrieks induced by a rubber snake. "That," she would say with a sigh, "would be Harry, then."

Yet Harry was anything but amused when William and Kate were seen quarreling in parked cars and on street corners. The issue: although Kate agreed reluctantly to stay under the radar, William was being linked to a number of attractive young women in the United Kingdom and abroad. Tongues wagged, for example, when he flew to Tennessee to spend time with Edinburgh University student Anna Sloan, an American heiress, at her family's 350-acre farm outside Nashville.

No one upset Kate more than Jecca Craig, William's old flame from Kenya. At his *Out of Africa* twenty-first-birthday soiree, at which Craig was an honored guest, there was rampant speculation in the press that Jecca was, in fact, The One. Even though Prince Charles went so far as to issue a statement denying that William and Jecca were anything more than friends, for two years in a row William insisted on returning to Africa to spend part of his summer vacation with Craig.

When he announced he intended to go a third time, Kate put her foot down. She felt, said a member of their tight group at St. Andrews, "threatened and humiliated." William, who had inherited a formidable stubborn streak from both parents, dug in. It wasn't until Harry cautioned his headstrong brother to consider Kate's hurt feelings that William grudgingly canceled his trip to Kenya. As it turned out, he didn't even have to leave the United Kingdom to see his old friend. The press took note that he and Jecca were both at the wedding of William's onetime *Alexander* yacht mate Davina Duckworth-Chad, and again at the nuptials of Edward van Cutsem. Both times, Kate was pointedly excluded.

Finally, Prince Charles stepped in to settle the matter. William was to stop seeing Jecca Craig—but not because the rumors hurt Kate. "You mustn't put her through that, William," Charles said. "It isn't fair to Jecca."

Whatever the reasoning behind it, Kate was grateful that Charles—and Harry—had intervened. Eventually a tender moment on a ski slope at Klosters was captured on camera, enough for a front-page *Sun* story sporting the headline "Finally: Wills Gets a Girl." The royal family was purportedly furious, and the Palace issued a statement accusing the *Sun* of breaching the media agreement to leave William alone until he graduated from St. Andrews.

The *Sun* countered that the photo was not taken by one of its photographers but by a veteran freelancer. "One of William's girlfriends could become Queen one day," the newspaper argued in an editorial. "Her subjects will be entitled to know all about her."

On one level, Kate and William were relieved. The charade was over. No longer would she have to go to great lengths to avoid detection while her prince was seen galivanting about with a bevy of beauties. Yet her emerging status as William's certified girlfriend meant, as the *Sun* made clear, that she would be subjected to scrutiny on a microscopic level because Britons "will be entitled to know all about her."

It also meant that, in the coming years, she would be run to ground as the Princess of Wales had been by Britain's no-holds-barred paparazzi. For now, however, the press ban technically remained in effect. This unusual arrangement, designed to allow Diana's motherless boys some measure of freedom as they grew into manhood, was set to expire once William graduated from St. Andrews and Harry received his commission in the army. Assuming, of course, that Harry could behave himself long enough to graduate from Sandhurst.

Down Under, Harry's antics did not go unnoticed. Following his three months fixing fences and rounding up steers on a forty-thousand-acre spread in Queensland, the Spare plunged headlong into Sydney's nightlife. Back home, a Buckingham Palace official told the *Times* of London there was concern that Harry "needs to be properly guided; otherwise he could go off the rails. When he is not committed to something serious, his thoughts turn to drink and girls, and he smokes endlessly."

With William ensconced with Kate and Fergus Boyd in new digs—Balgove House, a spacious farmhouse just outside St. Andrews—Harry was left to his own devices back in London while Charles decided how his youngest son should spend the remainder of his free time before entering Sandhurst. First stop: China White, where Harry partied until dawn with a woman who had once posed topless for a British tabloid.

Even stranger was the evening he spent cuddling up to willowy, doe-eyed Camilla Simon, whose mother, Kate, was none other than James Hewitt's erstwhile mistress. After getting as much information as he could out of Camilla concerning the current state of Hewitt's life—at the time, he faced mounting debts and was drinking heavily—Harry, clearly inebriated, proclaimed loudly that the gossip concerning his paternity was "total shit."

The fallout was instant—and brutal. "Spoiled and Lazy Harry Is One of a Kind," declared the *Daily Express*, which described him as "drinking and drugging" his way to becoming "a national disgrace." Harry, *Daily Express* writer Carol Sarler continued, "has rarely lifted a finger unless it's to feel up a cheap tart in a nightclub."

With Papa distracted by the repackaging of Camilla, it fell on William to suggest a way for Harry to silence his critics. Off to the tiny, landlocked South African kingdom of Lesotho for two months, Harry hauled water, built bridges, and played with AIDS-infected orphans. Just so that everyone back home got the point, a documentary crew from England's ITV channel was on hand to record it all.

"I believe I've got my mother in me," Harry explained, "and I just think she'd want us to do this—me and my brother. I want to carry on my mother's legacy as much as I can." But what of skeptics who labeled his do-good gap-year projects as self-serving publicity stunts? "I'd love to let it wash over me, but I can't," he replied with a shrug. "It is hard. But I'm not out here for a sympathy vote."

Besides, Harry was grateful just to be far from the usual Vesuvian spew of titillating gossip. This time Diana's voice coach Peter Settelen released videotapes he made with the princess in which she discussed many intimate details of her life, including how often she had sex with Charles (once every three weeks). For audio lovers, there were CDs of Diana telling all into a tape recorder for Andrew Morton's *Diana: Her True Story.* "Listening to their mother's voice as she talked about her depression and about Camilla, it was so terrible for William and Harry," Diana's friend Lucia Flecha de Lima said. "They wanted to put that all in the past, but no one would let them."

Yet nothing had more impact than the release of photographs of the princess in the final moments of her life—shocking images broadcast on American television that showed Diana lying with her eyes closed in the smoldering, crumpled wreckage. What upset the brothers was not merely the invasion of their mother's privacy and the sullying of her memory, but the stupefying realization that the paparazzi who chased her car into Paris's Alma tunnel did nothing to help her. "She was still very much alive in the backseat," Harry later said, "and those same people that caused the accident, instead of helping, were taking photographs of her while she was dying. They just stood there and watched her die. I will never forgive them."

William agreed. "Of course I blame the paparazzi for killing our mother," he stated. "It never would have happened if they hadn't pursued her relentlessly. They are totally to blame." But he also made it clear that he had no intention of being defined by her pointless death. "I wanted her to be proud of the person I would become," he said. "I didn't want her legacy to be that William or Harry were completely and utterly devastated by her death."

On that question, the jury was still out. Even before he left Africa, photos of Harry living it up on a Cape Town beach were accompanied by the tabloid headlines "Prince Feels No Pain" and "Harry's Just Wild

About Partying." Once again Harry seemed to brush off the negative press. "I can't control what other people think," he said, suggesting that "people just want to make my family look bad."

That June of 2004, Harry was fulfilling gap-year obligations in Botswana and geography major William was studying geological formations in Norway when they were suddenly called home. Their grandmother Frances Shand Kydd had died at the age of sixty-eight after a long battle with Parkinson's disease. "Gran Fran" had lived as a virtual recluse on the remote Scottish island of Seil for years, yet emotions ran high at the funeral when William and Harry—only Spencers were invited, no other members of the royal family allowed—stood to read passages of Scripture.

The boys were surprised to learn that Gran Fran, whom Diana had appointed principal guardian of her sons and executor of her estate, left them more than $1 million in her will. Together with the roughly $30 million Diana had bequeathed them—the bulk of which came from her divorce settlement with Charles—each boy now boasted a personal fortune of nearly $16 million that would grow to more than $30 million each by 2020. The princes' inheritance from their mother would eventually prove to be a godsend. But for the foreseeable future, they would be funded entirely by Papa and the Crown.

As unexpectedly moving as their grandmother's funeral was, three weeks later William and Harry again found themselves sitting next to each other and choking back tears at the dedication of the Diana Memorial Fountain in Hyde Park. Both brothers had wanted at the very least for a statue to be built in their mother's honor, but that idea was nixed out of hand. "To present a likeness seemed at best unnecessary," the Queen explained at the dedication, "for someone whose image continues to exert such a fascination the world over."

Once Her Majesty finished praising her late daughter-in-law as "a remarkable human being" and admitted that things were not always rosy between Diana and the rest of the royal family, the Queen acknowledged wistfully that her memories of the princess "had mellowed with the passing of the years. I am especially grateful for the happiness she gave to my two grandsons."

After the ceremony, the Queen, her purse slung over her left arm, toddled over to Earl Spencer. "I hope you feel satisfied by that," she asked the man who'd crucified the Windsors at his sister's funeral. "Yes, ma'am," he answered. "More than satisfied."

Moments like the one at the dedication of the Diana Memorial Fountain served to remind William and Harry of what lay at the heart of their unique relationship. "No one else has been through what we've been through together," William said. "We will always love each other and be there for each other."

Harry was no less convinced that theirs was an unbreakable bond. "We care for each other, no doubt," he said. "We are two different people with two different lives. But no one understands what it's like to be us. Sometimes it feels like all we've got is each other."

The following month, July 2004, while William and Kate lolled on the beach on the Indian Ocean island of Rodrigues, Harry stuck close to home getting ready for Sandhurst's demanding Regular Commissions Board test—a challenging combination of problem-solving tasks, interviews, written exams, and an obstacle course. Even though James Hewitt and the paternity rumors were back in the news—this time the once-dashing cavalry officer was arrested for cocaine possession— Harry managed to pass the grueling Sandhurst tests, but not without incurring a knee injury that would push back his admission to the military academy by nearly a year.

Harry had no trouble finding ways to amuse himself. Like William, he seemed to have found The One: tall, blond, curvaceous Chelsy Davy, the Zimbabwe-born daughter of a wealthy safari park owner and a former Miss Rhodesia. She and Harry had actually been introduced in 2003, when she was studying at Cheltenham College, not far from Highgrove. Davy had since returned home and was studying politics, philosophy, and economics at the University of Cape Town when Harry bumped into her again en route to Lesotho.

On his way back, Harry spent several more days with his new love, tooling up and down the South African coast with Davy at the wheel of her Mercedes convertible. According to his friend Gary Robinson, Harry was "quite besotted," and it was easy to see why: not only did she turn heads in her customary uniform of hip-hugging jeans, halter top, and sandals, but Chelsy also shared Harry's love of country pursuits and the outdoor life. "She's a sporty girl," Robinson continued. "No airs at all. And absolutely gorgeous, of course."

As he waited in London for a chance to reconnect with Chelsy, Harry woke up to find that he was being accused of cheating on his final art exam at Eton. His teacher released a tape recording in which Harry seemed to acknowledge that he had done little of the work that earned him his highest grade in four years at prep school: a B. While he would be cleared of cheating by an "exam board," as far as Harry was concerned the damage had been done. It was just one more dent in his already badly battered reputation.

With his royal protection officers hiding in plain sight at the bar or in a doorway—never more than twenty or thirty feet away—Harry plunged back into London nightlife. Drowning his frustrations at the usual hangouts—Purple, Boujis, China White—the Spare was leaving a nightclub called Pangaea at three thirty in the morning when suddenly he spun around and attacked press photographer Chris Uncle. "Why the fuck don't you just leave me alone!" he screamed as he pushed the camera into Uncle's face, cutting his lip. Realizing that the whole episode was being recorded by other paparazzi standing on the street, Harry fell into the back of a waiting car and cradled his head in his hands. "Christ, oh Christ," he muttered. "Now what have I done?"

What he had done was jeopardize his entire military career. Sandhurst's commandant, Major General Andrew Ritchie, stated flatly that he viewed "very dimly misbehaving over a weekend" and let it be known that he had his eye on Harry. "He is the same as everyone else," General Ritchie said. "I have removed certain cadets from Sandhurst, as their behavior is not up to Sandhurst's standards, and I would do it again."

No sooner did Harry apologize to his father—again—than he and Chelsy took off for two weeks at a ranch outside Buenos Aires. Although he spent virtually the entire time in Argentina playing polo with his South African girlfriend cheering him from the sidelines, false reports about Harry wreaking havoc at local bars inevitably made their way into the British press. It didn't help that newspapers in Buenos Aires proclaimed him *"el Príncipe Rebelde"*—"the Rebel Prince"—even before he arrived.

Harry phoned Clarence House to reassure his father that he was behaving himself but wondered aloud if it really mattered. "They'll say what they want to say about me. It's what sells, isn't it?" he protested. "I only hope it doesn't cost me getting into Sandhurst."

William, meanwhile, was also busy setting the record straight—this time about what he was and wasn't prepared to do after graduating from St. Andrews. As part of the bargain that would keep reporters at bay during his final year at the university, William agreed to another sit-down interview with the Press Association.

Was he losing sleep worrying about becoming king? "Frankly," he replied, "life's too short." He did worry, however, about whether or not he'd ever be allowed to fight alongside his fellow soldiers in Iraq. "The last thing I want is to be mollycoddled or wrapped up in cotton wool," he said, adding that he considered the idea of not being allowed to fight "humiliating" and that he didn't want to be kept out of combat "for being precious, or whatever."

Before any of those life-and-death decisions could be made, William revealed that he would be entering Sandhurst following graduation, presumably just as Harry was leaving. "That's why I put my brother in," he joked. "As a guinea pig!"

Harry wasted no time dashing back to the waiting arms of Chelsy, who, like Kate Middleton, brought a sense of calm to the life of her Prince Charming. They joined her family on the resort island of Bazaruto off the coast of Mozambique. At one point, the couple commandeered a motorboat and zipped off to a smaller, deserted island called Paradise. Just 1.8 miles long and 500 yards wide, it gave them a rare opportunity for solitude—with only one royal protection officer positioned discreetly at the far end of the beach.

Even as the couple spent hours snorkeling along a stunning coral reef that rings the tiny island, there were rumblings at home about Harry's girlfriend and her family. Chelsy's father, Charles Davy, who was believed to be Zimbabwe's largest landowner, was already coming under fire for his reported ties to the regime of that country's ruthless dictator, Robert Mugabe. Although Davy denied that he had ever even met Mugabe, Palace advisors cautioned Prince Charles and the Queen that the slightest hint of involvement with the notorious strongman could have far-reaching diplomatic consequences—particularly if Harry and Chelsy were to marry.

None of it mattered to Harry, who was already planning on taking Chelsy on a romantic ski holiday at Klosters in mid-January. But first he would spend Christmas at Sandringham, followed by an event that he and William had been looking forward to for weeks: a costume party to celebrate the twenty-second birthday of their friend Harry Meade, son of the Olympic equestrian Richard Meade.

The Heir and the Spare were both blithely unaware that they were about to unleash the biggest scandal of Harry's life thus far—a raging storm of controversy that imperiled his chances of ever having a future in the military and of ever being taken seriously as an adult, much less third in line to the throne.

With an eye on finding just the right costumes to fit Harry Meade's "Colonials and Natives" theme, the princes plowed through the racks at Maud's Cotswold Costumes near Highgrove. It didn't take long for William to decide to go as a lion, with big, floppy paws, ears, tail, black leggings, and furry feet. Just as quickly, Harry homed in on his choice: the short-sleeved khaki uniform of legendary Nazi field marshal Erwin "the Desert Fox" Rommel's Afrika Korps, which for a time early in World War II bedeviled Allied forces in North Africa. The outfit included a swastika armband and, on the chest, the eagle badge of the German armed forces, or Wehrmacht. Later, Harry would say that he was first attracted to the uniform because "guys with red hair always look good in khaki."

From the beginning, William had only words of praise for his brother's costume choice. "You look terrific, Harry," he told him at the shop. The princes were not so sure about their friend Guy Pelly's getup that evening. Pelly, who was perhaps unfairly chastised in the press for being a bad influence on his royal pals, was going as the Queen.

None of the 250 guests, many of whom also skirted the bounds of taste by wearing turbans, dreadlocks, Chinese "coolie" hats, and Native American dress, seemed bothered by Harry's Nazi uniform when the princes strolled into the party. Several thought it perfectly acceptable to join in the fun by clicking heels and delivering a "Heil Hitler" salute. For several hours, Harry mingled with the crowd, chain-smoking Marlboro Lights and polishing off one vodka tonic after another.

At one point, he was asked why he chose to wear a Nazi uniform. Harry drew a blank when the name Rommel was raised and looked nonplussed at the mention of the Desert Fox. Another guest recalled that "it was fairly obvious that Prince Harry did not have the slightest notion about swastikas or Nazis." For his part, William "seemed delighted with his brother's uniform" and "just as clueless" about the possible ramifications. After all, William had been instrumental in helping Harry choose his offensive attire. Incredibly, neither brother appeared particularly concerned that pictures of them were being taken by other guests. "I thought right at that moment that if it ever got out, it was going to land them both in trouble."

As it happened, it did get out, and quickly—but only one prince was held accountable. Harry alone was scolded by his infuriated father, flogged in the press, and denounced by political and religious leaders across the globe. Clarence House issued an official apology on Harry's behalf, stating that he apologized for "any offense or embarrassment" he may have caused. "He realizes," the brief statement concluded, "that it was a poor choice of costume."

Not enough, said Conservative Party leader Michael Howard. He, along with several other members of Parliament, demanded that Harry go on television and apologize directly to the people. There was also concern that Harry's gaffe could trigger a new wave of anti-Semitism. To head that off, Jewish leaders invited the young prince to visit Auschwitz. According to one former St. James's official, twenty-year-old Harry seemed puzzled by the invitation. "Auschwitz?" he allegedly replied with a quizzical look. "I got the distinct impression," the official said, "that he had no idea what that meant."

No one doubted that Harry's faux pas was entirely unintentional. But it did focus attention on what appeared to be a gaping hole in his education. Harry's family was a symbol of the fight against Fascism during World War II, but, astonishingly, he admitted to his Clarence House handlers that perhaps he did not know as much as he should. "Did he really know who Adolf Hitler was?" a St. James's official asked. "It was not clear to me at the time that he even knew that."

After branding Harry a "complete thicko," British commentator Tom Utley asked point-blank: "What the hell did they teach him during those five years at Eton? Prince Harry is a stupid young man who meant no harm, but we are not talking about an average level of stupidity. We are talking about stupidity on an absolutely monumental scale. It is the stupidity of a rather backward child of twelve."

On the floor of Parliament, there were calls for Harry to be barred from attending Sandhurst, but the Queen, through her courtiers, made it clear that she hoped the world-renowned military academy could whip Harry into shape. "Poor Harry just needs some direction," she told Margaret Rhodes. "He's a good boy, despite everything. He's a little lost."

Harry was, in a word, shattered. He also felt betrayed by the brother who could have spoken up publicly in his defense or at least assumed part of the blame for the Nazi fiasco. In private, William insisted that he saw nothing wrong with the costume choice and that the entire issue was being "blown out of all proportion." A mutual friend and Highgrove neighbor agreed that William "could have spoken up publicly, and maybe should have. But I think he was frightened about what that might mean for his family."

Indeed, as angry as Charles was with Harry, he was grateful that the focus of public outrage had been contained to the Spare. "Imagine if it had been William wearing the Nazi costume," journalist James Whitaker said. "It would have been a much bigger nightmare for the monarchy."

It was certainly bad timing for the Prince of Wales. Just three weeks earlier, Charles had asked for and received his sons' blessing to marry Camilla. If there were any lingering feelings of guilt over the fact that the woman who broke up their parents' marriage was replacing Diana, they just "melted away," said a friend from Gloucestershire. "William and Harry just wanted their father to be happy. They didn't feel they were betraying their mother."

The wedding of the Prince of Wales and his longtime mistress was supposed to be announced on February 14—Valentine's Day—but now he worried actively that his long-postponed marriage to the woman he had always loved could be derailed by another Harry-related public relations fiasco. By way of prevention, Charles hired a separate private secretary for William and Harry: forty-four-year-old Jamie Lowther-Pinkerton, a Gulf War–hardened major in the Irish Guards and former Special Forces officer who had served as the Queen Mother's equerry, or military aide.

Tall, patrician, and quietly authoritative, the father of three clicked instantly with both young princes. It helped that he shared their sense of humor. When asked what it was like being an aide to their

great-grandmother, the major recalled how at his first meeting with the
Queen Mother over lunch they discussed the best way of judging distance when flicking peas with a fork.

Over the next eight years, Lowther-Pinkerton would become not
only their most trusted advisor but also something of a father figure to
the boys, on call twenty-four hours a day with the advice and guidance
Charles had failed to provide. "Prince Charles never stepped in to take
the boys in hand the way Diana would have," Alan Hamilton observed.
"So it came as a relief to everyone when Lowther-Pinkerton came on
board."

In fairness, Charles had problems of his own. His engagement to
Camilla remained a secret for weeks—primarily due to the media's obsession with "Nazi Harry"—but that all changed once the Queen, as required by the Royal Marriage Act, informed Prime Minister Tony Blair
that wedding plans were in the works. That same afternoon word was
leaked to the press, and Clarence House was forced to make the announcement four days early. In a noticeably tepid statement of congratulations, the Queen and Prince Philip offered their "warmest good
wishes" to the happy couple. William and Harry, however, did not
want to leave any room for doubt about how they felt. In their joint
statement, the princes proclaimed flatly that they were behind the marriage that would make Camilla their stepmother "100 percent."

It could scarcely be said that the wedding itself went off without a
hitch. To start with, plans to hold the ceremony at Windsor had to be
abandoned when it was determined that if a license was issued to conduct the ceremony, anyone would have the right to be married at the
castle for the next three years. Instead, there would be a civil ceremony
at the town hall—Windsor Guildhall—followed by a blessing inside St.
George's Chapel.

Right away there was a challenge to the legality of a civil ceremony. Several scholars insisted that the future head of the Church of England must be married in an Anglican ceremony. The lord chancellor, Lord Falconer, shot down that objection. According to him, the Human Rights Act of 1998 allowed for any British citizen, including the heir to the throne, to be married in a civil ceremony.

None of which mattered to the Queen, who declared that despite Charles's pleading, she would not be among the thirty people attending the civil ceremony. She would, however, show up at the blessing ceremony that followed. Although her official excuse was that she did not want to eclipse the couple on their happy day, it was an obvious snub— one that reflected the country's general distaste for the union. Polls showed that more than nine out of ten Britons did not want Camilla as their next queen, and that 69 percent did not even want Charles as their next king; they preferred William instead.

For William and Harry, polls like these were a source of "immense distress," said a former Clarence House staffer, but for different reasons. "William and Harry both respected their father and hated to see him being treated so poorly. But, of course, for William there was also a sense that he was more the direct cause of his father's pain. He didn't like people comparing him to his father. He didn't think it was fair to either of them." Nor did he appreciate being "constantly reminded it was all going to be falling in his lap at some point. He wanted his own life."

Regardless of what the brothers felt, the drumbeat of opposition grew stronger, and Diana's friends led the charge. Vivienne Parry declared, "There is only one Princess of Wales in people's minds. And only when Prince William gets married . . . will it be time for another one." Another confidante of the late princess, Joan Berry, requested that the Queen call off the wedding "even at this late stage."

Charles scrambled to stanch the hemorrhaging. He promised that, once they were wed, Camilla would assume the title of Duchess of Cornwall and not be called Princess of Wales out of respect for William and Harry's late mother. Nor would she become Queen once he was crowned King. Instead, Charles pledged that she would assume the title of princess consort. This had a mollifying effect, although the fact remained that, by tradition and by law, Camilla would in reality be Princess of Wales *and* Queen—in that order.

Placating the public was one thing, but Prince Charles also had to convince the archbishop of Canterbury to conduct the forty-five-minute Service of Prayer and Dedication. Rowan Williams would agree only if Charles and Camilla made an overt act of contrition. Specifically, they would have to get down on their knees before the altar, then admit to and apologize for their flagrant adultery.

"Why are they doing this?" Charles complained to his long-suffering mistress. "Why does everyone want us to grovel?" The Prince of Wales had, it turned out, been griping in private about this for years. "I thought the British people were supposed to be compassionate," he confided to BBC-TV journalist Gavin Hewitt (no relation to James) while on a visit to Sofia, Bulgaria. "I don't see much of it." He went on to say that, for years, he had been "tortured" over his relationship with Camilla and that "all my life, people have been telling me what to do. I'm tired of it. I just want some peace."

Hewitt was surprised that Prince Charles was not just angry at the press but also at the people who were destined to become his subjects. "It was more than just an irritation," the journalist said. "I could sense he did not like the country that had so embraced Diana."

Sensing a major meltdown in the making, William and Harry took their father on a traditional "Stag Week" ski trip to Klosters. Unfortunately, it did little to brighten his mood. With open microphones just a few feet away, Harry and William smiled broadly as Charles eviscerated the reporters standing directly in front of him. "I can't bear that man," he said of the BBC's Nicholas Witchell. "He's so awful. He really is. Bloody people."

Realizing that their father's words were clearly audible, the brothers did what they could to keep Papa from digging an even bigger hole for himself. "Keep smiling," William murmured through his teeth. "Keep smiling." Trying his best to lighten the mood, the Heir said that he and his brother were "very happy, very pleased" about the wedding. "It will be a good day." All the while, their father "just sat there, fuming," said one of the photographers. "I wouldn't have been surprised if he got up and took a swing at one of us."

At least William was able to enjoy himself once Kate joined the party. Their masquerade over, the couple now felt free to canoodle on the slopes and afterward at the Chalet Eugenia. With Chelsy nowhere to be seen, Harry got drunk on Vodka Red Bull cocktails and began flirting with the young women who descended on Klosters—"always," in the words of the brothers' protection officer, "hovering about like fireflies." Still, Harry became emotional when a necklace Chelsy had given him broke, spilling beads all over the floor. "You don't understand," he said as he scrambled on all fours to retrieve the beads. "It's a gift from my girlfriend."

William and Harry were more than willing to see their father wed the woman everyone now acknowledged was the love of Prince Charles's life. But for all their professions of love, neither brother was quite ready yet to make that final leap into matrimony. At only twenty, Harry, who had yet to even begin his military career, was expected to play the field. But William had been seriously involved with one young woman for three years now, and he did not appreciate the pressure that was being brought to bear. "Look," he told a journalist shortly before his twenty-third birthday. "For God's sake, I'm too young to marry at my age. I don't want to get married until I am at least twenty-eight or maybe thirty."

Kate, who was six months older than William, harbored no illusions that a proposal would be coming any time. Nor was she eager to provoke speculation in the press by simply showing up at the wedding. So, while it came as a surprise to many, she was in fact relieved when her name was left off the guest list. From the comfort of their farmhouse at St. Andrews, she would study for final exams and watch events unfold on television.

At the brief civil ceremony, William fulfilled his one official obligation by producing the wedding rings. "Well, I'm happy with that," William told Camilla's son, Tom, as they waited outside for the couple to emerge. "Yup," Tom answered. "Me too."

Not so the Queen, who sat in surly silence throughout the subsequent blessing ceremony inside St. George's Chapel. "Cross," "sour," "sullen," and even "mean" were just a few of the adjectives used to describe Her Majesty's countenance throughout. She looked particularly perturbed when Charles and Camilla dropped to their knees in the transept to "bewail our manifold sins and wickedness, which we . . . most grievously have committed by thought, word, and deed against thy Divine Majesty, provoking most justly thy wrath and indignation against us."

Charles and Camilla had apparently not considered how irksome it would be for the racing-obsessed Queen to be torn from the Grand National Steeplechase, which was occurring the same day. Her Majesty made the best of it at the subsequent reception for eight hundred guests, likening the newlyweds to thoroughbreds who have "been over difficult jumps and all kinds of other terrible obstacles" but were finally "in the winners' enclosure."

The Queen and the Duke of Edinburgh reluctantly posed for the official wedding portraits, as did William and Harry—the first time any of them had ever been photographed with the once-notorious Mrs. Parker Bowles. The brothers also agreed that it was important they leave no doubt about how fond they were of their new stepmother. Even though Charles was never seen kissing his bride at any time during the day, William and Harry made a point of giving her a warm kiss on both cheeks as the happy couple left the reception. "It was," said royal family friend Santa Sebag Montefiore, "a real moment."

The boys had one more "real moment" up their collective sleeve. While guests nibbled on hors d'oeuvres and sipped champagne, William and Harry sneaked outside to decorate Charles's Bentley with Mylar balloons and scrawl graffiti across the windows and windshield reading "Just Married, C+C" and "Prince+Duchess." As the Balmoral-bound honeymooners walked arm in arm toward the waiting car, there was one more surprise: William and Harry lying in wait to ambush them with fistfuls of confetti.

Even at moments like these—or perhaps especially at moments like these—their mother's ghost was never far away. It seemed beyond imagining that, while Charles and Camilla finally pulled off their decades-in-the-making nuptials, a new investigation into Diana's death was gaining momentum. Mohamed Al Fayed was more vocal than ever in his assertion that Prince Philip ordered British intelligence to assassinate Diana and Dodi, and Operation Paget had been launched by Scotland Yard to look into this and other conspiracy theories.

Handpicked to head up the investigation was Metropolitan Police Commissioner John Stevens—Lord Stevens of Kirkwhelpington—who found himself in the unenviable position of having to grill both of Diana's sons on the subject of their mother's death. Even more daunting, Lord Stevens would have to ask Prince Charles and the famously irascible Prince Philip point-blank if they had conspired to murder the Princess of Wales.

As bizarre as the allegations may have appeared, there was ample cause to investigate them. There were the letters Diana had written to her lawyer, Lord Mishcon, in which she claimed her father-in-law was plotting with Britain's security services to kill her. "Prince Philip wants to see me dead," she told Lord Mishcon, adding that her murder would be staged to look like a helicopter or car crash. "They are going to get rid of me." She also told her friend Roberto Devorik that the Duke of Edinburgh "really hates me and would like to see me disappear." Then there was the letter handed to Paul Burrell in which she pointed the finger at Charles, claiming that her ex-husband was planning "an accident in my car, brake failure, and serious head injury" to clear the path for him to remarry.

Operation Paget would lumber on for two years before finally issuing its 832-page report confirming the findings of the original investigation in France: that the driver of the car in which Dodi and Diana were passengers on the night of August 31, 1997, was drunk; that paparazzi contributed to the crash; and that all three people who died that night failed to buckle up. But for now, William and Harry were dreading the prospect of being quizzed by investigators, not to mention the macabre possibility raised by royal coroner Michael Burgess that their mother's body might be exhumed for further toxicological tests. (In the end, such tests were deemed unnecessary.)

Distractions aside, on May 8, 2005, Harry reported for ten months of officer training at Sandhurst. Like his brother, the Spare's ultimate intention was to serve in the infantry—more specifically, on the front lines in Iraq and Afghanistan. "There's no way I'm going to put myself through Sandhurst," he insisted, "and then sit on my ass back home." But first he had to survive "five weeks of hell": boot camp. Soon Harry bragged that he was "being treated like a piece of dirt" by drill sergeants who called him "you 'orrible little prince." Harry lost twenty pounds and landed in the infirmary multiple times with blisters and the flu but insisted he was loving every minute of it. "I do enjoy running down a ditch full of mud, firing bullets. It's the way I am."

If all went according to plan, Harry would graduate and receive his commission as a lieutenant just as William was entering as a cadet. "Yes, I suppose I'll have to salute Harry," he told Peter Archer. "I'm sure he's looking forward to that. Terrible." But first Harry would have to step aside once again as William took his customary spot center stage—this time to receive his diploma from St. Andrews.

Seated front row center of the mezzanine in Younger Hall, Harry, Camilla, Prince Charles, Prince Philip, and the Queen leaned forward to see Kate Middleton step up to collect her degree in the history of art. Walking back to her seat, she exchanged smiles with William—a moment that elicited an approving nod from Her Majesty, who was won over by the auburn-haired commoner from the moment William first introduced them at Windsor. "Nice girl," she whispered to her husband before turning back to the main event.

No sooner had Dean of Arts Christopher Smith called the name "William Wales" than a roar went up from the crowd of graduating students and their families. With countless camera flashes illuminating the hall, William made his way to the stage and accepted his master of arts degree in geography.

All eyes were still on William and Kate when the school's vice chancellor, Brian Lang, launched into his well-worn commencement address. "I say this every year to all new graduates: you may have met your husband or wife," he proclaimed, as the world's most talked-about young couple sank deeper into their seats. "Our title as 'Top Matchmaking University in Britain' signifies so much that is good about St. Andrews, so we can rely on you to go forth and multiply."

Her Majesty took the hint. Determined to know more about Miss Middleton, the Queen invited her to tea while William was off to New Zealand on his first solo assignment as Her Majesty's representative at ceremonies marking the sixtieth anniversary of the end of World War II. Over the course of the summer of 2005, William and Kate dined privately with the Queen on three separate occasions—the clearest sign yet that an engagement was in the air. "The Queen," Camilla told a Wiltshire neighbor, "has obviously decided Miss Middleton is marriage material. She's checking her out," she added with more than a hint of sarcasm, "to see if she has the 'right stuff,' I suppose."

No one was bothering to check out Chelsy, who, despite her near-constant presence at Harry's side whenever the two were on the same continent, had met the Queen only once, and then only briefly. Yet "Haz," as Chelsy called him—he called her "Chedda"—was clearly besotted. And she was there to boost his morale whenever the press came down hard on him, most importantly as he suffered through his "Harry the Nazi" fiasco. "I would love to tell everyone how amazing she is," he said during his twenty-first-birthday interview. "I'm hugely protective of her. It's part of the baggage that comes with me, and she understands that. But I get to see how upset she gets, and I know the real her. Unfortunately, I can't turn around to the press and say, 'Listen, she's not like that—she's like *this*.' "

Harry had even fewer illusions about changing the public's perceptions of the Spare. "I'm never going to convince the general public of who I am," he said with a sigh, "because my image is always being portrayed as something else." Asked if he was a caring prince or a partying one, he replied, "Both! If that's a problem with anyone, then I'm very sorry."

In the same interview, Harry seized the opportunity to apologize fulsomely for having worn that Nazi uniform at Harry Meade's birthday party. As if to validate Harry's complaint, the *Sun* ran the front-page headline "*So Sorry*: Harry Opens His Heart over Nazi Gaffe," with the *S*'s in a Nazi SS-style lightning-bolt font.

In a revealing aside, Harry let it be known that as he grew to adulthood, he was feeling more and more anxiety over his position as third in the line of succession. Although extremely remote, there was no guarantee that William would agree to take on the job. The Heir often grumbled about not having control over his own destiny, and, after all, he would not be the first to throw up his hands and step aside—it had happened in spectacular fashion when King Edward VIII abdicated to marry Wallis Simpson in 1936. "He assures me," Harry said with a nervous laugh, "that he's not going to do that. I've had dreams . . ."

During his Sandhurst training, Harry and Chelsy bombarded each other with calls and texts throughout the day—even though cadets were supposedly allowed to use their cell phones only after they completed their official duties at ten in the evening. Such distractions aside, he still managed to graduate as planned on April 12, 2006. Among those present to watch Harry snap off a salute to his grandmother the Queen during the Sovereign's Parade: Prince Philip, Prince Charles, Camilla—and William, who had started his Sandhurst training three months earlier. In fact, as a mere cadet marching in the parade that day, William had to salute as he marched past his officer brother—"a moment which I really, really enjoyed," Harry confessed later.

Wearing a tan coat with fox-trimmed cuffs, the Queen told the 219 officer cadets that this was not only a "great occasion" but also "just the end of the beginning" of their military careers as they now awaited deployment. "My congratulations, my prayers, and my trust go with you all." While inspecting the cadets with their drawn sabers, the Queen and her grandson traded smiles when she stopped in front of Harry to give him a particularly intense once-over.

Chelsy did not show up at the passing-out ceremony—the Queen regarded this as strictly a family affair—but she did leave mouths agape with her entrance at the graduation ball that evening. Wearing a slinky, backless, turquoise silk dress, blond hair cascading over her bare shoulders, Chelsy drank champagne and danced with Harry until midnight—the moment at which, following tradition, he ripped the velvet strip off his jacket sleeve to reveal his lieutenant's stripes.

Since Harry could invite only eight guests to the ball, Kate graciously offered to bow out so that in addition to William and Chelsy, he could invite a few buddies from his Ludgrove and Eton days. Kate was there the following night when the princes continued celebrating at Boujis with the club's signature Crackbaby cocktail, a potent mixture of vodka, passion fruit juice, raspberry liqueur, and champagne served in a test tube.

Nine days later, there was even more cause for celebration, as twenty-five members of the royal family gathered to toast the Queen on her eightieth birthday at the newly refurbished Kew Palace, once home to King George III. While a twelve-piece string ensemble played selections from Handel's *Water Music*, the Queen chatted cheerfully with the two men seated on either side of her—Charles and William—

while guests dined on juniper-roast loin of Sandringham Estate venison and Hebridean smoked salmon.

Harry, seated far from the center of the action despite his high rank in the Firm, was his usual lively self. Having been relegated to the side-lines since childhood, he was well accustomed to not getting the sort of attention that was lavished on William at events like these. As an adult, however, there were signs that the entire unspoken arrangement was beginning to wear thin. "Prince Harry was all smiles and laughs," observed one of the Buckingham Palace footmen working at Kew Palace that night. "The Queen really is very fond of Harry, but, at family gatherings, he's often kept at a distance. You can see him glancing over, trying to read lips: 'Hmm, I wonder what they're saying.'"

Intent on making his own mark, Harry returned to Lesotho to team up with that country's Prince Seeiso to form Sentebale ("Forget Me Not"), a new charity for children orphaned by AIDS. No sooner did he arrive than Harry sought out Mutsu Potsane, the six-year-old boy he had struck up a relationship with during his visit two years earlier. As soon as his truck roared up to the entrance of the Mants'ase Children's Home, Harry jumped out, found the boy in the crowd, and swept him up in his arms.

"Do you remember me?" he asked Mutsu. The boy nodded shyly. "I've never seen him so quiet," Harry said. A nurse explained that the child was simply overwhelmed, adding, "He's been waiting for you." Then, with Mutsu center stage in the prince's lap, Harry beckoned the other children to lean in for a group shot. "Come back in twenty-five years," he said of his new charity. "You'll see a massive difference. As far as I'm concerned, I'm committed to this for the rest of my life." When someone asked if his mother would be proud, Harry took a moment to think. "I hope so," he answered with a smile.

Once Sentebale was launched, Harry and Chelsy flew off to Mozambique for another Paradise Island idyll—their last vacation before he began a ten-week course in tank warfare at the Bovington Camp in Dorset. Meanwhile, William and Kate escaped to Villa Hibiscus on the exclusive island enclave of Mustique in the Grenadines. Mustique had royal connections going back to the 1950s, when the high-living Princess Margaret built a lavish villa there. Mick Jagger bought a place on Mustique in 1971 and was soon joined by the likes of David Bowie and Richard Branson. Two other island residents—fashion moguls John and Belle Robinson, founders of the Jigsaw clothing chain—graciously waved the customary $14,000 weekly rental fee and lent Villa Hibiscus, their estate overlooking Macaroni Beach, to the young cadet and his girlfriend.

The couple spent a blissful week in unaccustomed solitude, playing beach volleyball, frolicking in the surf, and sipping mai tais at Basil's Bar. But once they arrived back in London, they realized that they had never really escaped the long lens of the paparazzi. In newspapers across the globe, people were getting a gander at the couple in their bathing suits, hosing themselves off on the deck of Branson's yacht.

FOR THE TIME BEING, William focused on protecting the girl he loved from the same forces that had destroyed his mother. Now that they had graduated, and the couple was no longer living together full-time, Fleet Street's gloves were off—and Kate was considered fair game. There was never a security problem whenever the prince stayed over on a free weekend at her family's stucco-fronted flat across from a Chelsea bus stop; his royal protection squad was always reliably close by—at times, annoyingly so. But for the most part, Kate lived there alone and unprotected; since there was no formal relationship between William and Kate, she was not entitled to her own officers from SO14, the Royalty Protection Group.

None of this mattered to the paparazzi who leapt out at her from behind parked cars, chased her down the street, or hid in the bushes outside her flat to ambush her as she left to go to the store. William threatened legal action and ordered St. James's Palace to badger newspaper editors with rebukes and reprimands. Not surprisingly, the press would have none of it. "Kate Middleton wants the privacy of a nun," editorialized the *Sun*, "yet she chooses to go out with Prince William. She can't have it both ways."

Yet calm, self-assured Kate had always shown herself to be remarkably adept at handling photographers even under the toughest circumstances. It was William who, in the ongoing struggle to find some measure of control over his own life, now felt increasingly powerless to head off what he saw as the inevitable.

For years, he and his brother had relived their mother's death in terrifyingly vivid technicolor dreams. As they grew into adulthood, the nightmares invaded their sleep less frequently. But now, as William confided to his father, as well as Harry and the most trusted members of his inner circle, the dreams were back—albeit with a difference. The car being chased by cars and motorcycles was not a Mercedes but a Bentley, and it careened through the streets of London, not Paris. Most chillingly, the young, female victim in the back passenger seat pleading for the driver to slow down was not the Princess of Wales. It was Kate.

Every year we get closer.
It's amazing how close we've become.
Ever since our mother died, obviously we were close,
but he is the one person on this earth who I can talk to
about anything. If I find myself in really hard times,
then at least I can turn to him, and vice versa,
and we can look after each other.

—Harry

It'll either make or break you, and I wouldn't let it break me.

—William, on dealing with grief and depression

FOUR

"THIS IS NOT RIGHT, THIS IS NOT NORMAL"

Westminster Abbey
April 29, 2011

I**T WAS A** sign from heaven, she later told them, and William and Harry knew better than to argue with their grandmother the Queen. The moment Kate Middleton stepped out of the 1977 Rolls-Royce Phantom VI, a shaft of sunlight pierced the dark clouds hanging over London and shone directly on her. The moment was abundant with meaning, and not only for the bride. Not long before, antimonarchists shouting, "Off with their heads!" had attacked the Prince of Wales and his wife, the Duchess of Cornwall, in this very same Phantom VI. Kate had always impressed William with her sense of history, but never more so than when she insisted that the battle-battered car be restored so that she and her father, Michael Middleton, could ride in it to the abbey—and make crystal clear to the world that the monarchy wasn't going anywhere.

Wearing a dress of ivory silk overlaid with lace by Alexander McQueen's Sarah Burton and a tiara loaned to her by the Queen, Kate waved to the cheering crowd and then walked with her father toward the abbey's west door. Gathering up the nine-foot train of her sister's bridal gown was Pippa, who was just as striking in a form-hugging white silk sheath.

Waiting inside with the 1,900 assembled guests were William and his best man: the groom dressed in the scarlet uniform of a colonel in the Irish Guards, and Harry in the black, gold-braided and medal-bedecked uniform of a captain in the Household Cavalry's Blues and Royals regiment. The bride was only halfway up the aisle when Harry, who was facing the altar with his brother, turned around to look, then whispered in William's ear. Once Kate finally arrived, William gazed adoringly at her. "You look beautiful," he said before turning to Michael Middleton. "I thought," he told the father of the bride, "this was supposed to be a small family affair."

In some respects, it still was. In addition to the billionaires, politicians, and aristocrats who had been invited by the Queen and Prince Charles were the newlyweds' childhood friends, schoolmates, and university pals. Also asked to attend were all twenty-seven of William's squadron members—he was now serving in the Royal Air Force as a search-and-rescue helicopter pilot—along with the survivors of fellow Sandhurst cadets killed in Afghanistan and Iraq. Representatives of several charities William supported were also there including the African wildlife group Tusk Trust, the London homeless shelter Centrepoint, the Child Bereavement Charity, and the wounded soldiers' organization Help for Heroes. Kate, wanting to thank the people she had known growing up in Bucklebury, invited the local mailman, grocer, butcher, several convenience store clerks, and the proprietor of their favorite Bucklebury pub, the Old Boot Inn.

A cheer went up outside the abbey when the archbishop of Canterbury pronounced William and Kate "man and wife," and an even bigger one when the newly minted Duke and Duchess of Cambridge—venerated titles the Queen had been holding on to for just this occasion—stepped outside and into the same horse-drawn open 1902 State Landau that carried Charles and Diana from their wedding at St. Paul's Cathedral thirty years earlier. "I'm so happy," Kate said as the carriage pulled away from the abbey and passed the one million well-wishers who lined the route to Buckingham Palace.

An hour later, William, Kate, Harry, and the rest of the royal wedding party were standing on the balcony waving at the half million people who gathered in front of Buckingham Palace. The newlyweds kissed quickly, then, sensing disappointment, did it again—this time with more enthusiasm. By way of a grand finale, soon everyone was squinting up at a thundering Royal Air Force flypast of Spitfires, Typhoons, Tornados, and Hawker Hurricanes.

The reception that night started in the Ballroom, the largest of Buckingham Palace's 775 rooms, then cascaded into the Blue Drawing Room, the White Drawing Room, and the State Drawing Room. In his best man's toast, Harry apologized to Kate "for having to marry a bald man," delivered spot-on impressions of William "cooing down the line at 'Babykins'" and Kate calling his brother "Billy," and referred to them repeatedly as "the dude and the duchess." There was one line the guests never got to hear. In singing his new sister-in-law's attributes, Harry was going to praise Kate's "killer legs"—a reference that Chelsy convinced him to cut on grounds of taste.

There were muffled sobs when Harry told his brother, "Our mother would be so very proud of you," and sighs when he said he loved Kate like a sister. At one point, the bride wiped away tears when her newly minted brother-in-law traded smiles with Chelsy and admitted that Kate and William's decadelong romance was his "inspiration."

Once the speeches were over, the action moved to the Throne Room, which maid of honor Pippa had transformed into a nightclub complete with disco, pulsating lights, a DJ, and giant bowls filled with Will and Kate's favorite Haribo candies. After the happy couple danced to the John Travolta–Olivia Newton-John hit "You're the One That I Want," friends lifted William and Kate up on their shoulders and carried them around the room—"like a scene," said one American guest, "from *Fiddler on the Roof*."

After one too many Crackbabies and glasses of Laurent-Perrier champagne, Harry had everyone in hysterics when he unbuttoned his dress shirt, climbed up onto a windowsill, and dove into the crowd. As fireworks signaled an end to the party at three in the morning, Harry put his arms around William and Kate and began to weep. Soon the best man and the bride were helping brush away each other's tears while a bemused and thoroughly dry-eyed William looked on. "People don't realize how much Harry and Kate love and help each other," another guest said of the moment. "It's key to this whole thing."

HAD IT NOT BEEN for Harry, "this whole thing"—the wedding of the century—might never have happened, even though it didn't seem inevitable as far back as the Sovereign's Parade marking Will's graduation from Sandhurst in December 2006. Back then, Kate and her parents watched from front-row VIP seats as William marched by. "I love the uniform," she whispered to her mother at the time. "It's so, so sexy." As she had with Harry the year before, the Queen reviewed the ramrod-straight troops and paused in front of Cadet William Wales just long enough to crack him up.

To the world at large, Kate's presence at William's passing-out ceremonies—an honor denied Chelsy Davy when Harry graduated— meant than an engagement announcement was imminent. "Her elegance, dignity, and beauty certainly make her the people's choice," proclaimed the *Sunday Times*'s Deirdre Fernand. "Kate is what we need." Bubbled Geordie Greig in the magazine *Tatler*: "She is perfect princess material—a Diana II."

But in truth, the couple were entering a perilous period in their relationship. On January 9, 2007, Kate turned twenty-five. It was also the day William reported for duty as a second lieutenant in the same regiment his brother belonged to, the Blues and Royals. By Valentine's Day, she expected an engagement ring but got a $17,000 diamond-encrusted Van Cleef & Arpels compact instead. A friend used one word to describe Kate's reaction: "crestfallen."

Not coincidentally, only days earlier Harry was told that in May he would be deployed to Iraq with the rest of his outfit. When he got the news, "Cornet Wales," as Harry was known in the army, cheered, leapt in the air, and waved his arms. "He was over the moon," recalled a fellow officer. "Haz," a worried Chelsy said, "is off to war."

William knew too well that the Queen would probably never put him in harm's way, but nonetheless gamely went off to spend the requisite ten weeks learning tank warfare in Dorset. Sadly for Kate, the more time Second Lieutenant Wales spent with his raucous army buddies off-hours, the more it became clear why his regiment was known throughout the British military as the "Booze and Royals." At a local hangout called Elements, a thoroughly soused William groped eighteen-year-old Brazilian student Ana Ferreira and wound up taking another student, nineteen-year-old Lisa Agar, back to his barracks for a nightcap. When Agar left shortly before dawn, she was under the impression that the prince was "depressed" about his relationship with Kate. "Strangely," she recalled, "I felt sorry for him."

Kate sensed it, too, telling her mother that somehow William had "changed." Indeed, for the first time in years they were spending weeks apart, and the physical distance, she reasoned, was taking an emotional toll. But it was worse than that. Spending time with his fellow officers had led the prince to question his relationship with Kate. He complained to his father that their arrangement now felt "claustrophobic." It hardly mattered that the eternally patient Miss Middleton—called "Waity Katy" in countless tabloid stories—said nothing when he ventured out on the town to dance the night away with other women.

There was something else. William still could not shake the deep and abiding fears he still harbored for her safety. The premonition that Kate would meet the same fate as Diana grew stronger, the recurring nightmares more terrifyingly vivid than ever. Now that he was embarking on a military career, William told his private secretary that leaving her at the mercy of the paparazzi was the same as "throwing her to the wolves."

William approached his father for advice, knowing how fond the Prince of Wales had grown of Kate over the years. Charles, who remembered all too well how Prince Philip pressured him to marry Lady Diana Spencer, asked his son if he intended "to marry her in the end." William responded that he was only twenty-five and not ready to commit himself to marry anyone. "Then end it now," Charles told him. Leading her on like this was "completely unfair to Kate."

In a matter of hours, William broke up with Kate in a tearful cell phone call. Devastated, she fled to her parents' home in Bucklebury to await the inevitable humiliating headlines. In terms of brevity and sheer shock value, the *Daily Mail* headline topped them all: "IT'S OVER." The news was so unsettling that Tony Blair was moved to issue a public statement from 10 Downing Street reassuring the British public that the Earth hadn't tilted on its axis. "They are a young couple," the prime minister said. "We've had the announcement. Fine. They should be left alone."

Not one to wallow, Kate put her head together with her mother and sister and came up with a strategy to win William back. Toward that end, she hit the clubs with a vengeance, sometimes with Pippa (they were now facetiously dubbed the "Wisteria Sisters" because of their "ferocious ability to climb") but even more often on the arm of one of the rich, titled, and handsome young bachelors she was now free to date. To make the point that she was now steering her own course, Kate also was photographed at the helm of a dragon boat, shouting orders to an all-women rowing crew called the Sisterhood.

Harry, who was stationed at Windsor while awaiting his deployment overseas, had initially said nothing about the breakup out of respect for his father. But now he told his brother point-blank: "Man, are you crazy? I don't care what Papa said, Kate is the best thing that ever happened to you!" Suddenly, according to their friend Jules Knight, it was obvious William "felt he had made a huge mistake."

Precisely six weeks after he told Kate they were through, William was pleading for her to forgive him. She did, instantly, but the public remained unaware of their reconciliation for another month. In the meantime, they got together privately to celebrate the fact that he was now turning twenty-five—a significant birthday because it meant he could begin collecting more than $600,000 in annual earnings from the money he had inherited from Diana. This was in addition to the expenses covered by Charles and the Queen as well as his own generous allowance.

The world would learn that William and Kate had patched things up on July 1, 2007, when sixty-three thousand people crammed into Wembley Stadium for the celebrity-packed Concert for Diana commemorating both her forty-sixth birthday and the tenth anniversary of her death. But even during the *Today* show exclusive interview they gave just days before, the brothers revealed nothing about the states of their respective relationships.

They did, however, provide the first real glimpse of their easygoing, warm, banter-filled rapport that had evolved in the decade since the world saw them walking behind their mother's coffin. They joked about William having "all the bright ideas" in planning the historic concert, while Harry's contribution was "nothing." Tellingly, they finished each other's sentences, even as the conversation moved on to the emotional scars that had yet to heal since Diana's death. "Not a day goes by when I don't think about it," William said. "For us, it's been very slow." Harry explained that, for the brothers, the situation was "weird because . . . there was never that sort of lull. There was never that sort of peace and quiet for any of us. Her face was always splattered on the papers the whole time. Over the last ten years, I personally feel she has always been there—a constant reminder to both of us." With his brother nodding in agreement, Harry also stressed that their goal was "to be as normal as possible" despite having "certain responsibilities." But he also conceded that "to a certain respect, we will never be normal."

At the concert, Kate was impossible to miss in a white skintight minidress as she took her place in the royal box—two rows behind Harry and Chelsy, the Spencer clan, royal sidekicks Guy Pelly and

Thomas van Straubenzee, and William. Kate struggled to control her emotions when the brothers, casually dressed in jeans and open-necked shirts, received a standing ovation as they rose to speak. "This event is about all that our mother loved in life," William told the television audience of one billion people in 120 countries. "Her music, her dancing, her charities, and her family and friends. We just want you to have an awesome time."

The courtship would continue at a glacial pace, as Kate realized she'd have to hang in there while William pursued his dreams of military service. As the future commander in chief of Britain's fighting forces, the Heir wanted to familiarize himself with all branches of the military by serving in the army, the Royal Air Force, and the Royal Navy. Yet it was doubtful that the prime minister, in consultation with Granny, would ever send the future monarch into battle. "There is simply no way," said a veteran diplomat, "they are going to put him at risk."

William saw an opening, however, after his younger brother finally got his wish to see action, in Afghanistan. Aware that Harry would be a prime target for kidnapping or assassination by enemy forces, the Palace agreed to send him to a war zone on one condition: that Fleet Street agree to sit on the story. Once there, Harry—known to the pilots he was directing from the ground only by the radio call name Widow Six Seven—was in the thick of it. Poring over maps and surveillance images, he identified targets and then called in drone strikes to take out pockets of Taliban fighters—a dozen or more at a time. Since he was keeping a video diary of his experiences, Harry's first firefight with the enemy was captured for posterity. "This is the first time," he said with a smile as he squeezed the trigger of a .50-caliber machine gun, "I've fired a fifty-cal."

Amazingly, the British press kept its promise. But Harry had to be spirited out of Afghanistan in February 2008 after the story was broken by the online news website the Drudge Report. As soon as his plane touched down in the United Kingdom, Harry was whisked off to an interview—part of the deal in exchange for the media blackout. William made sure he was on hand to protect his brother, who was clearly exhausted and, more important, disappointed.

"I didn't see it coming," Harry said of the decision to cut short his tour of duty out of fear that he would be killed or captured now that the Taliban knew he was close by. "It's a shame. Angry would be the wrong word to use. . . . I thought I could see it to the end and come back with our guys."

William stood up and cut the interview short when it was clear that Harry was physically and emotionally drained. "It was simply a young man realizing that at that point nothing was more important than his brother's welfare, and none of the other agreements mattered at that point," explained Defense Ministry spokesman Miguel Head, who would later serve as the princes' chief of staff. "And it says something about the closeness of the two brothers and their authenticity as well," he said. "They will not fake who they are simply to play a game or to go along with other people's expectations."

Two months later, the colonel in chief of the Blues and Royals, Princess Anne, pinned a service medal on her nephew's chest. William and Charles looked on, as did Chelsy, whose letters and satellite phone chats had boosted Harry's morale during his months in the desert. Although he often boasted to his comrades about the beautiful blond South African girl who awaited his return, Harry left no doubt that he wanted to get back to the front lines—and soon. "I don't want to sit around in Windsor," he said. "I generally don't like England that much, and, you know, it's nice to be away from the papers and all the general shit they write."

William was occasionally the target of such "general shit," to be sure. But Harry perceived rightly that there was a distinct difference in the way he and his brother were treated by both Fleet Street and Buckingham Palace's Men in Gray. Determined to become the fourth generation of Windsor men to earn pilot's wings (his great-grandfather George VI joined the Royal Air Force when it was founded in 1918), William reported to RAF Cranwell's Central Flying School in January 2008. Three months later, Flying Officer Wales was transferred to RAF Shawbury, a base 170 miles northwest of London, to take the controls of a helicopter for the first time.

Lauded by Commander Andy Lovell for his "natural handling ability," William moved on to RAF Odiham, just thirty-five miles southwest of London. Soon the Heir—along with an instructor and a crew of three—was buzzing friends and relatives in a $17 million twin-rotor Chinook troop carrier. After circling Highgrove, William moved on to Oak Acre, where Kate waved up to him from her bedroom window. Over a period of weeks, he used the Chinook to fly to a wedding, then to buzz the Queen at Sandringham—not realizing she was at Windsor at the time.

Kate looked on proudly as Charles, in his role as air chief marshal, presented his son with his provisional wings. The next day, William was off again in his Chinook—this time to pick up Harry at his barracks and fly on to a stag party on the Isle of Wight. By early spring, the total bill for His Royal Highness's five joyrides, all made at taxpayers' expense, topped $150,000.

Once Prince William's ongoing game of helicopter hopscotch became public, top brass was understandably peeved. "Sheer stupidity!"

were the words Air Chief Marshal Sir Glenn Torpy used to describe the unauthorized joyrides, which seemed particularly disrespectful given that British soldiers and airmen were fighting and dying in Iraq and Afghanistan. But by and large, in contrast to the brutal thrashings Harry suffered in print for his actions, the press chalked up William's antics to the natural exuberance of a young airman. Although no one could come up with an example of a twin-rotor Chinook transport being used to buzz a royal residence or attend a stag party, it was noted that an RAF pilot or two had been known to buzz a girlfriend's house.

More disturbing was the official report, which found no wrongdoing on the part of the future king: "All flights undertaken with Flying Officer Wales were planned, briefed, authorized, and flown by him . . . in accordance with extant regulations." Clarence House was willing to concede it was "a collective error of judgment," but Will was unfazed. Even as he was being called out for his "reckless" behavior on the floor of Parliament, the prince replaced his joyrides with a six-hundred-mile-an-hour thrill ride aboard a $50 million Tornado fighter jet—"the most awesome, most amazing experience of my life," he exulted later.

William's immediate superiors were not so thrilled when the army was accused of allowing him to use its aircraft as his personal taxi service. While the official line was that all officers had been absolved, it was later revealed that William's senior officers took the blame and were "counseled" for not stopping the headstrong royal. According to emails ricocheting up and down the chain of command, neither the prince nor his aides had actually told the officers about "the true nature" of his joyrides to weddings and stag parties. "Had the station commander known," complained one officer who took the rap, "the sorties would never have been flown."

As far as Will was concerned, none of it really mattered if he didn't get a chance to serve in a combat zone. In April 2008, though, he got his wish when the Queen green-lighted his deployment to Central Asia. The prince's sad mission was to pilot a C-17 Globemaster troop transport to Afghanistan to pick up the body of a slain British soldier. The entire mission took just thirty hours. Switched to train with the Royal Navy, William got another shot at adventure just two months later when, while serving aboard the frigate HMS *Iron Duke*, he piloted a Lynx helicopter that seized $70 million worth of cocaine from a speedboat in waters off Barbados.

IT WAS TIME, OR so Charles and the Queen thought, that William start his full duties with the Firm. After all, he had already been secretly helping to shape policy behind the scenes for nearly two years as a member of the Way Ahead Group, Her Majesty's tight-knit circle of family and anonymous advisors whose sole purpose was to chart a future course for the monarchy. Its members included Princes Charles, Andrew, and Edward, Princess Anne, and, of course, the Queen.

The details of what was said during their twice-yearly meetings remained strictly confidential, but the issues were of critical importance. The Queen's decisions to voluntarily pay income taxes, to mothball the royal yacht HMS *Britannia*, and to end primogeniture—the thousand-year-old rule stipulating that males have precedence over females in the line of succession—all grew out of Way Ahead Group deliberations.

Although Harry was third in line to the throne, he was not invited to join. Nor was he asked to participate in the decision-making process, much of which focused on ways to fulfill Prince Charles's vision of a more efficient, streamlined version of the monarchy. To accomplish this, several Windsor offspring would theoretically be demoted, stripped of their HRH standing, have their royal protection taken away, and—most alarming of all—kicked off the royal payroll. These changes, Charles suggested, would leave a new core team of royals to be the face of the Firm: the Queen and Prince Philip, Charles and Camilla, William and Kate—and Harry.

The Spare may have technically been included in the top tier, but he began to realize that it would "not always be thus," said a veteran courtier. "The 'slimmed-down' version of the monarchy that Prince Charles has in mind doesn't allow for many branches. It's a very narrow chain of command, with the power residing in the monarch and those in direct line: William and his children, then their children, and so on."

Despite Anne's own vaunted standing as princess royal (a title bestowed solely at the discretion of the monarch, there have been only seven princesses royal in all of British history), her children, Zara and Peter, were not automatically given titles at birth. But even after the Queen offered them, Anne turned down the titles to relieve her son and daughter from the burden of living their lives in the public eye. Edward's children were Lady Louise Windsor and James, Viscount Severn, although they might well have been entitled to be called Princess and Prince.

Prince Andrew, however, felt differently. He fought proposals that would have resulted in his daughters, Beatrice and Eugenie, being kicked off royal protection, forced to earn their own living, and downgraded from Princess to Lady—a suggestion that was shouted down in an angry confrontation between him and Charles—cautioning that it would then be only a matter of time before the next generations of secondary royals were similarly marginalized.

For all the string-pulling by others to ensure William's spot near the top of the Firm's power pyramid, the future monarch was hardly eager to begin a lifetime of tree plantings, ribbon cuttings, and working the rope line. Both he and Harry were now committed to a variety of causes and charities of their own choosing, and their philanthropic energy was beginning to rub off on Kate. More to the point, there were grumblings at the Palace that Miss Middleton had no charitable interests, and that if she wished to be part of the royal family, she'd have to get some.

Her first attempt was to raise money for a new surgical ward at Oxford Children's Hospital to be named after a mutual friend of hers and both princes, Tom Waley-Cohen, who'd been diagnosed with bone cancer as a teenager and died at age twenty. With encouragement from William and Harry, Kate organized the Day-Glo Midnight Roller Disco, and promptly flopped spread-eagle on the roller rink floor. Kate dissolved in hysterics as she was helped to her feet, but the unflattering tabloid photos that resulted had the Men in Gray fuming over such an "unseemly display." No matter, Kate's roller disco party raised $200,000 for Tom's Ward. "She threw herself into it," said Tom's brother Sam Waley-Cohen. "Literally!"

Not long after, the brothers revved up—again, literally—to raise money for several charities dear to their hearts: Sentebale, UNICEF, and the Nelson Mandela Children's Fund. They paid $3,000 each to race their Honda CRF 230 cc bikes against a hundred others in the Enduro Africa off-road motorcycle rally, choking on dust as they rocketed through a thousand miles of challenging terrain to raise nearly $300,000.

Adventure, excitement, risk taking—these were the things that made the Brothers Royal come alive. Yet there was little room for such things in the life of a working royal. "If they are going to do the things they really want to do, then they better do them now," said British-born entertainment journalist Robin Leach, "because that window is closing—fast."

That is precisely what William did. In defiance of Prince Charles, and without consulting anyone, he signed on in late 2008 for five years with the RAF as a search-and-rescue helicopter pilot. Fellow action man Harry cheered his brother's decision, and both pointed out to Charles that, after all, he had served in the navy and the RAF for five years. "My father's angry now," Harry told Guy Pelly, "but he understands. He and my grandfather are always saying being in the navy was the happiest time of their lives."

Early in 2009 William and Kate moved into a rented five-bedroom farmhouse just outside Blaenau Ffestiniog on the Welsh island of Anglesey, home of RAF Valley Air Base—making him the first member of the royal family to live in Wales since Henry VII some five hundred years before. Given the remote location, fifteen new royal protection officers were assigned to Prince William at an added annual cost to the British taxpayer of $2 million.

No one really noticed, in part because Harry was once again stirring public outrage. This time there was video of him three years earlier during military exercises on the island of Cyprus when he was still a Sandhurst cadet. At one point, Harry pans over his comrades resting in the RAF departure lounge while waiting for their flight. "Ah," Harry says as he zooms in on one cadet, "our little Paki friend Ahmed." The "little Paki friend" turned out to be Ahmed Raza Khan, by 2009 a captain in the British army. To another cadet wearing a camouflage hood: "It's Dan the man! Fuck me, you look like a raghead."

Both "Paki" (slang for Pakistani) and "raghead" (to denote anyone in a turban) are considered ethnic slurs. But that wasn't all. At one point, he kisses one soldier, then asks another if he feels "gay, queer, or 'on the side.'" A frequent refrain from Harry throughout: "All is good in the empire."

Reaction was swift. "It is obviously a completely unacceptable thing to say," declared Conservative Party leader David Cameron. The future prime minister went on to voice concern that Harry's comments undermined efforts to root out racism from the country's armed forces. On the other side of the aisle, Labour Party lawmaker Khalid Mahmood also blasted Harry for his remarks. "He needs to understand that this is not acceptable," Mahmood said, "especially as a member of the royal family." Mohammed Shafiq, director of the Ramadan Foundation, one of Britain's leading Muslim organizations, was more blunt: "Prince Harry's language is sickening, and he should be thoroughly ashamed of himself."

St. James's Palace swiftly issued an apology on Harry's behalf. "Prince Harry fully understands how offensive this term [Paki] can be and is extremely sorry for any offence his words might cause," the statement read. However, it went on to say that he used the term "without malice" and as a nickname for a "highly popular" member of his platoon. "There is no question that Prince Harry was in any way seeking to insult his friend." As for "raghead," the St. James's spokesman tried to explain that the term was widely used to describe a Taliban or Iraqi insurgent. In Pakistan, no one was buying it; government leaders in Islamabad went so far as to demand that Britain launch a formal investigation into Harry's behavior but were promptly rebuffed.

As calls for Harry to be formally reprimanded continued to mount, the Defense Ministry issued its own statement making clear that the British Army "takes all allegations of inappropriate behavior very seriously." But since none of his fellow soldiers had filed complaints, no action would be taken.

According to several Sandhurst graduates, such terminology was common among not only cadets but also the drill sergeants and other noncommissioned officers and enlisted men who trained them. "Oh, come on," scoffed one, "this is the army. Some of the things said about blacks, Asians, and women are far worse."

Beyond sparking outrage among Muslims, Harry's remarks also showed a callous disregard for the LGBTQ community, which in 2000 had won its fight to allow gays and bisexuals to serve openly in the British military. Then there was Harry's "All is good in the empire" mantra—an attempt at wry humor, clearly, but an insensitive one, given the seldom pretty history of British colonial rule. The fact that these casual references to the days of the British Empire were being made by the third in line to the British throne made them sound all the more misguided. As one longtime diplomat put it: "For more than sixty years, the Queen has worked tirelessly to make Commonwealth members forget they were once British colonies. This kind of thing certainly does not help the cause."

Adding to the awkwardness of the moment was the fact that Diana's last two lovers were Muslim—one of them Pakistani. The princess was so besotted with Pakistani heart surgeon Hasnat Khan, in fact, that she studied the Koran and flew to the city of Lahore to meet his parents. "Diana loved Muslim men—she thought they were the most handsome men in the world," said Oonagh Toffolo, who introduced Diana to Khan. "She would have been disappointed in Harry for saying such things, and she would have told him so, but she would have forgiven him. Diana loved military men, too. She certainly knew how they talked."

Now that his son was a decorated army officer, Charles no longer felt the need to scold Harry. Nor did the Queen, who was inclined to give her puckish grandson the benefit of the doubt—particularly in light of Prince Philip's long history of notoriously inappropriate comments.

William was another matter. Yet again, the one person whose support meant the most to Harry was conspicuous by his silence. Moreover, William knew better than anyone from his own military experience that his younger brother's remarks were not meant to wound. These were among the terms, many of which are not remotely acceptable outside locker rooms and barracks, that soldiers used to poke harmless fun at one another—all with the goal of relieving long stretches of boredom punctuated by moments of adrenaline-pumping tension.

Even the smallest gesture of solidarity between brothers could have made a huge difference in countering the public's growing perception of Harry as a buffoon, but none was forthcoming. "Prince William knows who he is, what role he has to fulfill, and what the consequences would be if it looked like he was minimizing what Harry said," observed Alan Hamilton of the *Times*. "They may be brothers, but William must play by a quite different set of rules."

Kate could certainly sympathize with Harry. Although she hated having her privacy invaded and winced every time she was depicted as long-suffering Waity Katy, William's girlfriend seldom came in for direct criticism. Her family was another matter. For starters, there were the persistent media reports depicting Carole as a gum-cracking, chain-smoking social climber who lacked both background and breeding—the very definition of nouveau riche. Then there were snapshots of her brother, James, both in drag and naked, and, perhaps most alarmingly, a stream of tabloid stories describing in excruciating detail the exploits of Kate's unapologetically foul-mouthed, cocaine-snorting uncle, tech magnate Gary Goldsmith.

After it was discovered that William and Kate had vacationed at Maison de Bang Bang, Goldsmith's indelicately named estate on the Spanish resort island of Ibiza, *News of the World* had a field day. "Kate Middleton Drug and Vice Shock," shouted the headline. "Tycoon Who Boasts of Hosting Will's Villa Holiday Supplies Cocaine and Fixes Hookers." Underlying the sordid details of Uncle Gary's libertine lifestyle were genuine concerns for the prince's safety voiced by his royal protection team. Yet, unlike Harry, who in all likelihood would have been roasted for having accepted Goldsmith's invitation, William received virtually no direct criticism in the media. (Incidentally, in 2017 Goldsmith changed the name of his infamous villa to the marginally more tasteful Villa Tesoro de Oro, or House of the Golden Treasure.)

It wasn't long before another royal scandal reared its very familiar head, taking some of the heat off Kate and her family. The same *News of the World* undercover team that trapped Gary Goldsmith released a hidden camera videotape of Sarah Ferguson soliciting a $700,000 bribe for access to her ex-spouse, Prince Andrew.

If anything, the negative stories about Kate's family seemed to bolster the public perception that Miss Middleton was just the breath of fresh air the monarchy needed. After the Queen dispatched William to Australia and New Zealand on his first tour abroad—sparking rumors that she was grooming him to succeed her in Charles's place—polls showed a startling 64 percent of the British public favoring William as their next king.

William did his best to discourage such speculation, praising his father as "a great man in his own right, but, unfortunately, not everyone sees that" and reminding people that Charles had raised hundreds of millions of dollars for a wide variety of causes through his Prince's Trust, the charity he founded in 1976. In this, Harry and his brother were in complete accord. "They are both totally loyal to Prince Charles and admire him tremendously," Dickie Arbiter said. "They hate it when it's made to look as if they're competing with their father." Besides, added a Clarence House staffer, "it's not as if either Prince William or Prince Harry relish the idea of becoming king. They'd rather go fight in a war."

Realizing that he was not likely to be sent back into harm's way, William still managed to get more than his share of action as the pilot of a Sea King Mk 3 search-and-rescue chopper—whether he was locating hikers stranded in the Snowdonia Mountains, plucking sick or injured workers off of oil rigs in the Irish Sea, or airlifting victims of horrific car crashes like the one that killed his mother to hospitals throughout Wales. To those who wanted him to put it all aside to fulfill his royal duties, William answered, "Work like this is worthwhile, valuable, and to me, there's an element of duty about it."

His brother approached the next assignment he was handed by the Queen in the same spirit. On May 28, 2009, Harry arrived in New York on his first overseas tour representing his grandmother. Toward that end, he assiduously avoided any activities that might embarrass the Crown. In other words, no clubbing, no women, no more alcohol than a glass of wine at a reception. "Quite frankly," said his private secretary Jamie Lowther-Pinkerton, "I think he will be cream-crackered and will want a good night's kip." Translation: Harry would probably be exhausted and want a good night's sleep.

Harry's whirlwind thirty-six-hour tour started with an emotional visit to Ground Zero in Lower Manhattan, where he met with the families of 9/11 victims and laid a wreath of peonies and yellow and white roses at the memorial construction site. Hundreds of New Yorkers strained to catch a glimpse of the prince from behind police barricades as he visited a firehouse across the street and then planted a tree at the British Memorial Garden in the city's financial district.

There was another emotionally charged item on the agenda: a visit to a school in Harlem, not far from the Harlem pediatric clinic where, in 1989, Diana was famously photographed hugging a little boy with AIDS—an act that helped break the stigma associated with the disease at that time. What even Harry had not known was that Diana did more than hug one little boy. She spent her visit hugging, cuddling, and chatting with more than a dozen pediatric AIDS patients. "Princess Diana made those children light up," said a nurse who was there. "Whatever she had, Harry has."

Harry's favorite stop on the tour was the Veuve Clicquot Polo Classic on Governors Island, where he competed to raise money for Sentebale. He used the occasion to tell the crowd that he set up the charity partly to honor his mother but also because "she loved this city, and it makes this occasion all the more poignant for me." Then he assisted in scoring the winning goal in the last seconds of the match, drawing the biggest cheer of the afternoon.

The trip was hailed as an enormous success on both sides of the Atlantic. Noting that "hard-partying Harry" had matured into a "regular Prince Charming," the *New York Post* declared that Harry "has swept the Big Apple off its feet."

There was talk among the Men in Gray that perhaps Harry should drop everything to join the Queen's team of traveling surrogates, but the Spare was far from ready to leave the military. He took his next step toward returning to the battlefield when he began training at RAF Shawbury to become an Apache attack helicopter pilot in 2009. Since

William had already been stationed there for months and was just finishing up when Harry arrived, the princes decided to forgo barracks living and share the rent on a small house just off the base.

"It's for the first time and the last time we'll be living together," Harry said during a joint press conference describing their roommate experience. "I assure you of that." William shot back, "Bearing in mind that I cook, I feed him every day, I think he's done very well. I do a fair bit of tidying up after him. He snores a bit and keeps me up all night long." Harry looked at his brother and rolled his eyes. "They're going to think we're sharing a bed now!" he cracked.

Chelsy Davy, who had just earned her law degree from the University of Leeds, was there the following May to see Harry receive his helicopter pilot's wings from a beaming Prince Charles. Sadly, it was the last time Chelsy and her Haz would be photographed as a couple.

They had split several times before. Not long after Harry helped William and Kate get back together in 2007, Chelsy changed her Facebook page status from "In a Relationship" to "Single," sending an unmistakable message to the world that she was tired of reading about Harry's skirt chasing. This time it was William to the relationship rescue, convincing his brother to apologize. There would be other rows and rough patches, usually stemming from Harry's roving eye. But by 2010, the specter of living the rest of her life in a royal fishbowl had finally proved too much. Chelsy called it quits and, for the time being, at least, fled home to Zimbabwe.

"Yes, it was tough," Chelsy later said of her roller-coaster six-year romance with Harry. "It was so full-on: crazy and scary and uncomfortable. I found it very difficult. . . . I couldn't cope. I was young. I was trying to be a normal kid, and it was horrible. It was nuts." Not so horrible and nuts that she didn't contemplate trying again. The following year, Chelsy would attend William and Kate's wedding, intending to see if the spark was still there. Instead, watching the Duchess of Cambridge walk down the aisle convinced her all the more that she was not willing to make the sacrifices Kate had made. "I still have feelings for Harry, of course I do," she told her parents. "But I can't live the rest of my life like that. It's just too much."

Too much for Harry as well. After it was duly noted what an attractive couple Pippa Middleton and Harry made as they left Westminster Abbey arm in arm in their roles as best man and maid of honor, he quickly snuffed rumors of a romance in the making. "Pippa? Ha! No, I am not seeing anyone at the moment," Harry told a reporter. "I'm one hundred percent single."

Around the time that Harry's love life was imploding, William finally decided to pop the question to Kate. But there was the matter of the engagement ring. Thirteen years before, when Paul Burrell took the young princes by the hand and led them through Kensington Palace so that they could pick out mementos of their mother, William selected the Cartier Tank watch that Diana's father had given her. It was Harry who chose her spectacular 18-carat sapphire-and-diamond engagement ring. Now William had to convince Harry to swap the ring for the watch. Understandably, Harry was reluctant at first. Diana's engagement ring—the most famous engagement ring in the world—symbolized so much. He had thought many times about slipping the ring on Chelsy's finger, but now that he was single, there seemed no point in withholding the ring from William—especially since he was marrying Kate. Harry joked with his brother that, under other circumstances, he might not be so willing to fork over the ring: "If it was any other girl . . ."

Carrying the ring in a blue velvet box that he stuffed in his backpack, William returned with Kate to the Lewa Wildlife Conservancy in northern Kenya. "Terrified about losing it the entire time," he admitted later. "I knew if it disappeared, I would be in a lot of trouble." Early one morning, he commandeered a helicopter and flew to the foothills of snow-covered Mount Kenya. Once there, he got down on one knee and proposed. Finally. As for the ring itself: "It was my way," William said, "of making sure my mother didn't miss out on today."

Harry didn't mince words when William and Kate flew home to England and called to tell him the engagement was official. "It took you fucking long enough!" he shouted.

IT HAD BEEN ONLY a little more than a year since the world pulled out to celebrate the nuptials of the future king and his strikingly beautiful wife—eventually to become England's first working-class, university-educated queen. Now, in 2012, Great Britain was getting ready to throw not one but two big parties—a Diamond Jubilee to mark Elizabeth II's sixty years on the throne, and the 2012 London Summer Olympics.

First up was the Diamond Jubilee—a monthslong series of tours and events culminating in June with a four-day nationwide blowout of garden parties, teas, country fairs, concerts, banquets, and receptions. Unlike the Silver Jubilee in 1977 and the Gold Jubilee in 2002, this time the Queen would rely heavily on surrogates to carry her message abroad. Starting in early February, Her Majesty and Prince Philip barnstormed Great Britain while her children and grandchildren crisscrossed the Commonwealth. The Prince of Wales and his wife, the Duchess of Cornwall, made stops in Canada, Australia, and New Zealand. Princess Anne was dispatched to Africa, while Andrew traveled to India and the Caribbean. William and Kate toured Singapore, Malaysia, and the South Pacific, while Harry, widely regarded as Her Majesty's most charismatic goodwill ambassador, charmed the locals in Belize, the Bahamas, and Jamaica. "We are in love with him—he's a wonderful person," said Jamaican prime minister Portia Simpson Miller, whom Harry greeted with kisses on both cheeks and the declaration that she was his "date for the night."

At one point during the Jubilee festivities, William, Kate, and Harry joined Prince Charles, Camilla, Philip, and the Queen aboard the *Spirit of Chartwell*, a 210-foot luxury cruiser that had been outfitted as a royal barge. While the vessel could easily accommodate the Queen's entire family, Her Majesty wanted to send a message by allowing only these seven principal members of the Firm who represented the future of the monarchy—the "Magnificent Seven"—aboard. Andrew, Anne, Edward, and their spouses and children were all consigned to much smaller boats.

Joined by more than a million spectators who lined the banks of the Thames, the royal party watched as more than a thousand vessels—from trawlers and tall ships to dragon boats and canoes—passed in review. Amazingly, the press still found time to focus on the fact that Kate had dared to try and "upstage" the Queen and Camilla by wearing a scarlet-red Alexander McQueen dress, in stark contrast to their coordinated white outfits. As always, Kate could rely on Harry to put everything in perspective. When the next morning's *Daily Mail* asked, "Oh Kate, what were you thinking?" he chided her by asking the same question: "Oh, Kate! What were you thinking? You wore a *red dress*! How *dare* you!" Kate told a Bucklebury friend, "Harry teases me all the time, and I absolutely love it! He keeps me sane, if you want to know the truth."

After a star-packed, three-hour pop concert, fireworks, a National Service of Thanksgiving at St. Paul's Cathedral, and a procession through the streets of London, the Magnificent Seven—and just the Magnificent Seven—walked out onto the balcony at Buckingham Palace to the thunderous cheers of an estimated one million people. Only one of the seven on the balcony that day knew he was expendable; it was only a matter of time before William and Kate had children, and Harry would be forced into the shadows along with his aunts and uncles and their families.

Harry admitted to an army buddy that he had always hated being called the Spare, but now he wasn't so sure. "You get used to things the way they are," the prince told him. "I don't know what they'll do with me."

Scarcely two months after the Diamond Jubilee drew to an end, William and Harry were shouting, "Go, Granny. Go!" as the Queen—or rather, a convincing stunt double—parachuted into Olympic Stadium to officially open the 2012 London Olympic Games. "We were kept completely in the dark about it; that's how big the secret was," William said during a press conference with his brother. "Both of us were slightly surprised," added Harry, "with our grandmother's secret hobby of parachuting."

Now that one of the busiest summers in memory was coming to an end, both brothers had proven beyond a shadow of a doubt that they were indispensable to the future of the monarchy. Their Kensington Palace digs had at long last been upgraded to the tune of $7.6 million, enabling the Cambridges to move into the palace's apartment 1A. The former home of Princess Margaret was, in fact, a twenty-room Georgian brick manor house complete with tennis courts and walled gardens. Similarly, $3 million was taken from the royal purse to reno-vate Anmer Hall, the sprawling country estate on the grounds of San-dringham that the Queen had given them as a wedding present.

For his part, the Spare seemed to have outgrown his hard-partying ways. Since William had been called back to duty with the RAF's Search and Rescue Force, the Queen asked Harry to step in and repre-sent the royal family at the closing ceremonies of the Olympic Games. Joined onstage by Kate, Harry gave a moving speech in which he pro-claimed that the London Olympics would "stay in the hearts and minds of people all over the world."

People all over the world were also beginning to take Harry seri-ously, and he liked it. He was even in a serious relationship, one that he had somehow managed to keep under wraps. For months, Harry had been quietly dating Cressida Bonas, a model and actress who also hap-pened to be the granddaughter of an earl and a close friend of the brothers' cousin Princess Eugenie. In fact, it was Eugenie who intro-duced them. Prince Charles believed that out of all his younger son's girlfriends, Cressida, who was accustomed to moving in royal circles, seemed overwhelmingly "most suitable" for marriage.

Perhaps, but for the time being neither Harry nor his new love had matrimony in mind. Having completed his training as an Apache attack helicopter pilot, his next step was to return to the battlefield in September. Before he shipped out, Harry decided he should enjoy a little R & R. With his entourage in tow, the Spare flew to Las Vegas and checked into a luxury VIP suite in the five-star Wynn Hotel. Two days later, all hell broke loose.

On August 21 the website TMZ released snapshots of the prince cavorting in the buff with a young woman during a game of strip bil-liards. Soon the snapshots, which showed Harry wearing nothing but a necklace and his Rolex watch, made their way onto tabloid pages across the globe. Harry was in a panic, and rightly so. Not only did he have Cressida and his senior officers to answer to, but his family, too.

"Heir It Is! Harry Grabs the Crown Jewels," blared the *Sun*, which ran a shot showing the prince doing just that in a clumsy attempt to conceal his genitals. More to the point was the headline in the *Daily Mail*: "Palace Fury at Harry Naked Photos." At first, that fury was aimed squarely at the press, which the Palace accused of violating Harry's right to privacy. Despite threats of action from Charles's legal team of Harbottle & Lewis, Fleet Street editors argued that there was clear public interest in the photos. Besides, they had already gone viral and been published in the United States and elsewhere.

There was still more fury to go around, however. Where were Harry's bodyguards? the Palace wanted to know. Why didn't they keep him from engaging in such reckless and potentially dangerous behavior? And why didn't they confiscate cell phones and other electronic devices at the door so that pictures wouldn't be taken in the first place?

As far as the military was concerned, Harry had done nothing wrong. To make their point, servicemen and -women posed naked online, deftly using helmets, flags, rifles, and whatever other gear they could find for cover. "Vegas was an epic party," said his troop commander Dickon Leigh-Wood, who first met Harry as a boy at Ludgrove. "Harry was about to go back to war. . . . He'd already survived the front line—he was alive and living it up! We all thought, 'Good for him!'"

For Harry, none of it mattered. The damage was done. Once again politicians took to the floor of Parliament to denounce the apparently unrehabilitated party boy prince for what one MP described as "a new low, even for the royal family."

Once again Harry rushed to Balmoral to apologize to his father and, most importantly, the Queen. He conceded later that he had been "too much army and not enough prince" and that once more he'd let himself and his family down. But for now, Harry refused to issue any sort of public apology. Instead, he commented ruefully on the fact that "there's no such thing as privacy now. You can't move an inch without someone judging you. That's just the way it goes."

IN NO TIME AT all, the paparazzi proved Harry right. His brother and his wife were in the middle of their nine-day extended Jubilee Tour of the Pacific and Southeast Asia when the French magazine *Closer* and the Italian magazine *Chi* published photos of Kate sunbathing topless while vacationing weeks earlier at a villa in Provence owned by Princess Margaret's son, Viscount Linley. "The future Queen of England," promised *Closer* on its cover, "such as you have never seen her . . . and such that you will never see her again!" Kate broke down when she saw the not-exactly-dignified images, which had been taken from a public road more than 1,500 feet away using a telephoto lens.

William, who along with his brother and father had earned a reputation in royal circles for having a volcanic temper, flew into a rage before ordering his lawyers to sue. In addition to seeking an injunction and damages in excess of $2 million, the couple's formidable legal team lodged a criminal complaint in France, where invasion of privacy could result in a one-year prison sentence. It would take five years for the case to wend its way laboriously through the French courts, and although no one went to jail, the courts ordered the defendants to cough up $250,000 in damages and fines.

As for Harry, once the dust from his Las Vegas scandal had settled, he returned to Afghanistan—this time deployed to Camp Bastion in Helmand Province as the pilot of an Apache attack helicopter. According to one of his instructors at Naval Air Facility El Centro in California, "Only the best of the best become Apache pilots. Harry is one of the very best of the very best." Over his full eighteen-week tour, Harry's combat unit averaged two Taliban "kills" per week, strafing and bombing enemy positions with extraordinary precision. Harry chalked this up to his skill with computer games. "It was a joy for me," he later said, "because I'm one of those people who loves playing PlayStation and Xbox. So, with my thumb, I like to think I'm pretty useful." Harry made no apologies for using the word "joy" in the context of killing people. "Take a life to save a life," he said. "That's what we revolve around. If there's people trying to do bad stuff to our guys, then we'll take them out of the game."

Once he returned home after his second tour of duty in Afghanistan, Harry plunged headlong back into his relationship with Cressida Bonas. Even with a little friendly guidance from an understanding Kate, Harry's girlfriend struggled to cope with the intense media scrutiny—and the inevitable comparisons between her and the Duchess of Cambridge. Predictably, there was talk of marriage and children. "I've longed for kids since I was very, very young," Harry told Katie Couric in an ABC-TV interview, "and so I'm just, I'm waiting to find the right person, someone who's willing to take on the job."

Yet Cressida knew what the public did not: that for all his bravado, Harry was emotionally fragile, frighteningly so. Harry conceded later that the two-year period following his brother's marriage was "total chaos. I just couldn't put my finger on it. I just didn't know what was wrong with me." He confessed to teetering on the edge of "a complete breakdown on numerous occasions, when all sorts of grief and sorts of lies and misconceptions and everything are coming to you from every angle."

Always "on the verge of punching someone," Harry channeled his aggression into boxing. "That really saved me . . . being able to punch someone in the ring was certainly easier." But the anxiety remained, and, for the first time, Harry told his brother that he intended to renounce his title and live out his life as a commoner serving in the military. "I wanted out," Harry recalled. "Pure and simple."

HAVING ENDURED THE SAME doubts, fears, and anxieties that plagued his brother, William urged Harry to seek professional help. "Look, this is not right, this is not normal," William said. "You need to talk about this stuff. It's okay." Harry finally began seeing a therapist and "actually, all of a sudden, all of this grief that I have never processed started to come to the forefront. . . . I sort of buried my head in the sand for many, many years," he said. "Losing my mum at the age of twelve, and therefore shutting down all of my emotions for the last twenty years, has had a quite serious effect not only on my personal life but my work as well."

Harry credited William with getting him the help he needed when no one else would—not Charles, the Queen, or his Palace handlers. "My brother, you know, bless him," Harry noted. "He was a huge support to me. . . . I owe him so much."

William had more than his brother's mental health in mind in 2013. That summer, one of the hottest on record, it was everyone else's turn to wait for Kate to give birth to the Cambridges' first child. Harry was particularly concerned about his sister-in-law's health, since she had suffered such severe morning sickness early in her pregnancy that she had to be hospitalized. Everyone breathed a sigh of relief when, one week past her due date and following twelve hours of labor with William at her side, Kate delivered an eight-pound, six-ounce boy on the afternoon of July 22.

The arrival of George Alexander Louis, His Royal Highness Prince George of Cambridge, was greeted with booming cannons and pealing cathedral bells. When it came time to leave St. Mary's Hospital in Paddington, William did what any first-time dad would do: he opened the rear door of his Range Rover, then fumbled awkwardly with the straps of the $160 Britax infant car seat before finally driving off.

Harry was there to greet them when they arrived at Kensington Palace. "It's fantastic to have an addition to the family," he had told the press. "I only hope my brother knows how expensive my babysitting charges are." It was not long before the Queen's green Bentley pulled into the drive, with William, Kate, and Harry standing there to greet her.

Inside, Prince George was waiting for his great-grandmother—the first time in 120 years that a reigning sovereign had met a third-generation heir. That last occurred in 1894, when Queen Victoria was alive at the same time as her son Edward VII, his son George V, and George V's son Edward VIII. (Victoria was also around to meet yet another great-grandson who would wear the crown. Edward VIII's brother Albert was born in 1895—six years before Victoria's death—and would become King George VI upon Edward VIII's abdication in 1936.)

As thrilled as he was to see William and Kate so happy in their new role as parents, Harry understood that George's birth did more than merely knock him from number three to number four in the monarchal pecking order. He was no longer the Spare, true, but he was also no longer tethered to the dreaded possibility—no matter that it had always been remote—that somehow the crushing responsibilities of kinghood might come crashing down on him.

Not surprisingly, the world was instantly smitten with the little prince. On his first royal tour Down Under, he proved himself to be every bit as beguiling as Willy Wombat had been thirty years earlier. That tour had an unintended impact on Harry's life as well. Watching television coverage of the Cambridges being met by cheering throngs in Australia and New Zealand, Cressida "freaked out. She couldn't handle it," said a mutual friend of Cressida and Princess Eugenie. "When she saw what her future could be, it scared the hell out of her." Moreover, Cressida wanted to pursue an acting career—something she knew would never happen if she married into the royal family.

When Cressida broke up with him over the phone, Harry pleaded with her to reconsider, but to no avail. For the second time, a woman he'd contemplated a future with couldn't tolerate the pressure. "It takes a special kind of woman to handle it," Harry told Guy Pelly. "A strong woman who can stand up to all this shit. A woman like Kate."

Harry had taken care to maintain his friendship with Chelsy after their breakup, and he did the same with Cressida. (When he finally did take the plunge, both women would be invited to his wedding.) "My life will never be 'normal,'" Harry admitted, "and, of course, neither will my brother's. That will never happen. We know that; we deal with that every day." But now that he had been burned twice romantically, he put that part of his life on hold to focus on what he called "the things that really matter."

Two years after the Las Vegas scandal that once again left his reputation in tatters, Harry set out to do something concrete for his fellow combat veterans. During the walk-up to the 2012 Olympics, he made a brief visit to the United States that included meeting with a group representing the Warrior Games, a Paralympic-style sports competition between servicemen and -women who had suffered major injuries on and off the battlefield. Noting that "it was such a good idea from the Americans that it had to be stolen," Harry took two years to put together what would become one of his most memorable achievements: the Invictus Games, a competition among hundreds of wounded, injured, and sick veterans from around the world.

Speaking at the first Invictus Games in 2014 at London's Queen Elizabeth Olympic Park, Harry said he hoped the competition would "have a long-lasting impact" on those who fought for their country. "Why do we need to do it?" he asked. "To demonstrate the power of sports, to inspire recovery, support rehabilitation, and to demonstrate life beyond disability. It really is as simple as that."

Fittingly, *invictus* is the Latin word meaning "undefeated," and Harry was determined to let the world know that he wasn't. The prince worked tirelessly to make the international competition a success and even managed to convince his new American friend, First Lady Michelle Obama, to record a video for the opening ceremony that was broadcast on giant screens around the stadium.

By the time they concluded five days later with a concert starring Bryan Adams, James Blunt, and the Foo Fighters, the Invictus Games were being hailed as a resounding success even by Harry's harshest critics. The prince had a new sense of purpose and, for the first time, felt he was conquering the panic attacks that had plagued him in recent years. Every time he was in a room "with loads of people, which is quite often, I was just pouring with sweat, like, heart beating boom, boom, boom, boom," he said, "literally just like a washing machine." He regarded the Invictus Games as "one hundred percent a cure for myself."

The next day, Harry turned thirty and in the process inherited complete control of the money that had been left to him in trust by his mother—now valued at close to $18 million. With his newfound confidence, Harry summoned the courage to finally take the leap into life as a full-time royal, something the Palace, Prince Charles, and his brother had been urging him to do. "It's time," Harry said he told himself. "You're Prince Harry. As long as you're not a total . . . You *can do this*. You have ten years' military experience behind you."

In March 2015 Kensington Palace announced that Harry, who had once said he would stay in the army until he could qualify for a pension—at least twenty years—would be leaving the armed forces in June. "Inevitably, most good things come to an end, and I am at a crossroads in my military career," he said, conceding that it was "one of the most difficult decisions of my life." But, he added on an upbeat note, "while I am finishing one part of my life, I am getting straight into a new chapter."

For William, Harry's abrupt decision to leave the military and take on the role of full-time royal was something of a godsend. The Heir was still managing to stave off royal duties after leaving the military, having signed up as a helicopter pilot with the East Anglian Air Ambulance service in Cambridgeshire, not far from Anmer Hall. For the next two years, the Cambridges would be just out of royal-duty reach, raising their young family in Norfolk while Harry remained behind in Kensington Palace's modest Nottingham Cottage ("Nott Cott"), very much available for tree plantings and walkabouts. "Suddenly more of the burden began to fall on Harry," said a St. James's Palace deputy private secretary. "I think he felt that was unfair."

Not that either brother was burning up the track in that department. In 2015 Charles, Camilla, and Princess Anne each racked up nearly five hundred official engagements, while the Queen and Prince Philip managed four hundred. William, Harry, and Kate? Only around two hundred appearances *combined*. Since William would one day be inheriting the top job, he received the brunt of the criticism for leaving so much of the hard work to the older folk—no matter that he was working ten-hour shifts, often risking his life to get people in remote areas the medical help they needed.

The need to pursue work outside the Firm was something Harry understood all too well: "I and William both feel as though we need to have a wage as well, to work with normal people, to keep us sane. To keep us ticking along."

William and Harry ticked along nicely as the patrons of more than one hundred charities, many dealing with issues that their mother was passionate about. The brothers had already set up their own Royal Foundation in 2009, raising millions of dollars for causes ranging from AIDS research, children's hospitals, and homeless shelters, to conservation groups, emergency responders, and mental health organizations. Kate came aboard five years later, turning what had been the brotherly Royal Foundation into the Royal Foundation of the Duke and Duchess of Cambridge and Prince Harry.

On May 2, 2015, Britain celebrated once again with sixty-two-round salutes, tolling church bells, and public fountains and monuments such as the London Eye and the Tower Bridge bathed in light—pink this time to herald the birth of eight-pound, three-ounce Charlotte Elizabeth Diana, Her Royal Highness Princess Charlotte of Cambridge. Charlotte made history just by being born. Now that primogeniture had been abolished, she became the first royal female to be treated the same way her male siblings would be treated—thus making her fourth in line for the throne behind George.

The new number five, Harry, was on an official trip Down Under when his niece was born. Moved by photos of the infant princess that William had sent from the hospital, Harry opened up for the first time about his own dreams of becoming a father. "Isn't that the same for everybody?" he asked. "Of course I would love to have kids right now, but there's a process to go through. It would be great to have someone else next to me to share the pressure, but, you know, the time will come, and whatever happens, happens."

Five weeks later, during Trooping the Colour ceremonies marking the monarch's official birthday, Harry took a backseat to twenty-two-month-old George, who was dressed in the same robin's-egg-blue romper that William had worn in 1984. "Prince George Steals the Show" was the headline in a half dozen newspapers and magazines, all of which also made the point that Kate looked "stunning" just six weeks after giving birth. Charlotte was at home in the care of her nanny, but it was just as well: the crowd went wild at the sight of William, dressed in the striking gold-and-scarlet uniform of a colonel in the Irish Guards, holding George with the radiant Duchess of Cambridge at his side.

Harry, pushed to the rear literally and figuratively, scowled through most of the proceedings. "He was obviously not his usual happy, chatty self up there," writer Wendy Leigh observed. "He was clearly distracted." He had a lot to think about: Harry was devoted to his family and doted on his nephew and niece. But William and Kate were no longer as available to him as they had been, and without someone like Chelsy or Cressida—or his army buddies—around for emotional support, he felt "cast adrift," as he put it to one of the women he dated briefly during this period. "Harry said he felt totally on his own now," she recalled. "There was resentment there, and bitterness, especially over being ignored by William. But you could tell he felt guilty about it."

Now even hard-core party animals like Guy Pelly and Tom "Skippy" Inskip, Harry's wingman during the Las Vegas fiasco, were either happily married or about to be. As much as Harry craved a family of his own, the obstacles were formidable. Worrying about the "massive invasion" on any potential girlfriend's privacy, he pointed out that "even if I talk to a girl, that person is then suddenly my wife, and people go knocking on her door."

There were plenty of attractive young women willing to overlook that particular inconvenience, including model Sarah Ann Macklin, Lady Natasha ("Tash") Howard, and actress Jenna Coleman, who starred in the sci-fi TV series *Dr. Who* and would go on to portray Harry's great-great-great-great-grandmother in the series *Victoria*, which aired on PBS. Unfortunately, none of these romances gained traction, and at thirty-two—a dozen years older than William was when he fell in love with Kate—Harry wondered if marriage was even in the cards for him.

Kate, even more than William, worried that Harry was becoming depressed about the failures of his personal relationships—and that his life might once again spiral out of control if something wasn't done to bolster his self-esteem. At her urging, William met privately with Harry at Kensington Palace to remind his brother about what their mother had told them: that someday they would both "find that someone who is everything to you. Once you've found that kind of love, you must hold on to it, no matter what or who gets in the way."

*We are very excited for Harry and Meghan.
It has been wonderful getting to know Meghan
and to see how happy she and Harry are together.*

—William and Kate's official reply to the news
of Harry and Meghan Markle's engagement

*It's not enough to just survive something.
That's not the point of life. You've got to thrive.
You've got to feel happy.*

—Meghan Markle

FIVE

"ALL THE STARS WERE ALIGNED, AND EVERYTHING WAS JUST PERFECT"

London
November 27, 2017

I WONDER WHAT THE children will look like?" Prince Charles mused to his wife over breakfast at Clarence House.

"Well, absolutely gorgeous, I'm certain," replied Camilla, taken aback somewhat by the question. "Is there any doubt? Look at them. Marvelous-looking couple."

"I mean," said the Prince of Wales, lowering his voice, "what do you suppose their children's *complexion* might be?"

"We'll find out eventually, I suppose, won't we?" the Duchess of Cornwall replied before changing the subject. Aware of the household staff members circulating within earshot, Camilla was significantly more circumspect than Charles—the result of decades spent master-minding their clandestine affair.

Still, had it been just two grandparents speculating on the appearance of their future grandchildren—particularly when the father was a redhead and the mother biracial—the exchange would have been innocent enough. But these weren't just any prospective grandparents, and the newly engaged couple they spoke of were at the epicenter of a royal romance that had captured the world's attention. The question posed by Charles was being echoed in a less innocent way throughout the halls of Buckingham Palace, as the Men in Gray voiced concern about how the royal family "will look to the rest of the world" once Prince Harry and his future wife, Meghan Markle, began having babies.

"It's not that the senior royals are racist per se," a former member of Prince Charles's senior staff said. "The Queen certainly isn't. But there are a few in the extended family who are, and the aristocracy as a whole is rife with racist thinking." As for the courtiers, bureaucrats, and advisors who actually keep the Firm up and running: "Most are not racist, but some are, and, unfortunately, at rather high levels. It's a sad reality, but they are more of a reflection of society as a whole."

It did not take long for Harry to be told by one of the Men in Gray that there were "apprehensions" about how dark a baby of his and Meghan Markle's might be—that if he or she was "too brown," it might look "strange." Soon, what might have begun as a benign question became the subject of intense conversation between Charles and Harry. "At the time," Harry later recalled, "it was awkward. I was a bit shocked." The Prince of Wales said that his son was perhaps being "overly sensitive about the matter," said a St. James's Palace staffer, "and when Harry went to his brother for help, William stood up for their father. The whole thing just got out of hand."

The conversations concerning how dark their offspring might be continued to ripple throughout the royal household. If anyone could have been counted on to make a racially insensitive comment, it was

Prince Philip. On one occasion, he asked an Australian aborigine if his people "still throw spears at each other," and when the president of Nigeria greeted him in flowing native robes, the Duke of Edinburgh chirped, "I see you're ready for bed." On a trip to China, he paused to tell a group of British students that if they stayed in the country too long, they'd "all be slitty eyed." (Harry was later quick to absolve both the Queen and Philip, the latter of whom had retired from royal duties in 2017 at the age of ninety-six.) But for all intents and purposes, Meghan recalled, the topic came up inside the Firm on numerous occasions. "It was always hard to see those," she later observed, "as compartmentalized conversations."

It was, they quickly discovered, only the beginning—and a far cry from anything they could have anticipated when their romance began. Harry described himself as being "in a good place" when he met Meghan in July 2016, and with reason. His second Invictus Games, held in Orlando, had been a huge success—proving, he said, that the first time "hadn't been a fluke." When his friends Barack and Michelle tweeted Harry to "bring it on" at the games, the prince even managed to convince the Queen to record a short video in which she replied to the Obamas' challenge with a dismissive "Oh, *really*."

At the closing ceremonies, Harry thanked everyone for the "hundreds of hours of grueling competition—and more smiles, tears, hugs, and cheers than you could ever count. . . . You are all Invictus. Spread the word. Never stop fighting. And do all you can to lift up everyone around you!" With his eye on the next games, which were to be held the following year in Canada, Harry bid the cheering crowd farewell: "See you in Toronto!"

Just four days later, Harry joined his brother and Kate to launch what became their biggest and most important joint initiative: Heads

Together, a campaign designed to end the stigma surrounding mental health. The brothers knew something about the subject, having not only witnessed their mother's battle against bulimia and suicidal depression but also having experienced grief on a scale that drove them both to despair. Each tackled a particular mental health issue: Harry, not surprisingly, focused on post-traumatic stress disorder (PTSD) in the military—the "invisible injuries" suffered on the battlefield. Kate concentrated on mental health in the schools, while William turned his attention to the soaring suicide rate, especially among young men.

One of the young men William had been noticing a change in—for the better—was his brother. The Cambridges knew that Harry had been yearning for the days when he lived at Nottingham Cottage, just across the cobblestone courtyard from Kensington Palace's apartment 1A, and could drop in anytime for dinner, a game night, or simply to watch television and kibitz. That all ended when William and Kate moved to Anmer Hall to focus on raising their children, and Harry's sense of loneliness was palpable. Now that he had found his voice, Harry seemed, as Prince Philip put it to them when William and Kate dropped in at Windsor, "less untethered." Harry agreed: "I am now fired up and energized and love charity stuff, meeting people, and making them laugh," he said. "I sometimes still feel I am living in a goldfish bowl, but I now manage it better."

That April, Harry and the Cambridges had an opportunity to reconnect with old friends when the trio cohosted a dinner for Barack and Michelle Obama at apartment 1A. In what would be a glimpse of the sort of racial-sensitivity issues Harry would soon confront, someone noticed only moments before the Obamas arrived that the huge 1660 old master painting by Dutch artist Aelbert Cuyp dominating the drawing room depicted a young black servant holding the reins of two horses. There was nothing they could do about the painting, but there was something that could be done with the large, gold plaque bearing the painting's title: *The Negro Page*. Worried that the Obamas might find the word *negro* offensive, aides scrambled frantically to position a large potted plant in front of the problematic nameplate.

William and Kate greeted their famous guests with handshakes, but Harry, who had worked with the Obamas on the Invictus Games, gave the American First Lady kisses on both cheeks. Photos of a cherub-cheeked Prince George greeting the Obamas in his gingham-blue pajamas and bathrobe, then riding the handcrafted rocking horse the Obamas gave him when he was born, delighted millions around the globe. Harry seemed lost in thought as he watched his nephew (Princess Charlotte was already asleep) play with a new toy brought by the First Couple—a plush, stuffed replica of the Obamas' dog Bo.

At one point, Michelle asked Harry half kiddingly when he was planning on settling down—a topic she'd brought up before—and this time Harry sounded serious. "Just have to find the right person," he said with a smile.

With a new and unfamiliar sense of self-worth, maturity, and calm, Harry made the conscious decision to settle down. "For the first time ever," he told British television personality Denise van Outen at a birthday party in May 2016, "I want to find a wife." Two months later, British fashion designer Misha Nonoo asked Harry if he'd be interested in going out on a blind date with a friend of hers who was starring in an American television series that filmed in Canada, *Suits*. Nonoo was not only the ex-wife of one of Harry's closest Eton pals, Paddle8 auction house founder Alexander Gilkes, but also counted among her royal friends Princesses Beatrice and Eugenie.

Harry was skeptical at first. "I'd never watched *Suits*; I'd never heard about Meghan before. I was like, right, 'Okay, give me some background. Like, what's going on here?'" Somewhat disingenuously, Meghan would claim later that she was just as unfamiliar with the prince, explaining that in the United States, "you don't grow up with the same understanding of the royal family." She had only one stipulation before agreeing to the setup. "I said, 'Well, is he nice?' Because if he wasn't kind, then it didn't seem like it would make sense."

Harry later said that, at least for him, it was love at first sight. "I was beautifully surprised when I walked into that room and saw her," he recalled of their first meeting for drinks at London's exclusive Soho House. "I was like, 'Okay, well, I'm really gonna have to up my game!'" According to Harry, "I knew she was the one the very first time we met."

Within minutes of meeting, they were checking the calendars on their cells phones to set up a second date. Over dinner the next night at Soho House's Dean Street Townhouse—which in its much earlier incarnation as the Gargoyle Club attracted such luminaries as Fred Astaire, Noël Coward, and Dylan Thomas—Harry and Meghan really got to know more about each other. "Everything that I learned about him I learned through him," she continued to insist, "as opposed to having grown up around different news stories or tabloids. . . . Anything that I learned about him and his family was what he would share with me, and vice versa. So for both of us, it was a very authentic and organic way to get to know each other."

Harry had a lot to unpack. Not only was Meghan an American, an actress, divorced, and the biracial descendant of slaves, but she was also three years older than he was. The Los Angeles–born daughter of Emmy-winning lighting director Thomas Markle Sr. and African American social worker Doria Ragland, Meghan grew up in LA's leafy

Woodland Hills district with her dad's children from his first marriage, Thomas Jr. and Samantha. Meghan's parents split when she was two, but even after her father moved out, they remained friendly, sharing meals and vacations together. "I never saw them fight," recalled Meghan, who described her parents as loving and supportive. "We were still so close-knit."

Still Harry, whose own childhood could not exactly be described as trouble free, was transfixed when Meghan told him about the day when what she thought was falling snow turned out to be ashes from buildings set afire during the race riots of 1992—the result of a jury verdict acquitting four Los Angeles police officers of savagely beating Rodney King—or the times her mother was reportedly referred to as "the maid" by Meghan's half sister. One of Meghan's most painful childhood encounters with racism occurred in Los Angeles, when her mother was called the N-word as they pulled out of a parking space. "My skin rushed with heat as I looked to my mom," she later wrote of the incident. "Her eyes welling with hateful tears, I could only breathe out a whisper of words, so hushed they were barely audible: 'It's okay, Mommy.'"

What Harry perhaps didn't hear about was Meghan's long-standing interest in the royal family from an early age—somewhat different from her later claim that she had never even Googled Harry or his relatives. As a girl, Meghan would visit the house of schoolmate Suzy Ardakani, and the two would watch a video of Charles and Diana's wedding over and over again. Sonia Ardakani, Suzy's mother, remembered giving Meghan a number of books about Diana, including Andrew Morton's *Diana: Her True Story*. Childhood best friend Ninaki Priddy, who posed with the future duchess in front of Buckingham Palace on a trip to London in 1996, said *The Princess Diaries* was one of Meghan's favorite films—the story "of a commoner who becomes part of the royal family. She was very taken with the idea."

Even as an adult, Meghan's deep interest in the Windsors was hardly something she tried to hide. Admitting that she'd dreamed about being a princess as a little girl, Meghan mused in 2014 on her lifestyle blog *The Tig* (named after her favorite Italian wine, Tignanello) about why "grown women seem to retain this childhood fantasy." She seemed particularly interested in the Cambridges. "Just look at the pomp and circumstance surrounding the royal wedding," Meghan wrote, "and endless conversation about Princess Kate." Priddy, who was maid of honor at Meghan's first wedding, to film producer Trevor Engelson, claimed to be "not at all shocked" to hear of Markle's romance with Prince Harry. "Meghan was always fascinated by the royal family," she said with a shrug. "She wants to be Princess Diana 2.0."

Perhaps, but Meghan was no intellectual lightweight. She double majored in theater and international studies at the Northwestern University School of Communication, and an internship at the US embassy in Buenos Aires led her to briefly consider a career in diplomacy. Instead, she returned to Los Angeles and began auditioning for roles, only to discover that because she was "ethnically ambiguous," she wasn't "black enough for the black roles" or "white enough for the white ones." Her first show business job was as one of the "briefcase girls" on the hit TV game show *Deal or No Deal*, followed by small parts in the films *Get Him to the Greek*, *Remember Me*, and *Horrible Bosses*, as well as on television in the soap opera *General Hospital* (where her father worked as the lighting director for thirty-five years) and the prime-time series *CSI: NY*.

Meghan dated Engelson for seven years before they married on a beach in Ocho Rios, Jamaica, in 2011—right before she landed the plum role of the ambitious paralegal-turned-legal-eagle Rachel (coincidentally Meghan's real first name) Zane in the USA Network series *Suits*. The series filmed in Toronto, which meant that Meghan had to divide her time between Canada and the couple's home in North Hollywood. The strain of the long-distance relationship took its toll, and after two years the marriage was over.

It was only a matter of months before Meghan, single and living in Toronto, moved in with good-looking, well-connected celebrity television chef Cory Vitiello. Markle would confess later that she had fallen in love with Vitiello, who eased her transition into Canadian society by introducing her to, among others, Prime Minister Justin Trudeau. But Vitiello wasn't interested in marriage or starting a family, and by the summer of 2016, she had fled to London in search of a new life—and a new love.

During those first two dates in London, Harry discovered that Meghan was more than just a radiant, charming, and intelligent American TV star. Sharing the prince's concern for servicemen and -women, Meghan signed on with the USO to entertain American troops in Afghanistan in 2014. Having taken up calligraphy to earn money between acting gigs early in her career, she put her artistic talent to work teaching kids in local Toronto schools how to paint watercolors. Meghan was also an outspoken feminist and in 2016 was appointed as an advocate for the United Nations Entity for Gender Equality and the Empowerment of Women.

Even more intriguing to Harry, she had been to Africa several times, most notably to pitch in digging wells as part of a fresh water project in Rwanda. As it happened, in a matter of weeks Harry was headed for Lesotho to see Sentebale's new children's center and then to Durban, South Africa, to address an AIDS conference. On the way, he planned to stop in Botswana to work on a wildlife conservation project—and do a shoot for *Town & Country* magazine. When he had finished his work, would she join him?

She did. For Harry, who set aside four to six weeks every summer to visit Africa, it was a "huge leap" to go on vacation there with someone he had met only twice and to stay "in the middle of nowhere" for five days. "We camped out with each other under the stars," Harry remembered, "sharing a tent and all that stuff. It was fantastic." It was then, he said, that they told each other, "We're going to change the world," and seriously started contemplating what the rest of their lives together would be like.

"The fact that I fell in love with Meghan so incredibly quickly was a sort of confirmation to me that all the stars were aligned, and everything was just perfect," Harry gushed. "This beautiful woman just sort of tripped and fell into my life; I fell into her life." The person he first shared his happy news with was William, who listened while Harry sang Meghan's praises. Like Harry, he had never seen *Suits* and had never heard of Meghan Markle. The Heir was happy for his brother, and if he had any initial qualms about her background—that she was American, an actress, divorced, and biracial—he kept those to himself. "Brother, she sounds absolutely amazing," he joked as Harry went on. "I think you're making her up."

At Harry's thirty-second birthday party, a shooting weekend at Balmoral, Meghan was introduced to Prince Charles, who found her "completely charming, absolutely delightful." The Prince of Wales, along with everyone present, agreed to keep the nascent relationship top secret. For nearly three months, Harry and Meghan somehow managed to fly under the radar as they pursued their transatlantic romance—he impulsively hopping aboard a jet and flying to Toronto to steal a few hours with Meghan, she spending a few days with her prince, then flying back to Canada and dashing from the airport straight to the set of *Suits*. It was important, they realized, to have this time to get to know each other without intrusions from the press, and they did—over cozy dinners at Kensington Palace, quiet weekends at getaways like the members-only club Soho Farmhouse in Oxfordshire (where they would soon buy a small retreat of their own), and intimate in-home get-togethers with a handful of Harry's closest friends.

"It was crucial to me to really get to know each other," Harry said. Without distractions, he added, they "went from zero to sixty in the first two months." Meghan agreed that their ability to keep things quiet and pursue their relationship with total privacy was "amazing . . . just to have so much time to connect. We never went longer than two weeks without seeing each other. We made it work."

To help make it work, they employed a number of the usual cloak-and-dagger tactics, from traveling under assumed names to meeting at unexpected, out-of-the-way places. Occasionally, they hid in plain sight. Early in the relationship, the two thought it would be fun to ren-dezvous at a supermarket. "Baseball cap on, looking down at the floor—all very clandestine," Harry recalled. They pretended not to know each other, texting from opposite sides of the aisle. Naturally, he was recognized anyway. "There's people looking at me, giving me all these weird looks, and coming up and saying 'hi.'"

Astoundingly, reporters never caught on—in part because there was so much else going on to distract them. That summer, Britons voted to exit the European Union, shaking the nation's political establishment and forcing Prime Minister David Cameron to resign. In the United States, Republican Donald Trump was squaring off against former American First Lady, senator, and secretary of state Hillary Clinton in one of the most bitterly fought presidential elections in modern history. Before Meghan met Harry, she made her feelings about Trump known in no uncertain terms. During the primary campaign, she went on television to say that she worked in Canada, and if Trump won the election, that's where she'd stay. Trump was more than a garden-variety misogynist, she said. He was dangerous. "You don't really want that kind of world that he's painting—if that's the reality we're talking about, come on, that's a real game changer."

Then there were Prince George and Princess Charlotte, gobbling up plenty of attention as they toured Canada with their parents—the Cambridges' first tour abroad as a family of four. No sooner were they back on home turf in mid-October than they were off to Manchester to, among other things, participate in an exhibition soccer match and visit a children's hospice center that had been opened by Princess Diana in 1991. Days later, Harry joined them at Buckingham Palace for a glittering evening reception hosted by the Queen and Prince Philip for British medalists from the 2016 Rio Olympics and Paralympic Games.

By the end of October, Harry had introduced Meghan not only to his father and a number of relatives on both sides of his family but also to friends such as Tom Inskip and Guy Pelly—yet not to his own brother, despite the fact that they lived only yards away from each other at Kensington Palace when William was in town. "He was frightened that for some reason William might not like her or wouldn't approve," said a mutual friend of Harry and Princess Eugenie. "William can be very stiff; a real traditionalist. But his opinion means everything to Harry."

Harry, still fearing that his brother might feel that Meghan did not fit the mold—or, worse, that she might simply be cravenly ambitious—was still dragging his feet when on October 30, 2016, the *Sunday Ex-*

press broke the story wide open. There were the inevitable comparisons with Wallis Simpson, the American divorcée who married Edward VIII in June 1937, six months after a constitutional crisis that ended with the king's abdication and landed Elizabeth's timid, stammering father, George VI, on the throne.

Yet Wallis Simpson did not have to contend with racist attacks. On its website, the *Daily Mail* ran the headline "Harry's Girl Is (Almost) Straight Outta Compton," while *Mail on Sunday* columnist Rachel Johnson (younger sister of controversial future British prime minister Boris Johnson) suggested that Meghan would "thicken" the royal family's "watery, thin blue blood and Spencer pale skin and ginger hair with some rich and exotic DNA."

Not all of the negative press was racial in nature: among other things, it was pointed out that both of Meghan's parents had filed for bankruptcy—Doria in 2002 over an outstanding $52,750 credit card bill, and Thomas in 1991, 1993, and 2016—despite at one point having won $750,000 in the California State Lottery. The London *Sun* took a different tack, running on its front page "Harry's Girl's on Pornhub"—failing to note that while someone had posted a *Suits* clip of Meghan's character having sex against a filing cabinet on the X-rated website, it was far from pornographic.

At the same time, reporters were now in hot pursuit of not only Harry and Meghan but also her family and friends on both sides of the Atlantic. Hounded by the press in much the same way the boys' mother had been—she and Harry were in Toronto when the story broke and had to seek refuge at the home of her friends Ben and Jessica Mulroney—Meghan was stunned by the ferocious tactics of the paparazzi and hurt by the lengths to which Fleet Street would go to distort the truth. She railed against "the misconception that because I am in the entertainment industry I'm used to this sort of thing. I've never been part of tabloid culture, so that was a really stark difference out of the gate. We were hit so hard at the beginning by a lot of mistruths that I made the choice not to read anything, positive or negative."

William had just read the *Daily Mail*'s "Straight Outta Compton" coverage when Harry and Meghan knocked on the door of apartment 1A. Meghan had been eager to meet the Heir but also "terrified the whole time" that she would be subjected to "the third degree." Even though she had cozied up to Princess Eugenie and others in the brothers' circle, Meghan was well aware that she existed far outside the bounds of what might normally be considered marriage material for a prince of the realm. She had also always expected William to be "protective," as she told a confidante, "like any good brother should be."

Now, however, she worried that Harry's brother might believe the savage stories being written about her. William had not yet had time to make up his mind. What he did know was that Meghan made his brother happier than he had been in years, and for that he was grateful. According to Harry, William threw open the door and bussed her on both cheeks. Then, pointing to Harry, the Heir said, "I want to meet the girl who put that silly grin on my brother's face."

Over tea in the kitchen, William put Meghan instantly at ease. He told her that Kate was also "desperate" to meet her, but for the time being had to remain at Anmer Hall with the children. Talk turned quickly to the pressing matter at hand—the storm of controversy that swirled around them. William was duly sympathetic to the couple's plight. More than any other royal, he had been willing to take legal action to prevent incursions on the privacy of his loved ones. Most recently, he had fired a warning shot over Fleet Street's bow after a photographer was found inside the trunk of a car across from a playground, waiting to jump out and snap a picture of Prince George. "A line has been crossed," the official statement from Clarence House read, "and any further escalation in tactics would represent a very real security risk."

William suggested waiting until their father returned from his tour of the Middle East before tackling the problem. Within a matter of days, however, it became clear that Harry could no longer resist Meghan's pleas that something be done. The salacious gossip, groundless rumors, and outright lies had, she said, left her feeling "violated."

Choking back angry tears, Harry called his father in Bahrain for permission to release a statement. In it, he, too, complained that "a line has been crossed" and that Meghan had been subjected to "a wave of abuse and harassment" that included a "smear on the front page of a national newspaper, the racial undertones of comment pieces, and the outright sexism and racism of social media trolls and web article comments." It all amounted to, in Harry's words, an intolerable "degree of pressure, scrutiny, and harassment from the media"—not unlike the "pressure, scrutiny, and harassment" that led to his mother's death.

William supported Harry in issuing the statement—reluctantly. There had long been resistance inside palace walls to taking any public stand in such matters; the Queen and her advisors felt it was preferable at all times, in the words of one courtier, "to sail above the fray." But in this particular instance, William understood that his brother was simply protecting his girlfriend—just as William had acted more than a decade earlier to safeguard Kate.

Yet there was a difference. Kate had been William's girlfriend for five years when he issued a statement warning the paparazzi to back off from harassing her. By then he knew not only Kate but the whole Middleton clan intimately. In contrast, Harry had known Meghan for

four months. Complicating matters further was Meghan's highly problematic family. Only days before Harry scolded the press, Samantha
Markle, who suffered from multiple sclerosis and was confined to a
wheelchair, described her half sister as a "shallow social climber" whose
behavior was "certainly not befitting of a royal family member." She
went on to say that "being a princess was something Meghan always
dreamed of as a little girl. She always preferred Harry—she has a soft
spot for gingers." Samantha also accused Meghan of failing to come to
the aid of their cash-strapped dad. The Windsors, she went on, would
be "*appalled* by what she's done to her own family."

Soon there were rumblings that the Men in Gray were having their
doubts about Ms. Markle, and that William was listening to them.
There was also a growing consensus among senior palace advisors that
Harry's statement upbraiding the press had gone too far, jeopardizing
what was essentially a symbiotic relationship between Fleet Street and
the Crown. "You can't call the press a bunch of racist thugs," said a former Clarence House press officer, "and expect them not to hit back."

After three weeks of mounting speculation that the Heir opposed
Harry's blistering declaration, William felt compelled to quell the chatter. "The Duke of Cambridge absolutely understands the situation concerning privacy," read the statement released by Kensington Palace,
"and supports the need for Prince Harry to support those closest to
him." Anything less explicit would have made it appear that a rift between the brothers did, in fact, exist—and that Harry's divorced American actress was the cause of it.

From his wearing of a Nazi uniform to using terms like "Paki" and
"raghead," Harry had a less than spotless past when it came to racial
and ethnic sensitivity. Now the hurtful comments about Meghan were
awakening him to the aristocracy's long history of racism. Birmingham

City University sociology professor Kehinde Andrews pointed out that the royal family is "so tied into the ideas of empire and colonialism, racial purity—they are probably the primary symbol of whiteness that we have."

Unlike her husband, the Queen had never been heard to utter a single racially or ethnically insensitive comment. And with the exception of the one time the Prince of Wales told a black person with dreadlocks that she didn't "look like" she was born in Manchester, Charles had similarly never made a misstep. The same could not be said for Princess Michael of Kent, wife of the Queen's first cousin Prince Michael. Princess Michael owned two black sheep at her farm in Gloucestershire that she named Venus and Serena, after the tennis-playing Williams sisters. She also once reportedly made a racist comment to two black diners in a New York restaurant—something she subsequently denied—and would cause a furor when she came to Meghan's first Christmas lunch with the Windsors wearing a large gold and jewel-encrusted Blackamoor brooch: a Rococo-era style of jewelry that depicts exoticized images of slaves in silks and turbans. (The following day, Princess Michael issued an official apology to Meghan, saying she was "very sorry and distressed.")

In mid-December Meghan flew to London on an impulse to spend at least a few days of the Christmas season with her prince. They understood it was too soon to wrangle an invitation to Sandringham from the Queen but went ahead and picked out their own six-foot-tall tree and spent an entire evening at Nott Cott decorating it. There was time to catch a play on London's West End—*The Curious Incident of the Dog in the Night-Time* at the Gielgud Theatre—and to take long walks through Soho admiring the Christmas lights before Meghan had to fly off to spend Christmas with her mother in California. She returned to

London in time to ring in the new year with Harry before the couple jetted off to Norway to see the northern lights—a trip arranged by an old friend of the prince, Norwegian adventure guide Inge Solheim. Inside the Arctic Circle and thousands of miles from the nearest paparazzi lens, they spent a week whale watching and dogsledding.

On January 10, 2017, Harry finally brought Meghan to apartment 1A to meet Kate. For two months, the Duchess of Cambridge had sidestepped the brothers' efforts to bring together the two most important women in their lives. Kate's initial reluctance "comes from a good place," explained a friend she has known since her days at Marlborough College. "She's always been a substitute big sister to Harry, watching out for him and making certain no one takes advantage. I think she was a little frightened by what she was reading."

At the same time, Kate knew what it was like to have family secrets exposed: the Middletons' dirty laundry—from James Middleton's nude romps to Uncle Gary's cocaine-fueled shenanigans—was hung out to dry by the tabloids. Kate was also in a unique position to empathize with Meghan over the hailstorm of criticism rained down on her mother. Both Doria Ragland, whose master's degree in social work from the University of Southern California was seldom mentioned, and Kate's self-made-multimillionaire mother, Carole, were mocked mercilessly for their working-class roots.

Yet Kate was also listening to her husband. William worried aloud that things were moving too fast and that, in a matter of a few months, Meghan had secured a degree of control over his brother that no other woman—certainly not Chelsy or Cressida—ever had. Harry was on the defensive whenever the subject of Meghan came up, leaving friends and family alike on tenterhooks. When he heard through the grapevine that one of his oldest Eton buddies made a crude joke about Doria, Harry flew into a rage and cut him off for good. Not even his very closest friends were immune from Harry's wrath when it came to Meghan. When Skippy Inskip dared to suggest that the prince might take more time to make sure Meghan was a good fit for the royal family, Harry refused to return his calls for months.

Whatever doubts she may have harbored, Kate kept them to herself when she threw open the door to apartment 1A and greeted Harry and Meghan with hugs. The duchess had celebrated her thirty-fifth birthday just the day before, so Meghan surprised her with a $295 leather Smythson Portobello notebook. She also charmed Kate by getting down on the floor to play with Princess Charlotte. Unfortunately, Meghan would have to meet Charlotte's brother some other time; it was a school day, and George was left at Anmer Hall in the care of his nanny, Maria Borrallo.

The get-together lasted less than an hour, and, as Meghan left, Kate told her to feel free to get in touch anytime if she needed "anything at all." If anyone could offer sound advice on how to navigate the treacherous waters of the monarchy, it was the ever-patient, transcendentally calm Waity Katy.

In the end, Meghan felt what she admitted later was a "profound sense of relief"—a feeling that she was being swept up in the welcoming arms of Harry's brother and sister-in-law. As working royals, William and Kate had mastered the art of concealing their true feelings, and while they reportedly harbored serious doubts about where this was all leading, the duke and duchess didn't let them show. Meghan and Harry, meanwhile, routinely stressed one word when asked how they'd been treated by the Cambridges: "They've been amazing," Harry and Meghan would say. *"Amazing."*

Later that month, Meghan spent five days in Delhi and Mumbai as

a "global ambassador" for the Christian humanitarian group World Vision, delving into some of the many problems facing India's poor.
When the fact-finding mission was over, she returned to the comforts
of life with her prince inside the walls of Kensington Palace. In March
they headed off to Montego Bay for the wedding of Skippy Inskip and
software developer Lara Hughes-Young—just up the coast from the resort where Meghan married Trevor Engelson in 2011. At the reception,
Harry was imitating Michael Jackson's famous moonwalk dance to the
cheers of onlookers when he suddenly collided with a waitress, sending
a tray of drinks flying. By all accounts, Harry was "mortified," said one
guest. "He couldn't apologize enough. Meghan and the bride were in
stitches."

MUCH OF THEIR TIME in Jamaica was spent trying—unsuccessfully—
to elude the paparazzi. Images of the couple frolicking in the aqua-
marine waters of the Caribbean accompanied front-page stories about
Harry and Meghan—and when they would tie the knot. Back in London, Kate worried that they would upstage Pippa's upcoming wedding
in May to ex–racing driver and hedge fund manager James Matthews,
who also happened to be heir to the Scottish feudal title of laird of
Glen Affric. "What can I do?" William asked. "They're on the guest list.
I can't ask them not to come."

Still, Kate's concerns were borne out when on the day of the wedding the *Sun* ran "It's Meghan v Pippa in the Wedding of the Rears" on
its front page. The article featured the memorable photo of Pippa's der-
riere taken when she was Kate's maid of honor, alongside a similarly
targeted shot of Meghan in tight yoga pants. Harry, aware of the com-
motion it would cause if he and his girlfriend arrived together, traveled

alone to the wedding ceremony at St. Mark's Church in Englefield, Berkshire, then returned with Meghan for the reception. To stump any photographers who might have been lurking in the hedges for the chance to take a rear-end shot, Meghan ditched the slinky number she was going to wear for a loose-fitting black crepe dress and matching black cloche. "Good luck," she joked to her table companion, "getting a sexy shot of me in this."

At the end of July, while media gossip concerning Harry and Meghan continued at a breakneck pace, William resigned quietly from the East Anglian Air Ambulance service. The decision was one of the most difficult he'd ever made, since it meant that, for the rest of his life, he would be in full-time service to the Crown.

What no one had fully appreciated was the toll it had taken on the prince. For two years, William had secretly been sinking into a deep well of depression as he spent twelve-hour days airlifting the victims of heart attacks, strokes, falls, workplace accidents, suicides, and horrific car crashes to hospital emergency rooms. "What the public doesn't know is that when you see so much death, it impacts how you see the world," he explained later. "You're exposed to such high levels of sadness, trauma, death that impacts your own life—and your family life. It's always there, and you're drawn into it. It stays with you for weeks on end. You see the world as a much more depressed, darker, blacker place."

There were times, Kate confided to a trusted friend since childhood, that William came home to Anmer Hall and wept when he told the stories of what he'd seen that day. Or worse, he remained silent, burying his feelings so that he could function both as a pilot and a senior member of the royal family. Then there was the occasional angry outburst. The shouting rows he had with Prince Charles over what he would and would not do for the Crown sent maids, staffers, and at times family members scurrying for cover. William had always checked his temper at the door when he came home, but Kate became emotional when she spoke of the anger and despair her husband kept "bottled up inside."

Both he and Harry had witnessed violence in the military, but it hadn't affected William in the same way. "It's different," the Heir explained, "because [in the military] there is an element of self-control." The stress encountered by emergency medical workers was of a different sort—even more intense, William claimed, and more personal. "When you see somebody at death's door with their family all around them, you share their pain." Now that he had children of his own, he felt that pain all the more keenly. "We're all human beings . . . with loved ones, it's only natural to become depressed when you're surrounded by such grief, such bereavement."

Turning those feelings off at the end of the day was not always possible. "There are some very dark moments," William said. "You try not to take it home, but sometimes . . . it can be quite difficult."

Like many of his fellow rescue workers, William reached a point, as he described it, where "you bear the brunt, and it leaves you with a very negative feeling where you think death is just around the corner everywhere I go. It's quite a burden to carry. . . . I could feel it brewing up inside me, and I could feel it was going to be a problem."

Kate agreed with her husband. At one point, William had descended into such a pit of despair there were deep concerns about where it all might lead.

Suicide was a subject William knew something about, and not just because his mother had spoken openly of the desperation that had caused her to try and end her life on multiple occasions. On his first assignment as an air ambulance pilot, William was called to the home of a young man who had taken his own life. "I was told there were five suicides or attempted suicides every day in East Anglia alone," William recalled. "When I looked into it, I was shocked by how bad this situation is—suicide is the biggest killer of men under forty-five in the UK—which is absolutely appalling."

To his credit, William was determined to use his voice to end the stigma associated with suicide and convince young males in particular to be open with others about whatever thoughts of self-harm they might be entertaining. He was also self-aware enough to recognize the dark feelings "brewing up" inside him, and to share his feelings with Kate. She, in turn, shared her fears for William's well-being with Harry. They both decided that out of love for his children and his overarching sense of duty to the Queen, William would never act on thoughts of suicide that might creep into his mind. That said, Kate and Harry staged an informal intervention, urging William to seek professional help—something both he and Harry had done before to come to grips with the still-unresolved feelings of grief caused by what happened to their mother in a Paris tunnel on August 31, 1997.

William's mental health concerns were likely among the triggers for the formation of Heads Together a year earlier, but even after courageously going public—to a very limited extent—about the ways in which Diana's death still haunted them, both brothers still struggled privately. What gradually came into focus was the likelihood that both of the princess's sons suffered from PTSD from 1997 onward, and that their subsequent experiences—in the military, William's air ambulance service, life as two of the most famous and aggressively pursued figures on the planet—exacerbated what was already a deep-seated psychological problem.

Yet Harry's focus from the summer of 2016 on was Meghan, not William's battle with depression or his own life-altering decision to assume the physically demanding and often soul-crushing burden of life as a full-time royal. Harry's obsession with his new love was, William told his father during a visit to Clarence House, "like something I've never seen." Then, with a wistful look, he uttered the words that summed up the ongoing seismic shift in their relationship: "I feel as if I've lost my best friend."

As with all things he undertook, William bore down on his new job. His calendar, annotated so sparsely during the years he spent as a family man at Anmer Hall, now filled up with appointments and official trips. "If I'm doing this," he told his private secretary, "then I'm doing it one hundred percent, full stop." But he had no intention of doing it without a full commitment from his very much distracted younger brother.

By September 2017, it had become abundantly clear to everyone that Harry and Meghan were headed for the altar. Over drinks at Kensington Palace, William told Harry what Skippy Inskip and others had already told him: "Kate and I think Meghan seems like a lovely girl, but why rush things? Does she really know what she's getting into? Take whatever time you need to really get to know this girl."

Much would be made of William's use of the term "this girl," but Harry often referred to Meghan as "this girl" when retelling the story of their romance. In fact, during their first official interview as a couple, Harry would tell the BBC: "I feel I know that I'm in love with this girl." What did irk Harry was William's tone, and the implication that she was simply not "suitable." Moreover, Harry resented William's presumptuous attitude—his belief that somehow he had a right to interfere in the private life of his now thirty-three-year-old brother. Their father had been completely won over by the magnetic Ms. Markle, as had Prince Philip and several Spencer family members. If any of them had misgivings, they had not made them known to Harry.

Harry's reaction was not unexpected. "Who the hell do you think you are, brother?" he demanded, rising to his feet. "I'm marrying Meghan, and nothing and no one is standing in our way." Harry was out the door. Searching for allies to press his case with Harry, William discarded the idea of asking their father to weigh in. Charles had no stomach for laying down the law where Harry was concerned.

Over the years, however, Earl Spencer had come to be regarded as a kind of benevolent godfather. Being outside the Windsor loop, Diana's brother offered a different perspective—one that Harry might find easier to accept. Spencer agreed to try, but all he did was make matters far worse; in the end, Harry was not upset with his well-intentioned uncle, but he was furious that his brother was actively seeking to have others interfere in his personal affairs.

Within minutes of his phone conversation with Earl Spencer, Harry began angling for a way to get over one last hurdle—the highest of them all. Late that September, just a few weeks after the Cambridges announced they were having a third child, Meghan and Harry were heading for Windsor's Royal Lodge to have lunch with Prince Andrew and his ex-wife, Fergie. Halfway there, they were told the Queen was actually at Windsor for a church service and would be at Royal Lodge when they arrived.

Meghan, though she denied ever having researched the royals, was so nervous about meeting the Queen that months earlier, while visiting her mother in California, she practiced the proper way to drink tea at a Pasadena tea shop called the Rose Tree Cottage. But there was one other thing: "Do you know how to curtsy?" Harry asked her. Meghan

claimed later that she thought this was a gesture for public consumption, and performed only outside. "I thought that was part of the fan-
fare," she said. "I didn't think that's what happens inside."

"But it's your grandmother," Meghan told Harry.

"It's the Queen!" he replied.

"And that was really the first moment that the penny dropped,"
Meghan recalled.

As soon as they got out of the car, Harry showed Meghan how to
curtsy—"deeply, to show respect." They practiced in front of Royal
Lodge until Fergie bolted out of the house and asked, "Are you ready?
Do you know how to curtsy?" Then, Fergie, who was renowned for her
very deep curtsies, demonstrated until Meghan got it right. Once inside, "Apparently I did a very deep curtsy," Meghan remembered, "and
we just sat there, and we chatted, and it was lovely and easy." Perhaps,
from that moment on, she realized that these "weren't just famous people like we Americans are used to. . . . This is a completely different ball
game."

They met the Queen again a few weeks later, and this time Meghan
clinched the deal. "The corgis took to you straightaway," Harry said of
Meghan, who had her own dogs—a rescue beagle named Guy and a
rescue Labrador-shepherd mix named Bogart. "For the last thirty-three
years, I've been barked at, and this one walks in, absolutely nothing,
just wagging tails." (Sadly, Meghan had to give Bogart away because, in
her words, the dog "did not take to Harry.")

Two months later at Nott Cott, on a lazy Sunday night with a
chicken roasting in the oven, Harry fingered the small ring box in his
pocket. The ring it contained was of his own design: two brilliant-cut
diamonds that Diana had left to him flanking a 3-carat cushion-cut
solitaire diamond from Botswana. The prince dropped to one knee and

asked Meghan to marry him. Before he could finish, she blurted out, "Can I say yes? Can I say yes?!"

Harry thought of his mother at that moment. "She would be over the moon," he said, "jumping up and down, you know, so excited for me." The Queen had already green-lighted the union, but it remained for her to give her formal approval via a signed Instrument of Consent the following year. In the meantime, Charles issued a formal announcement saying he was "thrilled," while Camilla cracked, "America's loss is our gain." Her Majesty released a statement declaring that she and Prince Philip were "delighted for the couple."

William and Kate also joined in, saying how "excited" they were at the news and how "wonderful" it had been getting to know Meghan. Neither, however, appeared to be going out of their way to make her transition to royal life any easier. Kate shared William's apprehension when it came to Meghan, and, despite Harry's oft-repeated suggestion to his sister-in-law that she might show this American newcomer the ropes, no such offers of assistance were forthcoming. Meghan told one of her closest Canadian confidantes that, at first, she expected to become fast friends with Kate because they were both "outsiders." Instead, she "walked away thinking that Kate was never going to reach out to her. Regardless of what they said publicly, William and Kate didn't think she was right for their Harry. They wanted a proper English rose."

The following February, William, Harry, Kate, and Meghan—dubbed "the Fab Four" by the press—made their first public appearance together for the purpose of launching their Royal Foundation Forum and to announce that Meghan was being made a trustee. The thrust of the conversation was mental health, although Meghan added that she wished to add the issue of female empowerment to the forum's list.

Putting their usual positive spin on an awkward moment, Harry said he was "incredibly proud and excited" that his future wife was joining the royal team, while William chimed in that he was nothing less than "delighted" by Meghan's presence among them. But when asked if they ever had disagreements, there was nervous laughter before William answered, "*Oooh*, yes!" Could Harry talk about the last one they had? "I can't remember," he tried to joke, "they come so thick and furious."

Well, said the interviewer, "you're putting on a great show."

Harry's mock-rueful answer: "Well, we're stuck together for the rest of our lives, so . . ."

Of the Fab Four, Kate—who now preferred to be called Catherine—was the most quiet and reserved, holding back as Meghan contributed as much to the conversation as the Windsor men. To be fair, the duchess was seven months pregnant at the time. On April 23, 2018, cannons thundered once again as crowds waited outside the Lindo Wing of St. Mary's Hospital to see Princess Charlotte holding her new brother, Prince Louis Arthur Charles. And Harry dropped another rung on the ladder of succession, from fifth to sixth.

No matter. With the exception of Louis's arrival, the spring of 2018 belonged to Prince Harry and his American bride. Over the months-long walk-up to the May 19 nuptials at St. George's Chapel in Windsor Castle, there was the usual breathless anticipation concerning everything from the guest list and flowers to the dress and the honeymoon.

Even these issues, however, created monumental tensions within palace walls. During one of the rehearsals, on a particularly humid day, there was a heated exchange between Kate and Meghan about whether or not the flower girls should wear tights. Charlotte was there and, following tradition, wore tights. When Meghan asked that all the little girls be bare legged, Kate demurred at first. "Princess Catherine thought it was gauche, and she told Meghan so," said an assistant who witnessed the argument. "Meghan made the point of it being so hot, and Princess Catherine kept saying, 'But it's just not *done*.' Both of them got very emotional."

Initially, Meghan was accused of having reduced the beloved Duchess of Cambridge to tears, but she would later go on record insisting that the reverse was true. "Yes," said Markle, Kate "was upset about the flower girls' dresses. It made *me* cry, and it really hurt my feelings." Later, according to Meghan, Kate brought her flowers and a note of apology. "It was a really hard week of the wedding, and she was upset about something, but she owned it," Meghan added. "And she did what I would do if I knew that I hurt someone."

There were apparently plenty of hurt feelings to go around. The escalating Markle family drama continued to mortify Harry and Meghan and horrify William. Now Thomas Markle Jr. joined Samantha in publicly bashing their half sister. "She is giving the greatest performance of her life," he told reporters. "She thinks she's another Princess Diana. She is acting phony. Maybe we embarrass her. There's a whole different side of her that has started to surface, and it's ugly to see."

"Maybe we embarrass her?" Ya think? When neither Thomas Jr. nor Samantha showed up on the guest list, they seemed genuinely surprised. "I'm not bitter, just baffled," Thomas Jr. said. "She's forgotten her own flesh and blood." He went on to plead with Charles and the Queen to intercede, but that wasn't happening. While the older royals seemed content to simply ignore the uncomfortable situation, William and Kate were alarmed by what they read. Even though there had been profoundly unflattering stories about the Middletons leading up to their wedding, not an unkind word was ever said about Kate. "I don't know what to believe," William told a press aide as he read what the Markles had to say.

Nevertheless, William was relieved when he was asked to be best man, just as Harry had been best man at his wedding seven years earlier. Back then it was a given. Not so today. "There's real tension between them now," Camilla told a Gloucestershire neighbor. "But the boys always come together for the important things."

Meghan was able to count on one relative: her mother, who traveled to England to help her daughter with wedding preparations and meet the in-laws. Thomas Markle Sr. was originally expected to be there as well. Meghan was close to her father and thanked him publicly for the "blood, sweat, and tears" he had invested in her future. Thomas Markle, she said, "believed in this grand dream of mine well before I could even see it as a possibility. I owe him so much."

But Meghan's father was a novice when it came to dealing with the media and had made the mistake of ignoring Harry's warnings about cooperating with the paparazzi. The "candid" shots that he wound up posing for showed the proud father of the bride trying on his tuxedo, leafing through books on Britain, and Googling the newlyweds. Markle was so embarrassed when it was revealed that he had posed willingly for the photos that he bowed out of the wedding.

"If you had listened to me, this would never have happened," Harry told Meghan's dad over the phone.

Markle, who was suffering severe chest pains and had checked into the hospital for tests, shot back, "Maybe it would be better for you guys if I was dead. Then you could pretend to be sad." At that point, Markle hung up on his future son-in-law.

A flurry of text messages ensued as Harry tried to lure Thomas to the wedding:

"Tom, Harry again! Really need to speak to u. U do not need to apologize, we understand the circumstances. . . . If u love Meg and want to make it right please call me. . . . And speaking to the press *will* backfire trust me Tom . . ."

Instead of responding, Tom went on TMZ to tell world he had suffered a heart attack and was about to undergo emergency surgery. Then he turned off his phone so that neither Harry nor Meghan could reach him.

Meghan, already under enormous pressure as the wedding approached, was desperate to find out if her father was okay: "I've been reaching out to you all weekend," she texted him just four days before the wedding. "Very concerned about your health and safety."

When Harry lambasted his future father-in-law in a text one last time for refusing to answer any of their more than twenty phone calls, Markle texted back, "I've done nothing to hurt you, Meghan, or anyone else. I'm sorry my heart attack is any inconvenience for you."

Hours later, Thomas Markle changed his mind and announced that he intended to give away his daughter—until a second heart attack forced him to cancel his plans to attend. Harry asked his father to step in, and Charles obliged eagerly.

On the day of the wedding, Markle called his daughter a little before five in the morning London time. She did not pick up. Meghan and the father she once adored have not spoken since.

Like the other 1.9 billion people watching the ceremony on television, Thomas Markle looked on from the United States as his daughter, true to form, broke tradition by walking down the first half of the St. George's Chapel aisle unescorted before being joined by Prince Charles. "I was thrilled to tears that he was doing that for me," Meghan's dad said. "I just wish it was my hand holding my daughter's, not his."

What Markle didn't know was that just three days earlier, Meghan and Harry asked the archbishop of Canterbury to marry them in their Nott Cott backyard. "Just getting down to basics," Meghan revealed later. "We just said, 'Look, this thing, this spectacle, is for the world, but we want our union between us.'" According to Meghan, the archbishop obliged, and with just the three of them present, she and Harry exchanged vows. Although the photo of that tiny ceremony is what they have framed on their wall at home, Archbishop Justin Welby claimed the legal ceremony was the big event at Windsor where he signed the wedding certificate, "which is a legal document. I would have committed a serious criminal offense if I signed it knowing it was false."

CASTING ASIDE ANY CONCERNS that she would be compared in any way to Pippa Middleton, Meghan wore a clinging white gown created by British fashion designer Clare Waight Keller of Givenchy. Much to the Queen's delight, her wedding veil was embroidered with flowers representing the countries of the Commonwealth, the California poppy (in honor of Meghan's California roots), and wintersweet, a flower that grows at Kensington Palace. Both Harry and his best man, William, were given permission by the Queen to wear the frock coat uniform of the Blues and Royals.

When Charles and Meghan reached the altar where the brothers were standing, Harry said, "Thank you, Pa." Lifting the bride's veil, he stared for a moment. "You look amazing," he said. "I'm so lucky."

Harry's dog-obsessed granny, who was photographed the day before riding in the backseat of her Rolls next to Meghan's beagle, Guy, on the way to Windsor, had already shown her faith in the marriage by bestowing titles on the newlyweds: Duke and Duchess of Sussex.

At the first of two receptions, the Prince of Wales got a laugh talking about how he used to change Harry's nappies (diapers) and praised Meghan before concluding with a heartfelt "My darling old Harry, I'm so happy for you." Intent on forging her own path, Meghan broke tradition again by giving a speech of her own. In it she thanked her mother for "always being there for me," and the royal family for being "so gracious and welcoming." Once the toasts were completed, William grabbed the microphone and asked, "Can anyone here play the piano?"—Elton John's cue to launch into a medley of, among other hits, "Tiny Dancer" and "I'm Still Standing."

The official wedding portraits taken after the ceremony said much about what impact Harry's choice of a bride would have on the monarchy. As an all-white dynasty, the royal family "influences perceptions of Britishness as white identity," author Afua Hirsch, whose father is British and whose mother came from Ghana, told the *Washington Post*. But having a senior member who is visibly of color will, Hirsch added, "change the subconscious messaging about what it means to be British."

Not that race was a subject that came up often in Britain, despite tone-deaf headlines like this one in the *Daily Mail*: "Now, That's Upwardly Mobile! How in 150 Years, Meghan Markle's Family Went from Cotton Slaves to Royalty Via Freedom in the US Civil War." Instead, Britons use the word "immigration" as a proxy for "race," said Nels Abbey, a former columnist for Britain's leading black newspaper, the *Voice*. "People will swear to high heaven that when they are talking about immigration they are not talking about race, when clearly they are. If you accept that the immigration debate is a racial debate, then Britain talks about race more than anything else," he added. "If you don't accept that, then Britain doesn't alk about race at all."

The Queen certainly wouldn't have accepted Abbey's premise, but that hardly meant she was racist. She wasted no time embracing Meghan into the royal family, inviting her on a June 14 overnight trip aboard the royal train to Chester, some two hundred miles north of London—sans Harry. The two women officially opened the Mersey Gateway Bridge and Chester's Storyhouse theater before attending a lunch as guests of the city council. They obviously enjoyed each other's company, chatting, smiling, and sharing inside jokes throughout the day. As they drove from one engagement to another, the Queen had a blanket across her knees. "It was chilly," Meghan recalled, "and she was like, 'Meghan, come on,' and put it over my knees as well. . . . It made me think of my grandmother." At the end of the trip, the Queen thanked Meghan with a gift: diamond-and-pearl earrings and a matching necklace.

Coverage of Meghan's first official solo trip with the Queen was overwhelmingly positive, focusing on the obvious rapport between the two women and the duchess's natural, Diana-like flair for pressing the flesh. None of this appeared to go over particularly well at Anmer Hall, however. Despite having known Kate for years, the Queen had waited eleven months before taking her on the road—at the time helping out on one of the legs of Her Majesty's Diamond Jubilee tour. "Yes, well, she has certainly charmed everyone," William said wearily when asked about Meghan during one of his walkabouts, "including my grandmother."

AVATAR OF CHANGE OR no, the newly minted Duchess of Sussex quickly learned to conform to the ways of the Firm. Months before the wedding, Archbishop Welby baptized Meghan into Harry's Anglican faith; the elaborate forty-five-minute ceremony at the St. James's Palace Chapel Royal was attended by Harry, Charles, and Camilla, but not the Queen or, to the Sussexes' great disappointment, William and Kate. Meghan had also begun the laborious, yearslong process of becoming a British citizen without it looking as if the Palace were leaning on authorities to speed up the process. (Meghan had planned to become a dual citizen but would abandon her UK citizenship plans after leaving the country in 2020.)

Yet it was not until her royal handlers demanded that Meghan turn over her passport, driver's license, and any other forms of personal identification that she realized she was handing over control of her life to the Men in Gray—that she was giving up her precious freedom. Meghan was also told that from now on, her every action would have to be run past Palace officials and approved first—be it a visit to the gym, a lunch date, or an official engagement. Ostensibly, all this was for security reasons, but the ultimate effect was to make the duchess feel "isolated, trapped, alone."

It went without saying that Meghan was no longer at liberty to speak out on political matters, as she had done when she denounced Donald Trump. Ever since Trump scored an upset victory against Hillary Clinton and became president in January 2017, the pomp- and pageantry-loving forty-fifth president had been angling for a way to make a state visit to England and meet the Queen. Britons threatened to take to the streets in protest if he came, which was fine with William and Harry. While they could not speak out directly against the US president, the brothers were aghast at Trump's comments about his campaign to date their mother. Trump had pursued Diana with florid letters and "oceans of flowers" after her divorce and insisted to a radio interviewer that he could have "nailed her if I wanted to"—but only if she passed an HIV test first.

As if that weren't enough, Trump felt it was necessary to weigh in on the successful legal battle the Cambridges waged against the publications that ran topless photos of Kate. "She shouldn't be sunbathing in the nude," he tweeted. "Only herself to blame." The brothers' response, according to one palace staffer: "torrents of profanity."

By the time Trump did make it to Windsor Castle for tea in July 2018, the Queen, who felt she was duty bound to be there as head of state, was the only royal willing to meet him. While Charles and Camilla tended to their roses at Highgrove, William and Harry—the latter fresh off his first foreign tour with Meghan, to Ireland—played in a charity polo match. Their wives had the perfect excuse, cheering on Meghan's good friend Serena Williams as she competed in the Women's Singles Final at Wimbledon (losing to Germany's Angelique Kerber). In spite of her ties to Serena, Meghan wasn't about to outshine Kate at the event; in 2016 the Duchess of Cambridge took over from the Queen as the royal patron of Wimbledon.

(When Her Majesty finally did pull out the stops to throw a Buckingham Palace banquet for Trump a year later, the Cambridges dutifully attended—Kate wearing Diana's favorite Lover's Knot tiara and dressed in white like the Queen and Camilla. The Sussexes were once again a no-show. Trump didn't take Meghan's attitude well. "I didn't know she was nasty," the US president remarked.)

Harry and Meghan, fresh from their long-postponed, top secret honeymoon (the precise destination unknown to even their closest confidantes), still faced unresolved family issues. Thomas Markle was at it again, complaining to any broadcast or print journalist who would listen that Meghan had cut off all ties with him and his family. He tossed around the idea of simply showing up on her doorstep. "I want to see my daughter," he insisted. "I don't care whether she is pissed off at me."

That August, Meghan tried to mend her relationship with her father by fedexing him a five-page letter. "Daddy, it is with a heavy heart that I write this," she began, adding that he had broken her heart "into a million pieces." (Meghan subsequently sued the *Mail on Sunday* for copyright violations when it published large portions of the letter without obtaining her permission, and won her case in 2021.) As for Meghan's half siblings, the chances for any sort of reconciliation seemed even slimmer. At one point, Thomas Jr. blamed Meghan for his unemployment and homelessness, and claimed his mere association with her "nearly destroyed" him. When Samantha showed up unannounced outside Kensington Palace with a photographer from the entertainment website Splash News, Meghan dismissed it as "just another publicity stunt." (Two years later, Samantha published a tell-all memoir that pretty much put an end to their relationship forever. Its title: *The Diary of Princess Pushy's Sister*.)

If Harry hoped to lean on his brother and sister-in-law for a little moral support, he was sorely disappointed. Not only did the Cambridges keep to their corner of Kensington Palace whenever the Sussexes were there, but Harry and Meghan's standing invitation to have them drop in anytime at their house in Oxfordshire went unanswered. "Please bring the children," Meghan wrote in a note to Kate. "We would so love to see them!"

It became increasingly clear to the Sussexes that if they wanted to be around children, they might as well have some of their own. On October 15, just as they were about to embark on a tour of Australia,

Fiji, Tonga, and New Zealand, the Sussexes announced that they were expecting their first child in the spring of 2019. Packing seventy-six engagements into sixteen days, Harry and Meghan drew massive, euphoric crowds wherever they went. In Sydney, they showed up to cheer for athletes at the fourth Invictus Games. Giving her only speech of the tour at the closing ceremonies, Meghan brought the audience of more than twelve thousand to its feet.

What the public didn't see were tensions behind the scenes. Several aides complained that the duchess occasionally snapped at them, and that the once-easygoing Harry was scrambling to make her happy. Just before delivering her Invictus speech, Meghan was reportedly giving orders to her hairdresser while at the same time someone was ironing the bottom of her dress. "All of Harry's staff have always thought he was fantastic," said longtime royal correspondent Duncan Larcombe, "but the two of them together are high maintenance." However, Larcombe understood the spot Harry was in. "Harry wants to be protective of Meghan," he continued. "If she's getting frustrated and stressed, he is the one reading the riot act to the staff. But you can't blame Meghan, either. She's gone into her biggest role yet, and she's put her heart and soul into it."

By any measure, the tour was a resounding success. Newspapers abroad and at home were rapturous in their praise, many drawing parallels between the fashion-forward, magnetic Meghan and her late mother-in-law. That was the problem. "That was the first time that the family got to see how incredible she is at the job," Harry later said. "And that brought back memories" of Diana's 1983 trip to Australia with Charles and toddler William—the first of many times when the princess upstaged her husband.

"I just wish that we would all learn from the past," he went on, alluding to the jockeying for attention that still goes on among the royals. "But to see how effortless it was for Meghan to . . . be able to connect with people. Really, here you have one of the greatest assets to the Commonwealth that the family could have ever wished for."

The Sussexes would mark this as an important turning point in their relationship with the Cambridges—and the beginning of an avalanche of stories leaked to the press for the sole purpose of discrediting Meghan. On November 10 the *Mail on Sunday* ran an article presumably based on information from a Kensington Palace source allied with the Cambridges that Meghan had driven her assistant Melissa Toubati to tears so many times that Toubati quit; this was the first in a series of stories painting Meghan as a bullying boss that would stretch into 2021. Then, more than six months after Meghan and Harry's wedding, the squabble between the duchesses over flower girl tights hit the proverbial media fan. "Meghan Made Kate Cry," stated the *Sun's* front-page headline, while the *Telegraph* reported that staffers were reeling from Meghan's five-in-the-morning wake-up calls and email "bombardments." At one point, according to veteran royal correspondent Robert Jobson, Harry allegedly told the staff, "What Meghan wants, Meghan gets."

There was more. While picking out jewelry for her wedding day, Meghan supposedly had her eye on an emerald tiara from the Royal Collection instead of the stunning Queen Mary bandeau tiara that Harry's grandmother had already picked out for her—the one she eventually wore and, by all subsequent accounts, loved.

Later, there were tabloid stories claiming that the Queen had barred Meghan from wearing jewelry that once belonged to Diana. The same article claimed that Kate had carte blanche from Her Majesty to wear whatever she wanted. The truth was that several of Diana's privately owned pieces were in the hands of her sons, to be worn by either duchess at her own discretion. Those major items famously worn by Diana but nevertheless belonging to either the Queen or the Crown—necklaces, brooches, earrings, bracelets, and tiaras—were lent by Elizabeth to whomever she pleased.

The attacks on Meghan continued unabated through early 2019: Her choice of dark nail polish was unacceptable. She crossed her legs at an event with the Queen, in violation of royal protocol. Her bra strap was visible for less than a second at a royal reception. She wore too much black. Her hand lingered too long on her pregnant stomach during a television appearance; "too showy," wrote one columnist, ignoring the fact that Kate was praised for cradling her baby bump in a similar fashion. When Meghan served avocado on toast for brunch, the *Daily Mail* ran a front-page story about how Mexican cartels are extorting money from avocado growers. The headline: "As the duchess serves avocado on toast . . . Is Meghan's favourite snack fueling drought and murder?" ("That's a really loaded piece of toast," Meghan commented when she saw the story. "I mean . . . you have to laugh at a certain point because it's just ridiculous.")

On a daily basis, Harry's pregnant wife was lambasted as "Hurricane Meghan," "Duchess Difficult," and the clumsy but still effectively degrading "Me-Gain." Then there were the unflattering comparisons to Kate, the third most popular member of the royal family after the Queen and William. "They really seemed to want a narrative," Meghan concluded, "of a hero and a villain. . . . So much of what I have seen play out is this idea of polarity. If you love me, you don't have to hate her. And if you love her, you don't need to hate me."

From the very beginning, Meghan was given her marching orders: whenever rumors surfaced, her response would be the same response given by every member of the royal family—no comment. If a rumor was so egregious that it required refuting, the Sussexes were reminded that the Palace would protect them. "I did anything they told me to do—of course I did," said Meghan, "because it was also through the lens of, 'And we'll protect you.' So, even as things started to roll out in the media that I didn't see—but my friends would call me and say, 'Meg, this is really bad'—because I didn't see it, I'd go, 'Don't worry. I'm being protected.'"

Not only was the Palace not setting the record straight, but it was clear to Harry and Meghan that the Men in Gray were spreading much of the salacious gossip to bolster the reputations of more important members of the family—principally the Cambridges. Meghan cited the flip-flop over who made who cry during the flower girl fiasco as a case in point. "I came to understand that they were willing to lie to protect other members of the family," she said, "but they weren't willing to tell the truth to protect me and my husband."

Harry and Meghan came in for more bad press when they moved out of Kensington Palace and into Frogmore Cottage in Windsor. A former retreat for George III's consort, Queen Charlotte, Frogmore had been refurbished by the Crown at a cost of about $3.4 million, ostensibly so that Prince Harry would have room for his growing family. Even the BBC struck an uncharacteristic note of outrage, questioning whether the Sussexes warranted such an outlay "in taxpayer funds." (By the fall of 2020, following their decision to step back from royal duties, Harry and Meghan had made good on their promise to repay the full amount.)

As Meghan's due date drew closer, Harry was called into a series of meetings with senior courtiers at Kensington Palace, Clarence House, and Buckingham Palace to discuss the future of his baby. When he reported to Meghan, she was shocked at what she was told: the child would not be automatically given a royal title of prince or princess at birth and would not have the HRH distinction.

Meghan, who also worried incorrectly that her child would not then be entitled to government-funded protection, was unaware that most great-grandchildren of the monarch were not given royal titles at birth. When the Queen issued a new letters patent (essentially a legal order from the sovereign) abolishing primogeniture in 2012, going forward she also gave all of the Heir's children—in this case, George, Charlotte, and Louis—titles and the HRH distinction because of their high ranks in the line of succession. Her Majesty could have done the same for Harry but didn't. Instead, the old rule from 1917 applied to the Sussexes: once Charles ascended to the throne, it was assumed that their offspring would all be offered royal titles and the HRH standing. However, since Harry and his family departed royal life in 2020, all that could change if Charles decided not to bestow a title on the Sussex children as part of his plan to slim down the Firm. For now, Harry and Meghan's firstborn would simply be known as Master Archie Harrison Mountbatten-Windsor. No title, no honorific, no HRH.

What couldn't be explained away were remarks purportedly made by members of the royal family about how light or dark the Sussexes' baby might be, or concerns voiced by others at the Palace about whether a mixed-race child might present "the right look" for the British monarchy abroad. With his heavily pregnant wife distraught to the point of tears, Harry was nevertheless reluctant to go to William for help. His brother had made his feelings about Meghan known early in the game, and the latent animosity between the two duchesses hadn't helped the situation. "Prince William complained about Meghan's whinging [whining]," said a Clarence House staffer, who added that the

Heir seemed to feel the Meghan "situation" was "driving a wedge" between the brothers. William also suggested that whatever comments being made about the baby's possible complexion might have been tactless, but not a sign of racism within the family. He could not say the same about the nonroyals who actually run the Firm.

Kept by their own pride from speaking frankly about what was going on, both brothers relied on communicating through their staffs—and on Palace gossip. The message being conveyed to Harry was that Meghan should stop complaining and that he was "oversensitive." Dismayed and hurt that his brother had not reached out to him, Harry seemed more wistful than angry. "William's the one person," he said, "I always thought I could count on."

In fairness to the Cambridges, they were distracted by persistent but baseless rumors that William was in the middle of an affair with the couple's longtime friend and Norfolk neighbor Rose Hanbury, Marchioness of Cholmondeley (pronounced "Chumley") and the married mother of three. After several months, the unfounded rumors died down—but only after William's legal team threatened action against several tabloids that had been spreading the story.

Even as Harry hoped for his brother's help, Meghan was in free fall. In late January 2019, the day before they were scheduled to attend the premiere of Cirque du Soleil's *Totem* show at the Royal Albert Hall in London, Harry told his six-months-pregnant wife she seemed too upset to go. "I can't be left alone," replied Meghan, who later revealed that at this point she was on the verge of taking her own life. "I was ashamed to have to admit it to Harry, especially because I know how much loss he's suffered. But I knew that if I didn't *say* it, I would *do* it. I just didn't want to be alive anymore. And that was a very clear and real and frightening constant thought. I didn't see a solution."

Harry cradled her as she wept that night, and as he would many other nights. But the next day, they went to Royal Albert Hall as planned. Photographs taken at the event show the couple beaming, but their hands are clasped so tightly that Harry's knuckles are white. Every time the lights went down in the royal box, Meghan sobbed.

The duchess did not want Harry to carry the burden of her psychological problems alone, but she didn't want her mother or close friends worried to distraction, either. Convinced that she needed immediate help from a mental health professional, Meghan approached senior officials at Buckingham Palace the day after the Royal Albert Hall event. "I need to go somewhere to get help," she told them. "I've never felt this way before."

The answer was immediate and succinct. "No, you can't," the duchess was told. "It wouldn't be good for the institution." She was also handed another disingenuous reason for not being offered any mental health services: because she was not technically a "paid employee" of the monarchy, she was not entitled to them. Meghan realized she was "supposed to be stronger than that." Instead, she continued to harbor suicidal thoughts. "I thought," she recalled later, "that it would be better if I just wasn't here."

At the time, Harry wasn't faring much better. "I went to a very dark place as well," said the prince, who conceded that he, too, needed help. Still, he said nothing to his brother or anyone in the family about the Sussexes' life-threatening mental health issues. "No, that's just not a conversation that would be had," he would try to explain. "I was ashamed of admitting it to them. I didn't have anyone to turn to."

Part of Harry's frustration stemmed from his family's abiding belief in the Queen's "Keep Calm and Carry On" credo. They failed to grasp that something new had been added to the equation: race, and the realization that the hate directed at them was also being directed at millions of others. "What was different for me was the race element," Harry later said. "Now it wasn't just about her, but it was about what she represents. It wasn't just affecting my wife, it was affecting so many other people as well."

In repeatedly considering taking her own life, Meghan must also have thought about what ending the life of her unborn child would mean. If that was part of a chilling rationale—that Meghan wished to spare the baby a lifetime of emotional pain as the royal family's first mixed-race child—then it spoke volumes about not only intolerance within the monarchy but also in Britain as a whole.

Concern for Harry is what stopped Meghan from killing herself. "The thing that stopped her from seeing it through," he said, "was how unfair it would be on me after everything that had happened to my mum and to now be put in a position of losing another woman in my life, with a baby inside of her—our baby."

Yet apart from race issues, Meghan's "clear, constant, frightening" thoughts of suicide were a haunting reminder of Diana's own battles with depression and her many attempts at seriously harming herself—including the day when, while pregnant with William, she threw herself down the stairs at Sandringham. "I understand now," Meghan told Harry, "what your mother went through."

In a situation rife with irony, nothing seemed more absurd than the idea that Meghan—who along with her husband, brother-in-law, and sister-in-law were now the world's most famously outspoken champions of addressing mental health issues—was being explicitly denied the help she so desperately needed.

THE SUSSEXES HAD KNOWN for months that they were having a boy, so they were ready with a name when he arrived at central London's Portland Hospital at 5:26 on the morning of May 6, 2019. Archie Harrison Mountbatten-Windsor weighed in at seven pounds, three ounces. "This little thing is absolutely to die for," Harry said of his newborn son. "So I'm just over the moon."

The happy trio barely had time to settle into Frogmore Cottage when the racist sniping began. Two days after Archie's birth, veteran BBC Radio 5 Live anchor Danny Baker posted on his Twitter account a photograph from 1925 showing a well-dressed couple holding the hand of an equally well-attired chimpanzee. He captioned it: "Royal baby leaves hospital." Baker offered an apology but was immediately fired.

The groundswell of blatant racism triggered by Archie's birth reflected much of what was happening in British society as a whole in the age of Brexit. That summer, the royals were forced to deal with an outrageously flamboyant home-grown populist, Boris Johnson, who took over the Conservative Party from Theresa May to become prime minister. The New York–born Johnson, like his friend Donald Trump, had been widely accused of being racist. When Barack Obama came out against Brexit, Johnson blasted "the part-Kenyan president's ancestral dislike of the British Empire." The new prime minister had also written op-ed pieces calling black people "piccaninnies with watermelon smiles."

Archie was eight days old when William and Kate dropped in to Frogmore Cottage to see their nephew. Charles, who was particularly fond of Meghan and Meghan's mother, Doria, came round twice to meet his new grandson. But, since she was only a stone's throw away, no one spent more time with Archie than "Gan-Gan"—his great-grandmother the Queen. This was all well and good, but before long Meghan, who was left to care for her infant son while her husband played at home and abroad in charity polo matches, began to feel the walls closing in. "Well, you can't do this because it'll look like that," Meghan recalled a deputy private secretary telling her. "You *can't*."

"Can I go and have lunch with my friends?" she asked in reply.

"No, no, no," she was told. "You're oversaturated, you're everywhere!"

When a royal family member suggested that Meghan "just lay low for a little while," she objected. "I've left the house twice in four months," the duchess said. "I'm everywhere, but I'm nowhere. Right now I could not feel lonelier."

Much of the pressure on both Harry and Meghan to "lay low" stemmed from the fact that they were in constant competition with Clarence House and, to an even greater extent, William and Kate. If the Sussexes had a project or charity they wanted to launch, and it conflicted in any way with what the others were doing, Harry and Meghan had to step aside.

Once again Harry, now convinced that none of the Firm's senior managers were looking after the Sussexes' interests, appealed directly to his brother, asking that he and Meghan be allowed to proceed with some of their own initiatives regardless of scheduling conflicts. In making his argument, Harry cited new polls showing that he, Meghan, and Archie were now responsible for more than 80 percent of new online interest in the monarchy.

If anything, Harry's argument offended William, who had gallantly downplayed polls that consistently showed that the overwhelming majority of Britons wanted him and Kate as their next king and queen, not Charles and certainly not Camilla. In the end, William reminded Harry that he, too, had to obey the rules of seniority. "That's just the way it is," William told his brother. "I don't see what your problem is."

That, in Harry's mind, *was* the problem. That, and the fact that their father controlled the purse strings through his revenue-gushing Duchy of Cornwall, forcing the brothers to compete for every pound spent by their respective households—including money for major projects, food, travel, staffs, and even their wives' wardrobes. "William and Harry were tired of working at cross-purposes," said a courtier. "They weren't getting anywhere, and they were no longer speaking to each other."

Speculation of a rift between the brothers was now rampant, and the Queen wanted something done. After an emergency meeting of the Firm's principal courtiers in June 2019, a decision was made: divorce, of a sort, was the only answer. Over the ten years since William and Harry created it, the Royal Foundation had kept their mother's philanthropic legacy alive by raising more than $11 million annually for some twenty-six charities—the most recent of which being the Royal Foundation Forum on mental health where the Fab Four made their debut only the year before.

On June 20, 2019, Buckingham Palace announced that the brothers were splitting up the foundation, and that the Queen and Prince Charles were creating a separate household for the Duke and Duchess of Sussex. While William and Kate took over complete control of the existing operation, Harry and Meghan were setting up their own organization targeting "global outreach." The following day was William's thirty-seventh birthday, and by way of rubbing salt into the wound, Harry and Meghan filed the necessary paperwork establishing the Sussex Royal Foundation for the Duke and Duchess of Sussex.

That summer, the Queen and Prince Philip waited eagerly for William and Harry to make their annual pilgrimage to Balmoral with the rest of the royals, but for the first time the Sussexes failed to show. Meghan and Harry's excuse was that Archie was still too young to travel to Scotland. The Queen was displeased to learn, then, that the Sussexes did manage that August to jet off for a few days in Spain and not long after take Archie along for a romp on the Côte d'Azur with Elton John and his husband, David Furnish.

As painful as the rupture between William and Harry was, the Queen had her hands full dealing with other brewing catastrophes—not the least of which was Prince Andrew's involvement in the salacious Jeffrey Epstein underage sex scandal. No one inside the family was paying attention to the Sussexes' plight—or to the stories with disquieting racial overtones that continued to portray "Me-Gain" as calculating and neurotic. They perked up, however, when, in *Harry and Meghan: An African Journey*—the television documentary filmed during the couple's trip to South Africa that September—the interviewer stopped talking about the Sussexes' charitable work to ask Meghan how she was doing. At this point in the tour, the duchess would later reveal, she was "fried" from exhaustion. "Thank you for asking," she replied as she fought to control her emotions, "because not many people have asked if I'm okay." When pressed if she was then "not really okay?" and if it had "really been a struggle," Meghan blinked back tears. "Yes," she answered.

The duchess didn't stop there. "It's not enough to just survive something, right?" she continued. "That's not the point of life. You've got to thrive, you've got to feel happy." She added that she had "really tried to adopt this sensibility of the British stiff upper lip," but concluded "that what that does internally is probably really damaging."

Not unexpectedly, the Palace took Meghan's unscripted remarks as

a swipe at the institution and what appeared to be her automaton-like in-laws. But Harry tossed his share of grenades as well, conceding for the first time that Diana's sons were barely speaking to each other. "Inevitably, stuff happens," he said in the documentary. "But, look, we are brothers; we will always be brothers. We are certainly on different paths at the moment, but I will always be there for him, and, as I know, he will always be there for me."

For whatever reasons, the Sussexes had used their Africa sojourn to launch attacks on a number of fronts—not the least of which was a major legal offensive against Fleet Street. In *An African Journey*, Harry pointed out that the daily presence of reporters in his life was a constant reminder of how his mother was hunted down by the press. "It's a wound that festers," he said. "I think being part of this family—in this role, in this job—every single time I see a camera, every single time I hear a click, every single time I see a flash, it takes me straight back."

With press coverage intensifying in the months following Archie's birth, Harry and Meghan announced that they were striking back at the "relentless propaganda" and "knowingly false and malicious" stories that the tabloid press was churning out on a near-continuous basis. "Unfortunately my wife has become one of the latest victims of a British tabloid press that wages campaigns against individuals with no thought to the consequences—a ruthless campaign that has escalated over the past year," read an official statement from Harry taking the British press to task. "Though we have continued to put on a brave face, I cannot begin to describe how painful it has been."

While their lawyers compiled a long list of "absurd" articles written about Meghan, the lawsuits filed by the Sussexes that day were targeted specifically at issues of invasion of privacy and copyright infringement. Harry filed lawsuits against the *Daily Mirror* and the *Sun* alleging that

they had intercepted his voice mail messages between 2001 and 2005, at the start of his military career. Meghan was bringing a separate copyright action against the *Mail on Sunday* for publishing extracts of the long, pleading letter she had sent to her father, seeking damages for "misuse of private information, copyright infringement and breach of the Data Protection Act."

Harry knew that if he had warned the Palace ahead of time, the Men in Gray would have tried to block him from taking on Britain's powerful, deep-pocketed press. Nor did he ask either his father or the Duke of Cambridge to weigh in; both Charles and William did not conceal their concern that this was an especially risky move. The Sussexes' legal action, Harry conceded, "may not be the safe one, but it is the right one." He went on to say that his "deepest fear is history repeating itself. I've seen what happens when someone I love is commoditized to the point where they are no longer treated or seen as a real person. I lost my mother, and now I watch my wife falling victim to the same powerful forces."

There was another powerful force, however, that the Sussexes had overlooked. By failing to secure the Queen's permission—something William and Kate had been careful to do when they brought their successful legal action over topless photographs taken of the Duchess of Cambridge in 2012—Harry and Meghan had broken a cardinal rule. As for complaints about being "commoditized," the Sussexes had also defied Her Majesty by applying to trademark hundreds of items, from jeans and T-shirts, to hoodies, bookmarks, pajamas, and socks under the Sussex Royal logo—all without her consent.

Shortly after spending Thanksgiving 2019 on Vancouver Island, Harry made it clear that he was willing to do whatever it took to make his wife happy—even if it meant forgoing the traditional holiday festivities at Sandringham. Instead, they would extend their holiday and spend Christmas in Canada with Meghan's mother. Her Majesty had understood on those rare occasions when other family members could not attend, but this was different. At a time when the brothers needed to come together to show their solidarity with each other and the rest of the family, Harry had chosen to stay away. "I think the Queen is very hurt by all that's going on," Kate told a friend from her days at St. Andrews. "Very hurt."

As she prepared to record her televised Christmas message in the Green Drawing Room at Windsor Castle, Elizabeth II looked over the table where the photographs she had so lovingly selected were arranged. All were fine except for one, she told the director as she pointed to a heartwarming portrait of Harry, Meghan, and eight-month-old Archie. "That one," said the Queen, surveying the other images of past and future monarchs and their families. "I suppose we don't need that one."

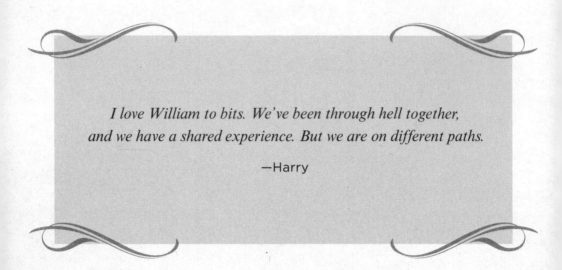

I love William to bits. We've been through hell together,
and we have a shared experience. But we are on different paths.

—Harry

SIX

"THINGS ARE QUITE BROKEN"/ "WE'RE STUCK TOGETHER FOR THE REST OF OUR LIVES"

ROYAL COMMUNICATIONS

13th January, 2020

STATEMENT FROM HER MAJESTY THE QUEEN

Today my family had very constructive discussions on the future of my grandson and his family.

My family and I are entirely supportive of Harry and Meghan's desire to create a new life as a young family. Although we would have preferred them to remain full-time working Members of the Royal Family, we respect and understand their wish to live a more independent life as a family while remaining a valued part of my family.

Harry and Meghan have made clear that they do not want to be reliant on public funds in their new lives.

It has therefore been agreed that there will be a period of transition in which the Sussexes will spend time in Canada and the UK.

These are complex matters for my family to resolve, and there is some more work to be done, but I have asked for final decisions to be reached in the coming days.

HARRY HAD ARRIVED at the Sandringham Summit as planned at 11:20 a.m.—more than two and a half hours before the scheduled conference so he could speak one-on-one with his grandmother before Charles, William, and senior staff arrived. He knew that, despite her special relationship with William, she'd always had a soft spot in her heart for the former Spare. "If we can just talk alone," he told Meghan, who remained in Canada with Archie, "I'm sure Granny will understand."

But Charles, fresh from attending the funeral of Oman's Sultan Qaboos bin Said, was already there when Harry arrived. The Prince of Wales made little effort to conceal his disappointment—or the resentment he felt toward the Sussexes for causing the Queen so much obvious heartache. After all, the Queen had fully embraced Harry's wife and child, visiting Frogmore Cottage more frequently than any other member of the royal family to check on Meghan and her great-grandson Archie. "I hate to see this happen," the Queen told Charles and Harry, adding that she saw no reason the Sussexes had to leave the United Kingdom to be "financially independent." More than once, she gave her headstrong grandson an opportunity to change his mind. "Are you absolutely sure there's no other way, Harry?"

Over lunch, the Prince of Wales cut right to the chase. He spoke of his vision for a pared-down, streamlined monarchy, and stressed that he had always seen a place for Harry and his family in it. But now that they were hell-bent on making their own way, there were cold, hard facts to consider. As much as 90 percent of the Sussexes' income came from Charles's Duchy of Cornwall, an estimated $4.8 million annually. If Harry and Meghan insisted on launching their own brand in another country, Prince Charles had no intention of continuing to prop them up. William, who was too angry to sit across from his brother over lunch, arrived just fifteen minutes before the summit began in Sandringham's book-lined Long Library. Seething, he agreed with their father that if Harry and Meghan insisted on going it alone, then it was a venture they themselves would ultimately have to finance.

After ninety minutes, during which it was agreed that concocting a blueprint for the Sussexes' future was going to be a complicated undertaking, the meeting broke up. Yet the unspoken mood in the Long Library was solemn and, in the monarch's case, anguished. Diana's friend and confidante journalist Richard Kay asked if the Queen could ever have written a "more poignant communique? Her message was clear that she will not stand in the couple's way, but it is with a heavy heart that she has agreed. In one sentence alone, her sadness about this incendiary situation shone through." The statement, Kay continued, was "laced with despair."

Yet there was also a rare sign of unity when, on the same day, William and Harry issued a joint statement denying a London *Sunday Times* story about tensions between the brothers. According to the piece, the Sussexes felt they were the victims of a "bullying" attitude by Prince William. "If you are Meghan and Harry, and you had two years of constantly being told your place," a source told the *Sunday Times*, "constantly bullied as they see it, constantly told what you can't do, Meghan has been thinking, 'This is just nuts. Why would anyone put up with this?' "

"I've put my arm around my brother all our lives, and I can't do that anymore," another friend of William's quoted the Heir as saying. "We're separate entities. I'm sad about that. All we can do is try and support them and hope that the time comes when we're all singing from the same page. I want everyone to play on the same team."

Tom Bradley, the director of *Harry and Meghan: An African Journey* and a friend of the couple, also suggested that Buckingham Palace had leaked the Sussexes' plan to move to North America to discredit them—an indication "of just how poisonous and, frankly, Machiavellian the modern House of Windsor has become. . . . There is no doubt Harry and Meghan feel they have been driven out."

What the brothers objected to was use of the buzzword 'bullying' to describe William's behavior. "Despite clear denials," read their joint statement issued right before the Sandringham Summit, "a false story ran in a UK newspaper today speculating about the relationship between the Duke of Sussex and the Duke of Cambridge. For brothers who care so deeply about the issues surrounding mental health, the use of language in this way is offensive and potentially harmful."

That William and Harry would come together publicly on anything was a positive sign, to be sure. However, for the brothers to express outrage based on their commitment to mental health, when Meghan was denied precisely that help and Harry was too proud to bring it up to the family, seemed specious. In addition, what the princes *didn't* say about their relationship—there was no express or implied denial that there were tensions between them—spoke volumes. "There's obviously been a very sad breakdown between William and Harry," said *Sunday Times* reporter Roya Nikkhah. "At the moment, things are quite broken . . . everyone is hopeful that at some point down the line, they'll reconcile." Toward that end, Nikkhah's sources were telling her that William was "very keen" on supporting his brother and sister-in-law "in their new lifestyle."

"The first round has gone to the Sussexes," said royal authority Ingrid Seward. "It feels that the royal family are bending over backwards to try and help." At home in the United Kingdom, however, the reaction to Megxit was predominantly negative. Broadcaster Piers Morgan, who had once been friendly with Meghan but had since had a well-documented falling-out with the Sussexes, claimed on ITV that Harry and Meghan had—here came that freighted word again—"*bullied* the Queen into letting them have their cake and eat it." Referring to Prince Andrew's stepping down from royal duties as a result of the Jeffrey Epstein affair, Morgan added, "The Queen's just had to fire her middle son, her ninety-eight-year-old husband is very sick, and these two little spoiled brats are holding her to ransom at the worst moment."

Although Americans were more inclined to side with the Sussexes, not everyone saw things their way—particularly the media. "It wasn't cool for Meghan and Harry to pants the ninety-three-year-old queen, defy her instructions, dump their Megxit plan on Instagram, and intensify the sad split between the brothers," wrote columnist Maureen Dowd in the *New York Times*. "What's the rush to give up real influence to be an Instagram influencer? Besides, who unfollows their own grandmother?"

In the end, it was Granny who decided that the Sussexes' original concept of being part-time, quasi-independent royals was untenable. Even though they were agreeing not to take money from the Sovereign Grant—the taxpayer-funded kitty that covers the expenses of running the monarchy—Meghan and Harry would still have to seek Palace approval for everything they wanted to do. There was also a Gordian knot of tax issues to untangle, not to mention the nagging question of the extent to which the Sussexes would be allowed to use the royal imprimatur to promote their personal brand.

After five more days of intense negotiations among all the palace staffs, the Queen handed down her verdict. Harry and Meghan were no longer to be working members of the royal family and were stepping back from all their royal duties. They would no longer be considered formal representatives of the Queen, and Harry would have to drop his role as Commonwealth Youth Ambassador, although both the duke and the duchess would be allowed to remain president and vice president, respectively, of the Queen's Commonwealth Trust (because, said the Palace, the trustees appointed Harry and Meghan to those positions and the Queen was not in a position to fire them). Harry would no longer be patron of the London Marathon Charitable Trust, the Rugby Football Union, and the Rugby Football League—duties he had taken over from the Queen—but the Sussexes would be permitted to hold on to their private patronages, including Sentebale and the Invictus Games. However, they could not use the term "royal" in any future nonprofit organizations they might launch.

For a time, it looked as if they might lose their titles, but a compromise was reached: the couple would technically retain their royal HRH status but agree not to "actively use" the titles going forward. As for military titles: "The honorary military appointments and Royal patronages held by the Duke and Duchess will therefore be returned to Her Majesty, before being redistributed among working members of the royal family." For Harry, being stripped of his honorary military titles was a major blow. The ten-year combat veteran was now told he could no longer wear the uniforms of an Honorary Air Force Commandant, Honorary Commodore-in-Chief of the Royal Navy's Small Ships and Diving Operations, and Captain General of the Royal Marines.

Knowing full well how devastated Harry was by the loss of his coveted military titles, the Queen reiterated in her statement outlining their exit plan that, above all else, she still adored her grandson: "While all are saddened by their decision, the duke and duchess remain much-loved members of the family."

On March 9, 2020, Harry and Meghan made their final royal appearance alongside the rest of the royal family at the nationally televised Commonwealth Day Service at Westminster Abbey. It was also the first time they had all seen one another since Megxit was formally announced. Right away there was trouble. Protocol had always dictated that after junior royals had taken their seats in the abbey, the Queen would walk down the aisle behind the Commonwealth flag with senior members—normally Charles and Camilla, William and Kate, and Harry and Meghan. But this time, Harry and Meghan were told they had not been invited to enter with the Queen and would instead be taking their seats alongside Prince Edward and his wife, Sophie. Incensed at the obvious slight, Harry complained to the Palace but got nowhere. It was left for William and Kate to take the high road, agreeing at the last minute to drop out of the royal procession and take their seats before the Queen made her grand entrance.

Yet the two thousand printed programs still showed the Cambridges entering with the Queen. Nor did it help that William and Kate took front-row seats directly in front of Harry and Meghan, not next to them. As they sat down, an unsmiling William exchanged a few words with Harry, who then turned to Meghan: "He literally said, 'Hello, Harry,' and that was it. He didn't say anything more than that!"

There was no concealing the tension in the air, or the obvious fact that William and Kate appeared to be snubbing the Sussexes. Throughout the service, Meghan sported a frozen smile and Harry looked grim. The service, with its mix of speeches and music, gave everyone in the abbey perfect cover for not talking to one another. When it was over, everyone went their separate ways. "People think when they're looking at William and Harry, they see anger," said a guest at the service. "What they see is hurt."

MEGHAN FLEW BACK TO Vancouver immediately after the Commonwealth Day debacle, and Harry followed suit soon after. But now even the legendarily laid-back Canadians appeared fed up with the Sussexes. In a blistering editorial, the country's most influential publication, the *Globe and Mail,* urged Prime Minister Justin Trudeau's government to uphold Canadian sovereignty by barring the Sussexes from migrating there permanently. "So long as you are senior royals, Canada cannot allow you to stay. It breaks an unspoken constitutional taboo," said the editorial. "If you are a senior member of the royal family, Canada cannot become your home."

It all became a moot point when, just two weeks after relocating there, they departed Vancouver for Los Angeles in the predawn hours of March 14, 2020, aboard movie producer–actor Tyler Perry's $150 million Embraer E-190 private jet. Once at their destination, they were whisked away to Perry's sprawling $18 million tiled-roof Mediterranean estate in Beverly Hills. The undercover move was masterminded by Oprah Winfrey, who had befriended the couple after reaching out to support Doria Ragland during Harry and Meghan's engagement.

The stealth mission to spirit the duke and duchess into the United States had been hastily arranged. Health experts had been sounding the alarm for weeks that a deadly new virus that began in China's Wuhan Province was spreading quickly through Europe and North America. To halt the spread of the coronavirus, Canada was beginning to close its borders. This could have made it impossible for the Sussexes to visit Doria in California. In addition, it might have also prevented Meghan, who had just finished narrating the Disney documentary *Elephant* to benefit the wildlife charity Elephants Without Borders, from networking with old entertainment industry friends and contacts.

Neither Harry nor Meghan could have known that just hours before they tiptoed into the United States, Prince Charles tested positive for the virus after lunching with Monaco's Prince Albert, who also tested positive. The Prince of Wales's schedule was abruptly cleared, but no reason was given at the time. Less than a month later, William, too, contracted the virus—something that would not be divulged for a full year. "There were important things going on," said William, who self-isolated with his family at Anmer Hall, "and I didn't want to worry anyone."

Both father and son experienced mild symptoms. Prime Minister Boris Johnson, however, was less fortunate. Early on in the pandemic, he had pooh-poohed precautions laid down by health experts, telling reporters he'd visited Covid-19 patients in a London hospital and "shook hands with everybody, you'll be pleased to know." Finally reacting to the sharp rise in cases, he ordered the nation to lock down on March 23. Three days later, Britain's problematic prime minister was diagnosed with the virus and would spend much of the next month battling for his life.

It was time for the government to put its biggest morale booster to work. On April 5, the Queen made a rare televised "special address" to the nation in which she thanked health care workers and rallied the country behind efforts to defeat the virus. Summoning the combative spirit of her favorite prime minister, Winston Churchill, she promised "better days will return. We will be with our friends again. We will be with our families again. We will meet again."

While the Queen and Prince Philip hunkered down at Windsor,

the Sussexes were holed up in their rambling new digs a world away in Beverly Hills. In keeping with their philanthropic spirit, they soon hit the streets to distribute food among several hundred needy families hard-hit by the pandemic.

That summer, there was good news for the Sussexes: Meghan was pregnant. Looking forward to the birth of their second child in early 2021, they began hunting in earnest for a permanent home—a place outside of Los Angeles, which Harry felt offered them little privacy. But tragedy struck in July when Meghan was changing Archie's diapers and suddenly "dropped to the floor in pain. I knew as I clutched my first-born child that I was losing my second," she wrote in a piece for the *New York Times.* "Hours later, I lay in a hospital bed, holding my husband's hand. I felt the clamminess of his palm and kissed his knuckles, wet from both our tears. Staring at the cold, white walls, my eyes glazed over. I tried to imagine how we'd heal."

Meghan was widely praised for going public about her own experience to raise awareness of the "almost unbearable grief" carried by women who suffer a miscarriage. Tommy's, a British charity that funds pioneering medical research and offers support to women who have suffered a miscarriage or stillbirth, lauded Meghan's openness. "Thank you, Meghan," the charity tweeted, "for #breakingthesilence." It would not be the last time.

In stark contrast, Buckingham Palace said next to nothing. "This is a deeply personal matter for the couple," read the official statement, reflecting the fact that Harry had told no one, not even his father and brother, about Meghan's miscarriage. Nonetheless, *Daily Mirror* royal editor Russell Myers called it "a huge, huge missed opportunity for the royal family. They should have made a public statement to say this is a really brave and honest thing to do. . . . It would have mended cracks in the relationship we've been talking about for months and months."

Sadly, the cracks only grew deeper and wider. According to Harry, it was in mid-2020 that Prince Charles stopped returning his phone calls and pulled the plug on him financially. "My family literally cut me off financially," he recalled of this period. "I've got what my mum left me. . . . I think she saw it coming." Without the millions inherited from Princess Diana, Harry added, it would have been impossible to afford a security detail for Archie.

Yet Charles did pay $3 million out of his own pocket to help with security costs in California, and there was evidence that the Prince of Wales had not completely stopped all Duchy of Cornwall funds from flowing to the Sussexes. As it happened, Harry and Meghan managed to plunk down $14.65 million that August for the Chateau of Riven Rock, their new 18,671-square-foot Mediterranean-style mansion north of Los Angeles in the pricey Santa Barbara County enclave of Montecito. The seven-acre estate, which got its name from an oak tree near the main gate that grew up through and split a large boulder, had belonged to Russian American billionaire businessman Sergey Grishin. It featured nine bedrooms, sixteen bathrooms, a two-bedroom guesthouse, tennis courts, pool, teahouse, arcade room, gym, library—and a chicken coop they promptly named "Archie's Chick Inn."

The Sussexes were confident they'd be able to afford it. For months, they had been in top secret talks with major US corporations such as Apple and Disney before announcing a $100 million deal to produce documentaries, children's programming, movies, and scripted series for Netflix. The Palace was anything but happy with news that one of the couple's planned projects for Netflix—the network responsible for the immensely popular, award-winning series *The Crown*—was a documentary on Princess Diana. (While Harry admitted to watching *The Crown* and went on record as saying it gave a "rough idea" of what royal life was like, his Windsor relatives followed the Queen's example and remained resolutely mum on the subject.)

When word got back to Montecito that William was "livid" about the Sussexes' Netflix deal, Harry defended the network's premier show. "They don't pretend to be news. It's fictional," he argued somewhat unconvincingly. "I am way more comfortable with *The Crown* than I am seeing the stories written about my family, my wife, or myself. I have a real issue with that."

Yet William's resentment over the exploitation of their mother grew when, to update the website for the Sussexes' Archewell nonprofit, Harry used a photo of himself riding on Diana's shoulders. Describing himself as "my mother's son," Harry wrote that he and Meghan had both experienced kindness and compassion "from our mothers and strangers alike." Neither William nor Charles were shown or mentioned.

Around the same time, Harry and Meghan also inked a deal with Oprah to produce a mental health docuseries and, in December, entered into a partnership with Spotify through their production company, Archewell Audio. Under the terms of the $25 million Spotify deal, Meghan and Harry agreed to produce and host podcasts. They had no trouble rounding up old friends for their first episode: a 2020 holiday special that featured appearances by, among others, actor and CBS late-night talk show host James Corden, Elton John, Tyler Perry, and author Deepak Chopra.

Still, there were reminders of what had been left behind. When Harry asked that a wreath be laid in his name alongside those of other family members at London's Cenotaph on Remembrance Day, the British equivalent of Veterans Day, the Queen said no. "The Queen is very firmly of the opinion," said a courtier, "that you can't pick and choose. Either you are in—or you are out."

Undeterred, the Sussexes enlisted celebrity photographer Lee Morgan to take pictures of them solemnly laying a wreath at the Los Angeles National Cemetery, then placing flowers from their garden at the gravesites of two Commonwealth soldiers, one who had served in the Royal Regiment of Canadian Artillery and another in the Royal Australian Air Force. Meghan and Harry were dressed appropriately for the occasion—she in a long, black coat and he in a dark-blue suit bearing a fistful of his military medals. Both the duke and duchess took off their black face masks to reveal expressions that veered from merely mournful to anguished. Harry's determination to honor the memory of the fallen was undoubtedly sincere—placing the wreath at London's Cenotaph had become a cherished annual ritual for him—but this time, the Sussexes were quickly taken to task for what was widely derided as a self-serving publicity stunt.

BY THE TIME HARRY went to work for a tech company in Silicon Valley, he and Meghan knew they were out—permanently out. A twelve-month "probation period" that had been part of the original separation agreement came and went, and, if anything, Harry was further apart from his Windsor relatives than ever. As strange as it seemed to hear that Prince Harry was joining the American workforce, he did seem a perfect fit for his new job: chief impact officer at BetterUp, a San Francisco–based firm offering professional and mental health coaching.

The issue of mental health was never far from either brother's mind. The princes had both dealt head-on with their own soul-trying feelings of grief and despair, and together they had fought to remove the stigma attached to seeking professional help. But as the heir to the throne, William was bound by a sense of duty, propriety, and loyalty—a conviction that he could only go so far in baring his soul to the world. Harry, no longer being chased through the streets by paparazzi and in control of his own destiny for the first time, felt no such compunction. The Duke and Duchess of Sussex were eager to tell all, and they did— to Oprah.

On Valentine's Day 2021 Harry and Meghan announced, "Archie is going to be a big brother. The Duke and Duchess of Sussex are over-joyed to be expecting their second child." Accompanying the an-nouncement was a black-and-white photo of the couple lying barefoot beneath a tree in their Montecito backyard. Five days later, Bucking-ham Palace would formally announce that Harry and Meghan had per-manently and completely withdrawn as full-time royals. While all this was going on, they sat down in a shaded stone courtyard to spill their feelings for over three hours to talk show legend and media mogul Oprah Winfrey. Ever since she attended their wedding in 2018, Oprah had been working to secure the interview for her Harpo Productions, which CBS paid a reported $9 million for broadcast rights.

While Oprah was busy editing down her interview to a compact ninety minutes, Harry jumped on an open-roofed double-decker bus ("This is the first time I've been on an open-top bus—not really al-lowed to") and tooled around Los Angeles with his old friend James Corden as part of a bit for *The Late Late Show with James Corden*. Along the way, they shared afternoon tea atop the bus as it sped down the freeway, stopped at the house where the popular 1990s TV series *The Fresh Prince of Bel-Air* had been filmed, FaceTimed Meghan (her nicknames for him were "Haz" and "H"; he called her "Meg"), and crawled on their bellies in the mud as they negotiated a Spartan Race Obstacle Course. But it wasn't all fun and games. "We all know what the British press can be like," Harry said, explaining why he moved to California. "It was destroying my mental health. It was like, this is toxic. So, I did what any husband and any father would do." Later, he told Corden his departure from full-time royal life "was never walking away. It was stepping back, rather than stepping down."

William, Charles, the Queen, and even the tetchy Men in Gray breathed a sigh of relief after Harry's lighthearted *Late Late Show* appearance. Fleet Street took the brunt of Harry's criticism, and the royal family had pretty much gotten off scot-free. But when the interview with Oprah aired just ten days later on March 7, 2021, shock waves from the megaton blast shattered crockery and knocked pictures off the walls at Anmer Hall, Highgrove, and the Queen's Windsor Castle drawing room.

More than sixty million viewers worldwide watched as Meghan and then Harry spewed one startling revelation after another: Her thoughts of suicide. ("You made a decision that certainly saved my life," Meghan told him, "and saved all of us.") The heartlessness and lies of conniving Palace officials. How Harry had two phone conversations with his father in 2020 "before he stopped returning my calls. There's a lot to work through there. There's a lot of hurt that's happened." How the family cut Harry off financially. That it was Kate who made Meghan cry, not the other way around. How Harry felt the tragedy of Diana "was repeating itself." As for William: "The relationship is 'space' at the moment," Harry said. "And time heals all things, hopefully."

There was good news, too: the Queen was kind, warm, and generous. ("I would never blindside my grandmother," Harry said when

Oprah asked if he had done just that by abruptly exiting the Firm. "I have too much respect for her.") Meghan and Harry felt they had finally carved out a peaceful, safe, happy life for themselves. And, best of all, the baby they were about to have was a girl. "To have a boy and then a girl, you know," gushed Harry, "what more can you ask for?"

Yet the impending birth of a second child underscored what was arguably the biggest bombshell—aside from Meghan's assertion that she'd nearly been driven to taking her own life—detonated during the interview: the revelation that, beginning early in their marriage, "concerns" were raised about what a child of theirs might look like— how dark the baby's skin might be and "what that means" for the institution. Harry described several such conversations, but as Oprah sat gobsmacked, declined to name names. Neither did Meghan, claiming that identifying the parties involved would be "very damaging to them." (Following the broadcast, Harry quickly called another friend, *CBS This Morning* host Gayle King, to insist that the Queen and the most logical suspect, Prince Philip, were not the culprits.)

One of the most poignant comments during the interview came from Harry, who on earlier occasions had said that "nobody, including William, wants to be king." Now he seemed to realize something more sinister was afoot. "I was trapped," he told Oprah, "but I didn't *know* I was trapped. Trapped within the system like the rest of the family. My father and my brother are trapped. They don't get to leave, and I have huge compassion for that."

Predictably, the Oprah interview was compared to Diana's earth-shattering 1995 *Panorama* tell-all. It touched on many of the same topics: the omnipotent power of the insidious Men in Gray, the lack of privacy and a vanishing sense of self, self-destructive thoughts. But there were also important differences. There was no talk of marital

infidelity on both sides—a key component of Diana's *Panorama* interview. Also, the *Panorama* interview had nothing whatsoever to do with
race. In that sense, Harry and Meghan's televised confessional may have
had an even greater impact, calling attention to systemic racism in a
country that is famous for avoiding the topic altogether.

After watching the entire interview in her private sitting room at
Windsor Castle, the Queen crafted a statement with her private secretary, Sir Edward Young. "The whole family is saddened to learn the full
extent of how challenging the last few years have been for Harry and
Meghan," it read. "The issues raised, particularly that of race, are concerning. While some recollections may vary, they are taken very seriously and will be addressed by the family privately. Harry, Meghan and
Archie will always be much-loved family members."

At an event with Kate, William confronted one issue head-on when
a reporter asked him if the royal family was racist. "We are very much
not a racist family," he replied.

For the princes, there seemed little hope of reconciliation in the
late spring of 2021. Charles remained aloof from the son he first derided for having "rusty hair," telling American friends visiting Highgrove that he was "hurt and disappointed" by Harry's actions. William
also felt wounded by his brother's remarks, particularly Harry's statement that both heirs to the crown were "trapped" by the system. William took it as an insult to their father, who had spent his seventy-two
years on the planet dutifully waiting to take on the one job he was
born to do—the job he must someday do. Yet a few days after the
Oprah interview aired, William and Harry did briefly connect, though
not for long. Worried that their conversations were being leaked to the
US media (perhaps by Harry himself), William stopped returning his
brother's calls and the standoff resumed.

Harry's hopes for reuniting with his brother now hung on flying to London to celebrate Prince Philip's hundredth birthday on June 10, just a few days before the monarch's official birthday parade. But when Trooping the Colour was canceled due to the pandemic for a second year in a row, plans to mark the Duke of Edinburgh's milestone birthday with some sort of public event were thrown in doubt.

Not that Philip would have minded. Despite the fact that he was the oldest male in the history of Britain's royal family and was poised to become the first to reach a hundred, the Queen's husband hated birthday parties—especially his. There was also the issue of his declining health. He had been in and out of hospitals in recent years, and, after being treated for an infection in February 2021, returned the following month to undergo a heart procedure. Covid restrictions on hospital visits meant that even members of the royal family had to keep visitors few and the length of visits brief—the perfect excuse for Philip, who detested what he called "fuss," to tell the Queen and other members not to bother. Prince Charles was surprised, however, when his father summoned him from Highgrove, presumably so that the Prince of Wales could report back to the Queen. From that point on, Charles was in what he called "constant contact" with his father, serving as the conduit between Philip and the rest of the family.

WILLIAM AND HARRY BOTH called their grandfather several times over this period, and when Meghan learned in the middle of her Oprah interview that Philip had been readmitted to the hospital, she "picked up the phone and called the Queen just to check in. That's what we do." Philip was reported in "good spirits" when he returned to Windsor Castle on March 15, but his condition continued to deteriorate. On the morning of April 9, with the Queen at his side, the man who had been her "strength and stay" for seventy-four years and the longest-serving consort in British history, passed away. Official cause, as listed on the death certificate: "old age."

It hardly came as a surprise, but both William and Harry knew it would still come as a significant blow to the Queen. It hadn't helped that Her Majesty had also been coping with fallout from the Sussexes' jaw-dropping Oprah interview as well as the Palace's decision to hire an outside law firm to investigate accusations that Meghan bullied her staff. The duchess replied that she was "saddened by this latest attack" on her character, "particularly as someone who has been the target of bullying myself." Behind the scenes, Meghan was undone by the accusations, which she viewed as another calculated broadside by the Palace. Harry was, he recalled, "woken up in the middle of the night to her crying into her pillow because she doesn't want to wake me up, because I'm already carrying too much. That's heartbreaking. I held her. We talked. She cried and she cried and she cried."

Now the brothers' staffs put together a coordinated response, with Kensington Palace issuing William's statement praising his grandfather at two in the afternoon, and Harry's statement being made public a half hour later on the Sussexes' Archewell website. The princes' divergent personalities were evident in how they expressed their affection for the Duke of Edinburgh.

"My grandfather's century of life was defined by service—to his country and Commonwealth, to his wife and Queen, and to our family," said William, who included with his statement a photograph of Philip with Prince George in the duke's horse-drawn carriage. "I will never take for granted the special memories my children will always have of their great-grandpa coming to collect them in his carriage and

seeing for themselves his infectious sense of adventure and his mischievous sense of humor! I will miss my grandpa," he concluded, "but I
know he would want us to get on with the job."

By contrast, Harry's statement was decidedly more, well, irreverent.
"My grandfather was authentically himself," he said, "with a seriously
sharp wit, and could hold the attention of any room due to his
charm—and also because you never knew what he might say next. . . .
To me, he was my grandpa: master of the barbecue, legend of banter,
and cheeky right 'til the end. . . . I know that right now he would say to
all of us, beer in hand, 'Oh, do get on with it!'" He ended with *"Per
Mare, Per Terram,"* a Latin term used by the British marines that means
"by sea, by land." This was especially poignant, since Harry had taken
over the ceremonial rank of Captain General of the Royal Marines
when his grandfather retired in 2017—a rank he had now lost.

SPECULATION QUICKLY TURNED TO Philip's funeral. Given her
previous miscarriage and the dangers of taking a transatlantic flight at
the height of a global pandemic, Meghan was under strict orders from
her doctors not to travel at this late point in her pregnancy. Besides, it
seemed highly unlikely that she would go even if she could. Harry wasn't
eager to go, either, since he had long regarded London—the scene of
his mother's funeral—as an emotional "trigger. . . . For most of my life
I always felt worried, concerned, a bit tense and uptight whenever I fly
back into the UK." As he planned to return for his beloved grandfather's
funeral, Harry was "worried about it, afraid about it . . . because of what
happened to my mum and what happened to me."

Even before he departed for London, the issue of whether or not
Harry would be allowed to wear a uniform was raised. The Queen

quickly defused the matter: to avoid embarrassing her grandson, she ordered that only civilian attire be worn by mourners—including Charles
and William, who had originally planned to wear their gold-braided,
medal-bedecked best in honor of the decorated World War II navy
veteran.

Intent on strictly obeying Covid rules, Harry self-isolated at Frogmore Cottage before heading to the memorial service at Windsor.
Once there, in a scene reminiscent of their walk behind Diana's coffin
twenty-four years earlier, William and Harry joined their cousins, uncles, and aunt in the procession behind the military-green Land Rover
Defender TD 130 that carried Philip's coffin to St. George's Chapel.
This time, as before, the brothers were separated; funeral planners had
put their cousin Peter Phillips between them, apparently to avoid tensions or any awkward appearances.

The ceremony itself, like funerals everywhere in the midst of the
deadly pandemic, was a dramatically scaled-down affair. Only a handful of mourners—thirty close family members—were spaced out in
pews lining the sides of the chapel, which accommodated six hundred
guests when Harry and Meghan were married there. The Queen, a
small, solitary, and heartrendingly sad figure, sat closest to the stan-
dard-covered coffin, on top of which rested her husband's naval cap
and sword. Ten feet to her left was Prince Andrew, and farther down
sat Harry, who faced William and Kate on the opposite side of the
chapel.

The moving fifty-minute ceremony included trumpeters, buglers,
and a lone piper, and when it was over, everyone filed out into the sun-
shine. As the Queen stepped into her Rolls-Royce for the short ride to
the castle itself, everyone else took off their masks and strolled leisurely
up the hill. When she saw that William and Harry had drifted together

and begun to talk, Kate broke away to speak with Prince Edward's wife, Sophie.

If there was any animosity or rancor between William and Harry, it did not show at that moment. The two brothers leaned into each other and chatted amiably. They praised the music and prayer readings and agreed that the service was what Philip wanted—and they were right. Philip had planned his own funeral down to the very last detail. So, as was the case with all senior royals, had William and Harry.

Meghan had watched the funeral on television in Montecito, and, like everyone else, she hoped that somehow that brief conversation between the brothers as they strolled up Castle Hill would bring about a truce. If so, then Harry might stay for the Queen's ninety-fifth birthday to work on repairing the damage that had been done to the relationship. Unfortunately, the world had read too much into what was only a fleeting, cordial chat. Later that same day, William and Charles agreed to a face-to-face meeting with Harry on the grounds of the castle, but only if all three were present; in a move that reflected how deep the rift still was, his brother and father insisted on meeting with Harry together so that there would be no misunderstanding afterward about what had been said. That meeting apparently went nowhere, and three days later—the day before Her Majesty's milestone birthday—Harry flew back to California.

Harry was not going to make it easy for his family to forgive him. On a podcast in mid-May 2021, he inexplicably lambasted his father's parenting skills. "He's treated me the way that he was treated," he said of Prince Charles. "There's a lot of genetic pain and suffering that gets passed on anyway. Isn't life about breaking the cycle?" He went on to compare life in the Firm to "a mixture between *The Truman Show* and being in a zoo. I've seen behind the curtain," he continued. "I've seen the business model. I know how this operation runs. I don't want to be part of this."

The Duke of Sussex doubled down in a mental health docuseries he and Meghan coproduced with Oprah, *The Me You Can't See*. "Family members have just said play the game and your life will be easier," Harry told Winfrey. "But I have a hell of a lot of my mum in me. I feel as though I am outside of the system, but I'm still stuck there." Any attempt to seek help for the post-traumatic stress disorder he suffered after Diana's death was "squashed" by the royal family, said Harry, who recalled years of self-medicating with alcohol and drugs. As for seeking help when Meghan contemplated suicide: "I felt completely helpless," he said. "I thought my family would help—but every single ask, request, warning, whatever it is, just got met with total silence or total neglect."

Yet, in the same *The Me You Can't See* documentary, Harry revealed that in the middle of an intense argument with Meghan in 2017, she insisted that he see a therapist. He did, and in fact, had been in therapy ever since. Princess Margaret, Prince Charles, and Prince William also sought mental health counseling in the past. Clearly, the same option was available to Meghan. Harry had been involved with mental health issues for years and had even been hired by a Silicon Valley mental health firm to be its chief impact officer. He knew how to get his wife the help she needed, and, given the fact that she had convinced *him* to enter therapy, so did she.

Whatever the truth, one thing was certain: the Queen was heartbroken by Megxit and the firestorm of controversy unleashed by her rebel grandson and his disgruntled wife. It remained to be seen if Charles could ever forgive Harry for what he viewed as wanton acts of betrayal. In the United States and Canada, Meghan had her own posse to turn to: longtime pals like producer-actress Lindsay Roth, fashion stylist Jessica Mulroney, and Serena Williams spoke out to defend the embattled duchess. "Meghan Markle, my selfless friend, lives her life and leads by example with empathy and compassion," the tennis star said. "She teaches me every day what it means to be truly noble." Mulroney, whose longtime best-friendship with Meghan had reportedly cooled, was equally effusive in her praise of how the duchess was handling bullying allegations. "In the face of it all," Mulroney wrote, "I have never seen her waver from kindness, empathy, and love." Not long after, Meghan, by way of signaling a rapprochement, sent Jessica a bouquet of pink roses on Mulroney's forty-first birthday— which Mulroney promptly shared on her Instagram account. The caption read: "Luckiest Friends Xxxx. Thx Mm."

In Harry's case, few comparable words of support were forthcoming from his tight circle of friends. Not that some of them weren't sympathetic. In fact, many of the friends he made during his army career and in the course of raising money for charities such as Sentebale, the Invictus Games, and Heads Together felt strongly that he and Meghan had done the right thing in baring their soul on American media.

"It was powerful, it was honest, it was sometimes uncomfortable, but it humanized the couple," Dean Stott said of the Oprah interview. Stott, Harry's old army training partner, had remained a close friend. "Here Harry had his heart on his sleeve. It was difficult to watch at times, but I understand why they've done what they've done. Harry talks about the parallels between his mother and Meghan, and he saw history repeating itself, and he doesn't want to be following another coffin, so he took action."

The brothers' celebrity friends—the ones they'd known before

Harry met Meghan—either kept their opinions to themselves or waltzed around the topic. Actor George Clooney had bonded with Harry long ago over their shared passion for motorcycles, and he and his activist-lawyer wife, Amal, had hosted the Sussexes at their estate in Berkshire and at Villa Oleandra, their eighteenth-century mansion on Italy's Lake Como. Yet this time, the Clooneys, along with mutual pals David and Victoria Beckham, stayed silent. So did actor Tom Hardy, singer James Blunt, and James Corden. High-profile pals of both William and Harry—including actor and Eton classmate Eddie Redmayne, singer Joss Stone, Elton John, and the Obamas—were just as inclined not to get in the middle of the dispute between brothers. Michelle Obama did concede that what the Sussexes revealed in the Oprah interview was "heartbreaking to hear" and added, "I just pray that there is forgiveness and there is clarity and love and resolve at some point in time, because there's nothing more important than family."

Harry's older chums, the ones he had grown up with at Ludgrove, Eton, and within the aristocracy, were, if anything, even more cautious. All were part of the tight circle that included William and Kate as well—people like Guy Pelly, Skippy Inskip, Jake Warren, Arthur Landon, Hugh Grosvenor, and Thomas and Charlie van Straubenzee. In fact, the Van Straubenzees were a perfect case in point: two brothers who found their own brotherly bond being tested because of the strains between William and Harry. Tom was Charlotte's godfather, while Charlie shared godfather duties for Archie with Harry's mentor Mark Dyer. As the royal brothers drew further apart, William leaned more heavily on Tom for support, while Harry turned increasingly to Charlie.

"Not everyone sees eye to eye," said the mother of one of the boys' Eton pals. "Most, I would say, don't understand why Harry is saying all these horrible things. He has to know how it is hurting his father and the Queen, and William." The overarching concern among friends of the dukes is that the rift between brothers "might never be mended, and what a tragedy that would be. William and Harry have always been so terribly close." In the meantime, those closest to the brothers were careful not to take sides—something even the outspokenly pro-Sussex Dean Stott understood. "You can't," said Stott, "go against one or the other."

For most of those young men and women who grew up basking in the reflected glory of the modern world's most celebrated princelings, it seemed inconceivable that their brotherly bond had been irrevocably broken. "They come as a pair," said one. "We don't even think about one without the other." With good reason. As they have both said repeatedly over the years in one way or another, no one has been through what they've been through. Nobody knows what it's like to be them.

YET EVEN THE BIRTH of the Sussexes' second child was not enough to entirely breach the widening gap between William and Harry. Lilibet "Lili" Diana Mountbatten-Windsor was born at Santa Barbara Cottage Hospital on the morning of June 4, 2021, weighing seven pounds, eleven ounces. In their official statement, the proud parents explained that their daughter's name was a nod to both the Queen, whose childhood nickname was "Lilibet," and to the late Princess of Wales. Although the Cambridges had done something similar in naming their daughter Charlotte Elizabeth Diana, Harry and Meghan were criticized for not getting the Queen's permission to name the baby Lilibet—a claim that the Sussexes were quick to refute. After the baby's birth, the Queen was the first person Harry called with the news. It was at that point, before the new arrival's name was announced, that the Sussexes broached the notion of naming her Lilibet—and found the Queen to be on board with the idea. To drive home the point, Harry and Meghan had their law firm, Schillings, write a letter to several British publishers and broadcasters saying an early BBC report that the Queen was not asked for permission to use the name Lilibet was false and defamatory and should not be repeated.

"We are all delighted by the happy news of the arrival of baby Lili," the Cambridges wrote on their official Instagram account, along with a photo of the couple holding their two-year-old son. "Congratulations to Harry, Meghan and Archie." Aside from the pro forma announcement, nothing more was said until a week later—and only then in response to a reporter's question. While touring a primary school in West Cornwall with visiting US First Lady Jill Biden, Kate was asked if she had any wishes for Lilibet. "I wish her all the very best," Kate replied. "I can't wait to meet her, because we haven't yet met her. So, hopefully, that will be soon." But apparently it wasn't. Despite her efforts—over the next several weeks, Kate sent notes and gifts to Meghan in an effort to repair their relationship—it did not appear that Lilibet's birth alone was enough to bring the brothers and their wives back together.

THE BROTHERS WERE ABLE to agree on one thing: that the underhanded tactics used by the BBC to secure its historic 1995 *Panorama* interview with their mother had set in motion a series of events that were unspooling to this day. When the official report was released on May 20, 2021, and the BBC offered a "full and unconditional apology"

to the princes, a visibly incensed William stepped before the cameras to lambast the network anyway. "It brings indescribable sadness to know," he said, that the interview with Diana "contributed significantly to her fear, paranoia, and isolation that I remember from those final years." He went on to argue that the interview "established a false narrative" and "should never be aired again."

"Our mother lost her life because of this," Harry added in his own searing statement, "and nothing has changed. By protecting her legacy, we protect everyone, and uphold the dignity with which she lived her life." Given the emotion of the moment and their understandable resentment of the press, both brothers overlooked the fact that no one was disputing the content of the interview itself, in which the globally adored Princess of Wales bravely laid bare the sad truths about her complicated, tormented life in mesmerizing detail—the first serving royal ever to do so. On that score, Harry tugged hearts when he pleaded, "Let's remember who she was and what she stood for."

DESPITE HARRY'S ACT OF rebellion and William's steadfast allegiance to The Firm, there was one more chance on the horizon for reconciliation: the dedication of a statue of their mother in the Sunken Garden at Kensington Palace on July 1, 2021, what would have been Diana's sixtieth birthday. Her sons had been working together on getting the statue done for four years, and Harry had a two-word response when asked if he would skip the unveiling: "No way."

Yet, when the moment came, it became quickly and painfully evident that nothing had changed. The brothers chatted amiably enough as they entered the Sunken Garden together, and greeted the thirteen guests in attendance. Diana's sisters, Lady Sarah McCorquodale and

Lady Jane Fellowes, were there, along with Earl Spencer. But neither Charles nor the Queen chose to attend, and the complete absence of anyone from the royal family other than William and Harry was jarring. Kate also chose not to be there out of deference to Meghan, who, less than a month after giving birth, understandably remained in California. It seemed particularly sad that none of the Cambridge children were there with their father and Uncle Harry; William and Kate had made a point of frequently talking to George, Charlotte, and Louis about their Grandma Diana, and the children were even encouraged to write loving letters to her as a way to keep her memory alive.

Even during the unveiling itself, William and Harry kept their distance from each other. Gingerly pulling two cords, the brothers watched as the green tarpaulin dropped to reveal a bronze statue of Diana surrounded by three children who, according to a Kensington Palace press release, "represent the universality and generational impact of the Princess' work."

"Every day," the brothers said in a joint statement, "we wish she were still with us." Then, having chosen to forgo this singular opportunity for a cathartic public reconciliation, William and Harry went to their separate corners—from all accounts, still barely on speaking terms.

It was impossible to imagine a more poignant and fitting moment for the Heir and Spare to come together than at the unveiling of her statue. Diana had nearly toppled the monarchy once, but what she wanted most in her life was for her sons—princes she had molded from an early age into down-to-earth, charismatic, caring human beings—to ultimately save the hidebound institution from itself. Only time would tell if William, who has always needed Harry as much as Harry needed him, would join with his maverick brother in making Diana's dream a reality.

For his part, Harry was not making the prospect of reconciliation any easier. Not long after Meghan released *The Bench*, a children's book about the bond between fathers and sons featuring touching illustrations of Harry and Archie, the rebel prince announced that he would be publishing an "accurate and wholly truthful" memoir of his own in late 2022. "I'm writing this not as the prince I was born," Harry said in a press release, "but as the man I have become." He promised that proceeds from his reported $20 million book deal with Penguin Random House would go to charity, but the fact remained that he had been working on the book for more than a year and waited until the very last minute to spring it on his unsuspecting relatives. Understandably, there was once again panic in the Palace as royal family members and courtiers alike braced themselves for a probable new onslaught of headline-making revelations. This time the Sussexes had truly crossed the Rubicon. There would be no turning back.

Whatever the future held, there was one promise to the brothers that, in the end, the People's Princess couldn't keep. "William and Harry will be properly prepared," Diana had once naively said. "I am making sure of this. I don't want them suffering the way I did."

ACKNOWLEDGMENTS

Y OU CAN'T MAKE this stuff up, as the saying goes. And luckily, with Britain's royal family you don't have to.

When *Diana's Boys* was first published in 2001, it made headlines around the world. Readers were shocked to learn—among other things—how the boys had been used as pawns in their parents' tempestuous marriage, how they struggled to cope in the immediate aftermath of their mother's death, of Buckingham Palace's efforts to cut the Princess of Wales's family and friends out of the young princes' lives, and of Charles's campaign to win his sons' acceptance of Camilla as their stepmother.

There were always hints of trouble on the monarchy's horizon, but not for the brothers themselves; theirs seemed to be an unbreakable bond, a union of hearts and minds forged by the simple fact that no one else on the planet had experienced exactly what they experienced. No one could have anticipated the twists and turns of fate that led Harry to exit his life as a full-time royal, precipitating the monarchy's most serious crisis since Diana perished in a Paris tunnel nearly a quarter century earlier.

From the perspective of someone who has covered the royal family for nearly fifty years—first as a staff writer for *Time*, then as the senior editor responsible for *People* magazine's royals coverage in the 1970s and 1980s and later as the author of six *New York Times* bestselling books on the Windsors—it seemed that the modern history of The Firm could be divided into two parts: B.D. (Before Diana) and A.D. (After Diana). Then came Meghan.

Notwithstanding the fact that William's commoner bride, Kate Middleton, was the daughter of a former flight attendant and the descendant of coal miners, Harry's marriage to a divorced, biracial American actress turned out to be the proverbial game-changer—and not simply because their children, Archie Harrison Mountbatten-Windsor and Lilibet Diana Mountbatten-Windsor, were the first nonwhite members of Britain's royal family. Suicidal depression, bullying, and yes, racism, would be just a few of the issues raised as the Sussexes maneuvered to free themselves from what they saw as shackles of servitude to the Crown.

It's not as if there weren't other things going on in the world. In the wake of one of the most hard-fought presidential campaigns in U.S. history, insurrectionists staged a bloody attack on the Capitol. A global pandemic shut down countries and killed an estimated 3.8 million people over the course of just eighteen months. Yet the public was still riveted by the drama unfolding behind palace walls—the captivating saga of a wayward prince and his unhappy wife gone rogue, the private sorrow of a Queen who must bid farewell to both a husband of seventy-three years and a beloved grandson, the sting of betrayal felt by two future kings—in the end, a glittering fairy tale gone terribly wrong.

It is such a privilege to be working with the great team at Gallery. My editor, Gallery's editorial director, Aimée Bell, is not only the consummate pro and a great pleasure to work with, but also someone who is as spellbound by the House of Windsor as I am. My thanks as well to Jennifer Bergstrom, Jennifer Long, Jennifer Robinson, Sally Marvin, Max Meltzer, Lisa Rivlin, Lisa Litwack, Davina Mock-Maniscalco, Caroline Pallotta, Natasha Simons, Felice Javit, Paul O'Halloran, and Molly Gregory.

Brothers and Wives marks my thirty-sixth book and thirty-ninth year with Ellen Levine—peerless literary agent, steadfast champion of authors, and dear friend. Ellen has always managed to make each of her many clients feel as if he or she is her *only* client—a remarkable feat, considering just how demanding we writers can be. My thanks to Ellen's exceptionally gifted team at Trident Media Group, including Martha Wydysh, Nicole Robson, Alexa Stark, and Nora Rawn.

Many years ago, I had the privilege of interviewing Henry Fonda at his town house on Manhattan's Upper East Side. When he couldn't find his wallet, Fonda sighed, "Good Lord, I need a guardian," in that trademark man-of-the-people, *Grapes of Wrath* cadence of his. I knew perfectly well what he meant. For the past half century, my wife, Valerie, has put up with my absentmindedness and worse. We met as undergraduates at UC Berkeley in 1967, and ever since—as an international and commercial banker, elected official, civic leader, wife, mother, and grandmother—she has taken on every challenge with grace, generosity, and humor. A ludicrous amount of humor, in fact. Valerie has also been indispensable as both literary advisor and all-important "first reader" not only to me but to our Washington-based daughter, Kate Andersen Brower, veteran journalist, CNN contributor, respected historian, lecturer, author of five nonfiction bestsellers—and resolutely cheerful mother of three.

Kate's younger sister, Kelly, meanwhile, is a talented artist with a master's degree in contemporary art from the University of Manchester/

Sotheby's Institute of Art in London. In pursuit of a museum career, she has worked at the Guggenheim as well as New York's Neue Galerie. She is knowledgeable on a whole range of subjects, and brings a unique perspective to the work we do as writers. It's less surprising that Kate's husband, who has to put up with constant talk of books and publishing, makes a valuable contribution to the family publishing enterprise. A highly respected senior news executive at CNN in Washington, Brooke is very much in the thick of it practically round the clock—and yet is the kind of hands-on doting dad that grandparents can only dream about. As lucky as we are to have Brooke in our family, he would not want us to forget our four-legged family member, Chance the Wonder Wheaten.

I have mentioned my parents in every single book I've written, and I'm not about to stop now. My father, Commander Edward F. Andersen, was a decorated career navy pilot who flew dive bombers off of aircraft carriers during World War II and was shot down in Manilla Bay. Undaunted, he went on to serve in Korea and Vietnam. My mother, Jeanette, was Dad's "strength and stay," as the Queen once said of Prince Philip. Like the Queen, my mother was a proud navy wife, but she was more—innately curious, witty, well read, and someone who would have loved to have had her own career in the writing game.

Additional thanks to Alan Hamilton, Lady Margaret Rhodes, the 2nd Countess Mountbatten, Lord Mishcon, Lady Elsa Bowker, Richard Kay, Peter Archer, Lady Yolanda Joseph, Jules Knight, Vivienne Parry, Winston Spencer-Churchill, Mimi Massy-Birch, James Whitaker, the Countess of Romanones, Raine Spencer, Norman Parkinson, Guy Pelly, Alexandra ("Tiggy") Legge-Bourke Pettifer, Beatrice Humbert, Penny Walker, Mark Shand, Janet Jenkins, Janet Lizop, Hamish

Barne, James Whitaker, Lord Bathurst, Lucia Flecha de Lima, Max Clifford, Mary Skone Roberts, Jo Aldridge, Harold Brooks-Baker, the Earl of Powis, Elizabeth d'Erlanger, Muriel Hartwick, Mary Roberts, Claude Garrick, Jeanne Lecorcher, Miriam Lefort, Lord Carnarvon, Dr. Frederic Maillez, Richard Greene, Emma Sayle, Gered Mankowitz, Aileen Mehle, Andy Radford, Lord Glenconner, Amber Weitz, Michael Cantlebury, Tim Graham, Tom Freeman, Adrian Munsey, Jeanette Peterson, Patrick Demarchelier, Penny Russell-Smith, Lynn Redgrave, Thierry Meresse, Ezra Zilkha, Wendy Leigh, Simone Dibley, Sharman Douglas, Charles Furneaux, Paula Dranov, Tasha Hannah, Hilary Hard, Barry Schenck, Matthew Lutts, Geoffrey Bignelli, Joan Rivers, Peter Allen, Delissa Needham, Hugh Massy-Birch, Jules de Rosee, Lady Elizabeth Longman, Rhoda Prelic, Rosemary McClure, Susan Crimp, Laura Watts, Katrina Kochneva, Tom Corby, Rachel Whitburn, Jessica Hogan, Elizabeth Whiddett, Tom Sykes, Mark Butt, Dudley Freeman, Fred Hauptfuhrer, Tom Wolfe, Yvette Reyes, Mark Halpern, Gary Gunderson, Hazel Southam, Elizabeth Loth, Pierre Suu, Simone Dibley, Bill Diehl, Betty Kelly Sargent, Everett Raymond Kinstler, Kyle Cowser, David McGough, Jesse Birnbaum, Tiffany Miller, Cranston Jones, Marcel Turgot, Julie Cammer, Mary Beth Whelan, Scott Burkhead, Michelle Lapautre, Jasen Cook, Mick Magsino, Mark Bluey, Ian McKay, John Goodman, Michael Mandel, Tucker DiEdwardo, Philip Bashe, Samantha Hoback, Ludgrove School, Eton College, Marlborough College, the Royal Military Academy Sandhurst, the University of St. Andrews, the Press Association, Channel Four Television Ltd., the BBC, ITV, Sky News, Buckingham Palace, St. James's Palace, Kensington Palace, the *Guardian*, *Times* of London, *Daily Mail*, *Daily Telegraph*, *Sunday Times*, *Mail on Sunday*, *Financial Times*, the *Sun*, *Daily Express*, *New York Times*, *Wall Street Journal*, *Washington Post*, *London*

Evening Standard, *Vanity Fair*, the Bodleian Library Oxford, the New York Public Library, Northwestern University, the Athenaeum, the Lansdowne Club, the Reform Club, the East India Club, the Lotos Club, the Associated Press, Bloomberg News, CNN, MSNBC, Reuters, Getty Images, Shutterstock, Zuma Press, and Alpha Press.

SOURCES AND CHAPTER NOTES

THE FOLLOWING CHAPTER notes have been compiled to give an overview of the sources drawn upon in the writing of *Brothers and Wives*. Certain key sources at Buckingham Palace, St. James's Palace, Clarence House, and Kensington Palace, as well as at the University of St. Andrews, Sandhurst, Scotland Yard, and Britain's Ministry of Defense—professional colleagues, former classmates, close friends, and relatives among them—agreed to cooperate only if they were allowed to remain anonymous. These are, in many cases, the same unimpeachable inside sources I have relied on over the decades to provide highly detailed and accurate information on the inner workings of the Firm. The author has respected their wishes and therefore has not listed them here or elsewhere in the text. It is worth pointing out that with comparatively few exceptions, everything in *Brothers and Wives* is on the record.

Millions of words have been written about William and Harry since their mother's tragic death in 1997, and millions more undoubtedly will be. Among those British publications that at times seem to have chronicled the princes' every waking moment are British newspapers such as the *Times*, the *Daily Mail* and the *Mail on Sunday*, the *Guardian* (UK edition), the *Daily Telegraph*, and the *Daily Express*, while in the United States, the *New York Times*, the *Washington Post*, the *Wall Street Journal*, *Newsweek*, *Time*, *People*, the *Boston Globe*, the *Los Angeles Times*, the *Chicago Tribune*, the *Detroit News*, the New York *Daily News*, and *Vanity Fair*—not to mention the wire services such as AP, Bloomberg, and Reuters—cover Britain's royal family as avidly as if it were their own. Add to this the flood of TV network, internet, and social media royals coverage, and it becomes impossible to imagine that the Cambridges and the Sussexes—not to mention the Queen and Prince Charles—have any secrets left.

CHAPTERS 1 AND 2

Interviews and conversations for these chapters included Richard Kay, Lady Margaret Rhodes, Alan Hamilton, Frederick Maillez, Jules Knight, Richard Greene, Lord Mishcon, Alexandra ("Tiggy") Legge-Bourke Pettifer, the 2nd Countess Mountbatten, Beatrice Humbert, Lady Emma Bowker, Janet Lizop, Guy Pelly, Josy Duclos, Peter Archer, Jeanne Lecorcher, Judy Wade, Claude Garreck, Lady Yolanda Joseph, Andy Radford, Cecile Zilkha, Oonagh Toffolo, Mimi Massy-Birch, Lynn Redgrave, Remi Gaston-Dreyfus, Miriam Lefort, Alex Shirley-Smith, and Penny Walker.

Published sources included Omid Scobie and Carolyn Durand, *Finding Freedom: Harry and Meghan and the Making of a Modern Royal Family* (New York: William Morrow, 2020); Sarah Bradford, *Elizabeth* (New York: Riverhead Books, 1996); Simone Simmons, *Diana: The Last Word* (New York: St. Martin's Press, 2005); Wendy Berry, *The Housekeeper's Diary* (New York: Barricade Books, 1995); Danny Danziger, *Eton Voices* (London: Viking, 1989); Max Clifford and Angela Levin, *Max Clifford: Read All About It* (London, Virgin, 2005); Nicholas Davies, *William: The Inside Story of the Man Who Will Be King*

(New York: St. Martin's Press, 1998); Paul Burrell, *A Royal Duty* (New York: New American Library, 2004); Ken Wharfe, with Robert Jobson, *Diana: Closely Guarded Secret* (London: Michael O'Mara Books, 2003); Andrew Morton, *Diana: Her True Story* (New York: Simon & Schuster, 1997); Christopher Andersen, *The Day Diana Died* (New York: William Morrow, 1998); Anna Pasternak, *Princess in Love* (London: Bloomsbury, 1994); Sally Bedell Smith, *Diana in Search of Herself* (New York: Signet, 2000); James Hewitt, *Love and War* (London: John Blake, 1999); Kate Snell, *Diana: Her Last Love* (London: Granada Media, 2000); Valentine Low, "Harry and Meghan Quit Roles Amid Palace Split," *Times* of London, January 9, 2020; Rebecca English, Sam Greenhill, and Sebastian Murphy-Bates, "Royal Bombshell Special Issue: Queen's Fury as Meghan and Harry Say 'We Quit,'" *Daily Mail* (UK), January 8, 2020; Graham Russell, "'Queen's Fury': What the Papers Say About Harry and Meghan's Bombshell," *Guardian* (UK), January 8, 2020; Russell Myers, "They Didn't Even Tell the Queen," *Daily Mirror* (UK), January 8, 2020; Erin Hill, "The Queen Responds to Prince Harry and Meghan Markle's Decision to Step Back as 'Senior' Royals," *People*, January 8, 2020; Mark Landler, "'Megxit' Is the New Brexit in a Britain Split by Age and Politics," *New York Times*, January 15, 2020; Richard Kay, Jack Elsom, Danyal Hussain, and Terri-Anne William, "Inside the Megxit Summit: Harry Talked to the Queen Alone to Give Her His Side of the Story," *Daily Mail* (UK), January 13, 2020; Rebecca Cope, "Inside the Sandringham Summit," *Tatler*, January 13, 2020; Jim Ross, "Could 'Megxit' Be a Royal Fairy Tale for Canada?," *New York Times*, January 22, 2020; Martin Robinson, Richard Kay, and Rebecca English, "'Deeply Hurt' Queen Gathers Royals for Megxit Crisis Summit," *Daily Mail* (UK), January 12, 2020; Michael Barbero, "Harry and Meghan: And Why Their Saga Matters," *New York Times*,

January 23, 2020; John Sharman and Harriet Hall, "Prince Harry and Meghan Markle Quit Senior Royal Duties," *Independent* (UK), January 8, 2020; Katie Nicholl, "Why the Queen Failed to Convince Harry and Meghan to Change Their Minds," *Vanity Fair* online, last modified January 14, 2020, https://www.vanityfair.com/style/2020/01/meghan -harry-sandringham-summit-call; Laurel Wamsley, "Meghan and Prince Harry to 'Step Back' as Senior Royals," NPR online, last modified January 8, 2020, https://www.npr.org/2020/01/08/794642642/meghan -and-harry-to-step-back-as-senior-royals; Richard Kay, "Meaningless. Cliched. And 5,000 Miles Away from Queen's Wisdom," *Daily Mail* (UK), March 19, 2020; Richard Alleyne, "Royal Chef Reveals the Queen's Favorite Meals," *Telegraph* (UK), May 3, 2012; Rachel Cooke, "What the Royals Eat at Home," *Guardian* (UK), May 19, 2012; Iliana Magra, "Harry, Meghan, and Britain: When Did the Fairy Tale Go Sour?," *New York Times*, January 11, 2020; Victoria Murphy, "Meghan Markle and Prince Harry Open Up About Their Visit to Canada with Baby Archie," *Town & Country* online, last modified January 7, 2020, https://www.townandcountrymag.com/society/tradition/a30430126 /meghan-markle-prince-harry-return-to-work-2020-canada-house-visit/; Stephanie Fillion, "As Harry and Meghan Arrive, Canadians Wonder If They Should Dump the Queen," *Foreign Policy*, March 5, 2020; Elise Taylor, "It's Official: Prince Harry and Meghan Markle Are Moving to Canada," *Vogue* online, last modified January 13, 2020, https://www .vogue.com/article/prince-harry-meghan-markle-moving-to-canada; Chantal Da Silva, "Prince Harry and Meghan Won't Get Queen's 'Special Treatment' If They Try to Stay in Canada, Expert Says," *Newsweek*, January 15, 2020; Alan Hamilton, Andrew Pierce, and Philip Webster, "Royal Family Is 'Deeply Touched' by Public Support," *Times* of London, September 4, 1997; Anthony Holden, "Why Royals Must Express

Remorse," *Daily Express* (UK), September 3, 1997; Robert Hardman, "Princes' Last Minutes with Mother," *Daily Telegraph* (UK), September 3, 1997; Angela Levin, "Exclusive: Prince Harry on Chaos After Diana's Death and Why the World Needs 'the Magic' of the Royal Family," *Newsweek*, June 21, 2017; "William Injured by Golf Club," Associated Press, June 4, 1991; "Earl Spencer 'Lied to' over Princes Following Diana's Coffin," BBC News, July 26, 2017; "Diana, Princess of Wales, 1961–1997," *The Week*, September 6, 1997; HRH the Princess of Wales, interview by Martin Bashir, BBC One, November 20, 1995; Mark Landler, "25 Years Later, BBC Apologizes for Diana Interview," *New York Times*, May 20, 2021; "Balmoral: Why the Royals Love Spending Time There," *Hello!*, September 7, 2016; John Simpson, "Goodbye England's Rose: A Nation Says Farewell," *Sunday Telegraph* (UK), September 7, 1997; "The Nation Unites Against Tradition," *Observer* (UK), September 7, 1997; Tess Rock and Natalie Symonds, "Our Diana Diaries," *Sunday Mirror* (UK), November 16, 1997; "Driver Was Drunk," *Le Monde* (Paris), September 3, 1997; Robert Jobson and Greg Swift, "Look After William and Harry," *Daily Express* (UK), December 22, 1997; Jo Thomas, "The Early Education of a Future King," *New York Times*, April 13, 1986; Marianne Macdonald, "A Rift Death Can't Heal," *Observer* (UK), September 14, 1997; David Ward, "Prince's Pride in His Sons," *Guardian* (UK), September 20, 1997; Sue Ryan, "Here's Harry!," *Mail on Sunday* (UK), October 14, 1984; William E. Schmidt, "Charles and Diana Are Separating 'Amicably,'" *New York Times,* December 9, 1992; Matilda Battersby, "A Day That Shook the World: Windsor Castle Fire," *Independent* (UK), November 18, 2010; "The Princes' Final Farewell," *Sunday Times* of London, September 7, 1997; Howard Chua-Eoan, Steve Wulf, Jeffrey Kluger, Christopher Redman, and David Van Biema, "A Death in Paris: The Passing of

Diana," *Time*, September 13, 1997; "Charles Escorts Diana Back to a Grieving Britain," *New York Times*, September 1, 1997; Dominick Dunne, "Diana's Secrets," *Vanity Fair*, January 2003; Jerome Dupuis, "Diana: The Unpublished Report of Witnesses at the Ritz," *L'Express*, March 12, 1998; Rosa Monckton, "Time to End False Rumors," *Newsweek*, March 2, 1998; *Diana, 7 Days*, television documentary special, BBC One, August 27, 2017; Queen Elizabeth II, "Speech by the Queen on the Fortieth Anniversary of Her Succession" (Annus Horribilis Speech, November 24, 1992), The Royal Family, accessed December 2, 2020, https://www.royal.uk/annus-horribilis-speech.

CHAPTERS 3 AND 4

For these chapters, the author drew in part on past conversations with Peter Archer, Lady Emma Bowker, Thierry Meresse, Janet Jenkins, Alan Hamilton, Emma Sayle, Lord Mishcon, Patricia Knatchbull, Lady Elsa Bowker, Hamish Barne, the Duchess of Alba, Hugh Massy-Birch, Alice Tomlinson, Prince Rupert Loewenstein, Charles Furneaux, Jules Knight, James Whitaker, Lady Yolanda Joseph, Tom Sykes, Fred Hauptfuhrer, Delissa Needham, Pat Charman, Pierre Suu, Earl McGrath, Sioned Compton, Richard Greene, Guy Pelly, Geoffrey Bignell, Penny Walker, Natalie Symonds, Mark Butt, Barry Schenck, Tess Rock, Jules de Rosee, Richard Kay, Farris Rookstool, Wendy Leigh, Colin St. John Wilson, Evelyn Phillips, Susan Crimp, Kitty Carlisle Hart, Elizabeth Widdett, Janet Allison, and Mary Robertson.

Published sources included Caroline Graham, *Camilla and Charles: The Love Story* (London: Blake, 2005); Robert Jobson, *Harry's War: The True Story of the Soldier Prince* (London: John Blake, 2008) and *The New Royal Family: Prince George, William and Kate, The Next Generation* (London: John Blake, 2013); Katie Nicholl, *William and Harry:*

Behind the Palace Walls (New York: Weinstein Books, 2010); Christopher Andersen, *William and Kate and Baby George: Royal Baby Edition* (New York: Gallery Books, 2013); Andrew Pierce, " 'I'm Sorry for Wearing Nazi Swastika,' Says Prince Harry," *Times* of London, January 13, 2005; Neil Tweedie and Michael Kallenbach, "Prince Harry Faces Outcry at Nazi Outfit," *Daily Telegraph* (UK), January 14, 2005; Jamie Turner, "Harry's Choice of Costume Was Lazy," *Times* of London, January 15, 2005; Christopher Morgan and David Leppard, "Party Girl in William's Circle Snorted Cocaine," *Sunday Times* of London, February 26, 2000; David Leppard and Christopher Morgan, "Police Fears over William's Friends," *Sunday Times* of London, February 27, 2000; Andrew Pierce and Simon de Bruxelles, "Our Mother Was Betrayed," *Times* of London, September 30, 2000; Richard Kay, "William Stalked by His Uncle's TV Crew," *Daily Mail* (UK), September 27, 2001; Ben Summerskill, "The Trouble with Harry," *Observer* (UK), January 13, 2002; J. F. O. McAllister, "Once Upon a Time, There Was a Pot-Smoking Prince," *Time*, January 28, 2002; Christopher Andersen, "The Divided Prince," *Vanity Fair*, September 2003; Antony Barnett, "Prince Taken to Drink and Drugs Rehab Clinic," *Observer* (UK), January 13, 2002; Ellen Tumosky and Corky Siemaszko, "Look to Put the Lid on Pot Prince," New York *Daily News*, January 15, 2002; Warren Hoge, "Charles's Response to Use of Drugs by Son Is Praised," *New York Times*, January 14, 2002; Richard Price, "Hewitt Wanted 10 Million Pounds for Letters from Diana," *Daily Mail* (UK), December 16, 2002; Burhan Wazir and Shekhar Bhatia, "Royals Covered Up 'Rape,' Says Victim," *Guardian* (UK), November 9, 2002; Paul Henderson, "I Was Raped by Charles' Manservant," *Mail on Sunday* (UK), November 10, 2002; Warren Hoge, "Royal Palace Roiled Again in New Round of Revelations," *New York Times*, November 11, 2002; Tom Rawstorne,

"William in His Own Words," *Daily Mail* (UK), May 30, 2003; Robert Hardman, "Just (Call Me) William," *Daily Telegraph* (UK), June 9, 2000; Richard Kay and Mike Pflanz, "Prince Harry, a Stunning Heiress, and the Hewitt Connection," *Daily Mail* (UK), February 12, 2004; Jacqueline Malley, "$75,000 Damages for Teacher Who Accused Prince Harry of Cheating," *Guardian* (UK), February 14, 2006; Brian Dakks, "Ex-Guard Speaks Out About Di Tapes," CBS News online, last modified November 30, 2004, https://www.cbsnews.com/news/ex-guard-speaks-out-about-di-tapes/; Roxanne Roberts, "Fairy Tale for Grown-Ups: Charles and Camilla Once upon a Time," *Washington Post*, February 11, 2005; Thomas Fields-Meyer and Pam Lambert, "Royal Stepmum," *People*, February 28, 2005; Patrick Jephson, "Everybody Loves a Royal Wedding . . . Usually," *Sunday Telegraph* (UK), March 27, 2005; Hamish Bowles, "At Long Last Love," *Vogue*, April 2005; Barbara Kantrowitz, "Legal: At Last," *Newsweek*, April 18, 2005; Andrew Alderson, "Husband and Wife—At Last," *Sunday Telegraph* (UK), April 10, 2005; Simon Freeman, "The Royal Wedding Day, Minute by Minute," *Times* of London, April 9, 2005; Nicola Methven, "Hyno-Di-Sed: Hewitt Put in Trance," *Mirror* (UK), September 19, 2005; Michelle Green, "Is She the One?," *People*, October 17, 2005; Robert Stansfield, "Harry the Hangover," *Mirror* (UK), June 16, 2006; Andra Varin, "Party Time Is Over for Playboy Prince Harry," ABC News online, last modified January 6, 2006, https://abcnews.go.com /International/story?id=732952&page=1; "Queen at Harry's Army Graduation," CNN.com, last modified April 12, 2006, http://www .cnn.com/2006/WORLD/europe/04/12/uk.harry/index.html; Nicholas Witchell, "William Graduates from Sandhurst," BBC News online, last modified December 15, 2006, https://www.bbc.com/news/av/uk-125 05885; Alex Tresniowski and Ashley Williams, "Will and Kate: The

Perfect Match," *People*, December 11, 2006; "The Battle to Protect Kate," *Evening Standard* (UK), January 9, 2007; Kira Cochrane, "In Diana's Footsteps," *Guardian* (UK), January 9, 2007; Oliver Marre, "Girl, Interrupted," *Observer* (UK), March 18, 2007; Duncan Larcombe, "Wills & Kate Split," *Sun* (UK), April 14, 2007; David Smith, "Royal Relationships: The Breakup," *Guardian* (UK), April 1, 2007; Rajeev Syal, "Tony Blair: 'Let Them Be, They Are Young,'" *Times* of London, April 16, 2007; Zoe Griffin and Grant Hodgson, "Wills & Kate 2002–2007: The Fairytale's Over," *Sunday Mirror* (UK), April 15, 2007; Victoria White and Stephen White, "Life After William," *Mirror* (UK), April 21, 2007; Karen Rockett, "It's Back On," *Sunday Mirror* (UK), June 24, 2007; Sarah Knapton, "Prince Denounces 'Aggressive' Paparazzi Pursuit," *Guardian* (UK), October 6, 2007; Andrew Alderson, "Prince Eyes Legal Action," *Sunday Telegraph* (UK), October 7, 2007; Andrew Pierce, "Prince's Lawyers Warn Paparazzi Off Stalking Middleton," *Daily Telegraph* (UK), February 23, 2008; Aislinn Simpson, "William Flies into a Storm," *Daily Telegraph* (UK), April 21, 2008; Rebecca English, "William Lands His Air Force Helicopter in Kate's Garden," *Daily Mail* (UK), April 21, 2008; "William and RAF Sorry for Prince's *Five* Chinook Joyrides," BBC News, April 23, 2008; Lucy Cockcroft, "Prince William's Chinook Flight to Stag Party Costs 8,716 Pounds," *Daily Telegraph* (UK), June 30, 2008; Richard Kay, Geoffrey Levy, and Katie Glass, "Wild Side of Kate's Family," *Daily Mail* (UK), August 9, 2008; Paul Majendie, "Prince Harry Back from Afghan Frontline," Reuters, March 1, 2008; Sarah Lyall, "Prince Harry Withdrawn from Afghanistan," *New York Times*, February 29, 2008; "Prince Harry Wins Wings and Is on Course for Afghanistan," *Evening Standard* (UK), May 7, 2010; Simon Perry, "Chelsy Davy Steps Out to Support Prince Harry," *People*, May 7, 2010; Amelia Hill, "Politicians

Condemn Prince Harry over 'Racist' Remark," *Guardian* (UK), January 11, 2009; Peter Hunt, "Prince's Apology for Racist Term," BBC News online, last modified January 11, 2009, http://news.bbc.co.uk/2 /hi/uk_news/7822574.stm; Vicky Ward, "Will's Cup of Tea," *Vanity Fair*, November 2008; Geoffrey Levy and Richard Kay, "How Many More Skeletons in Kate's Closet?," *Daily Mail* (UK), July 22, 2009; David Stringer, "Prince William Makes First Royal Rescue for RAF," Associated Press, October 5, 2010; Lee Ferran, "Prince William Proposes to Kate Middleton with Princess Diana's Engagement Ring," ABC News, November 14, 2010; Chloe Foussianes, "Prince William Talks About Proposing to Kate Middleton in a Speech at a Buckingham Palace Reception," *Town & Country*, January 21, 2020; Anthony Faiola, "William and Kate's Royal Wedding: Britain's Monarchy's New Era Sealed with a Kiss," *Washington Post*, April 29, 2011; Sarah Lyall, "A Traditional Royal Wedding, but for the 3 Billion Witnesses," *New York Times*, April 29, 2011; Katie Nicholl, "Harry Pays Tribute to William 'The Dude' . . . in Best Man Speech," *Daily Mail* (UK), April 29, 2011; Kayleigh Roberts, "Prince Harry Made Kate Middleton Cry During Her Royal Wedding in 2011," *Marie Claire* online, last modified March 3, 2019, https://www.marieclaire.com/celebrity/a26607559 /prince-harry-made-kate-middleton-cry-royal-wedding-2011/; Prince Harry: Naked Photos During Vegas Rager Leaked," TMZ, last modified August 22, 2012, https://www.tmz.com/2012/08/21/prince-harry -naked-photos-nude-vegas-hotel-party/; *Us Weekly* Staff, "Prince Harry Naked Photos Emerge After He Parties in Las Vegas," *Us* online, last modified August 22, 2012, https://www.usmagazine.com/celebrity -news/news/prince-harry-naked-photos-emerge-after-he-parties-in -las-vegas-2012218/; Rebecca English, "Palace Fury at Harry Naked Photos," *Daily Mail* (UK), August 22, 2012; Katie Kindelan, "Prince

Harry Returns to England, with His Clothes On," *Yahoo! News*, last modified August 23, 2012, https://abcnews.go.com/blogs/entertainment/2012/08/prince-harry-returns-to-england-with-his-clothes-on; Catriona Harvey-Jenner, "Prince Harry Just Discussed Those 2012 Naked Las Vegas Photos and the 'Great Body' He Had at the Time," *Cosmopolitan* online, last modified May 14, 2021, https://www.cosmopolitan.com/uk/reports/a36427362/prince-harry-naked-las-vegas-photos/; Julia Neel, "Topless Photos Cause Royal Furor: French Magazine Shows Royal Couple Sunbathing," *WWD*, September 14, 2012; Nick Hopkins and Caroline Davies, "Prince Harry: I've Killed in Afghanistan but Dad Wants Me to Act Like a Prince," *Guardian* (UK), January 21, 2013; "Royal Baby: Kate and William Visited by Prince Charles," BBC News online, last modified July 23, 2013, https://www.bbc.com/news/uk-23421388; Sylvia Hui and Jill Lawless, "Prince Charming: Kate Gives Birth to Boy, Home by Suppertime," Associated Press, April 23, 2018; Valentine Low, "Duke and Duchess of Cambridge Formally Register Birth of Prince George," *Times* of London, August 3, 2013; Lesley Messer, "Prince Harry on Being an Uncle: I'll 'Make Sure He Has Fun,'" ABC News, July 25, 2013; Maria Puente, "Prince Harry Launches 'Invictus Games' for Wounded Vets," *USA Today*, March 6, 2014; "Prince George Makes Friends on Royal Tour of New Zealand," Reuters, April 9, 2014; Nicholas Witchell, "Royal Tour: Prince George Steals the Show as Support for Monarchy Rises," BBC News online, last modified April 25, 2014, https://www.bbc.com/news/uk-27139389; Queen Elizabeth II, "A Speech by the Queen at the Opening of a Memorial Fountain to the Late Diana, Princess of Wales" (July 6, 2004), The Royal Family, accessed January 12, 2020, https://www.royal.uk/opening-memorial-fountain-late-diana-princess-wales-6-july-2004; "The Christening of Prince George of Cambridge"

(September 27, 2013), The Royal Family, accessed November 4, 2020, https://www.royal.uk/christening-prince-george-cambridge; live coverage by the BBC, CNN, Fox News (on which the author offered live commentary), and MSNBC on the wedding of Prince Charles and Camilla Parker Bowles; *The Operation Paget Inquiry Report into the Allegation of Conspiracy to Murder Diana, Princess of Wales, and Emad El-Din Mohamed Abdel Moneim Fayed* (London: Great Britain Metropolitan Police Service, December 14, 2006), http://downloads.bbc.co.uk/news /nol/shared/bsp/hi/pdfs/14_12_06_diana_report.pdf.

CHAPTERS 5 AND 6

Information and background for these chapters was based in part on conversations with Alan Hamilton, Lady Margaret Rhodes, Countess Mountbatten, Richard Kay, Lord Bathurst, Oonagh Toffolo, Lady Yolanda Joseph, James Whitaker, Tom Sykes, Cecile Thibaud, Mark Shand, Liz Smith, Jules Knight, Ezra Zilkha, Robin Leach, Wendy Leigh, Harold Brooks-Baker, Elizabeth d'Erlanger, Alex Kidson, Aileen Mehle, Muriel Hartwick, Philip Higgs, Joan Rivers, Penny Russell-Smith, Gered Mankowitz, the Countess of Romanones, Peter Allen, Janet Allison, Norman Parkinson, Lucia Flecha de Lima, John Marion, and David McGough.

Published sources included Robert Lacey, *Battle of Brothers: William and Harry—The Inside Story of a Family in Tumult* (New York: Harper-Collins, 2020); Halima Sadat, *Harry & Meghan: The Royal Wedding Album* (New York: Sterling, 2018); Simon Perry, "A Perfect Princess! Kate and William Announce the Arrival of Their Baby Girl," *People*, May 2, 2015; Cecilia Rodriguez, "Kate Middleton Gives Birth to a Baby Girl, the New Royal Princess," *Forbes*, May 2, 2015; Melissa Chan, "The Invictus Games: Prince Harry and Michelle Obama Discuss Queen Elizabeth's Trash Talk," *Time*, May 9, 2016; Josh Duboff, "Princess Charlotte Makes Her Palace Balcony Debut at the Queen's Birthday Parade," *Vanity Fair*, June 11, 2016; Danny Boyle, "Who Is Meghan Markle? Everything We Know About Prince Harry's Girlfriend," *Daily Telegraph* (UK), November 12, 2016; Tom Sykes, "Why Prince William and Kate Middleton Have a Work Problem," Daily Beast, last modified April 11, 2017, https://www.thedailybeast.com/why-prince-william-and-kate-middleton-have-a-work-problem; Emmeline Saunders, "Prince Harry Admits Wanting to Punch Someone in the Wake of Mum Princess Diana's Death," *Mirror* (UK), April 17, 2017; "Duchess Gives Birth to Baby Boy," BBC News, April 23, 2018; "Royal Baby: Duke and Duchess of Cambridge Name Their Baby Son Louis," Press Association, April 27, 2018; Maria Puente, "How Does Duchess Kate Do It? From Giving Birth to Camera-Ready in Heels in Under 8 Hours," *USA Today*, April 23, 2018; Megan Fisher, "When Prince Harry Met Meghan Markle: A Royal Romance," BBC News, November 27, 2017; Tara John, "Meet Meghan Markle, Prince Harry's Fiancée and Britain's Newest Royal-to-Be," *Time*, November 27, 2017; "Prince Harry 'Thrilled' to Marry Girlfriend Meghan Markle Next Year," BBC News, November 27, 2017; Robert Booth, "Meghan Markle Could Shake Up Monarchy, Says Noam Chomsky," *Guardian* (UK), December 1, 2017; "Meghan Markle and Prince Harry: A Timeline of How Their Lives Collided," *Sunday Times* of London, May 20, 2018; Caroline Davies, "The Royal In-Laws: Meghan Markle's Family," *Guardian* (UK), July 10, 2018; Elise Taylor, "How Prince Harry Met Meghan Markle," *Vogue*, May 19, 2020; Richard Palmer, "Meghan's Dad Not Going to Wedding," *Daily Express* (UK), May 15, 2018; Jennifer Earl, "Meghan Markle's Family Drama Pre-Royal Wedding, from Staged Paparazzi Pics to Prince Harry's Shocking Letter," Fox News,

May 20, 2018; Marina Pitofsky, "Meghan Says Tabloid Reports She Made Kate Cry Were False and the 'Reverse Happened,'" *Hill*, March 7, 2021; Kate Storey, "Prince William Got 'Revenge' on Prince Harry with a 'Naughty' Best Man Speech," *Town & Country*, May 20, 2018; Carly Ledbetter, "Thomas Markle Attacks Meghan Markle, Royal Family in Brutal Interview," *Harper's Bazaar*, July 30, 2018; Amy Mackelden, "Why Meghan Markle's First Solo Royal Event with the Queen Is So Significant," *Harper's Bazaar*, June 14, 2018; "Prince William Speaks About 'Traumatic' Air Ambulance Callouts," BBC News, November 2018; Hannah Furness, Phoebe Southworth, and Samantha Herbert, "Royal Baby: Prince Harry Says Birth of Son Is 'the Most Amazing Experience' as World Waits for First Sighting," *Telegraph* (UK), May 6, 2019; Sharnaz Shahid, "Fab Four Reunited! Prince William, Kate, Harry and Meghan, Join Forces Once More," *Hello!*, October 7, 2019; Kathy Campbell, "Prince Harry Confirms Rift with Brother Prince William: 'We're Certainly on Different Paths,'" *Us*, October 20, 2019; Meadhbh McGrath, "Royal Rift: Why Are William and Harry on 'Different Paths'?," *Independent* (UK), October 27, 2019; Kate Whitfield, "Royal Rift: William and Harry Are on Different Paths 'For One Very Good Reason,'" *Daily Express* (UK), October 31, 2019; Aimee Lewis, "Prince Andrew Sparks Near-Universal Condemnation with TV Interview," CNN, November 17, 2019; "Prince Andrew's Links to Jeffrey Epstein," BBC News online, last modified November 16, 2019, https://www.bbc.com/news/uk-49411215; Camilla Tominey and Victoria Ward, "Queen Did Not Approve Prince Andrew's Excruciating Newsnight Interview," *Sunday Telegraph* (UK), November 17, 2019; Jack Royston, "Prince Andrew Should Lose Royal Titles, Face Extradition: Poll," *Newsweek*, June 26, 2020; Jeetendr Sehdev, "The Queen Bans Prince Harry and Meghan Markle from Using 'Sussex

Royal' Brand—Here's Why That's a Bad Idea," *Forbes*, February 19, 2020; Rosemary Feitelberg, "Harry and Meghan Withdraw 'Sussex Royal' Trademark Applications," *WWD*, February 21, 2020; "Harry and Meghan to End Use of 'Sussex Royal' Brand," BBC News, February 22, 2020; Ryan Parry, Ruth Styles, and Cheyenne Roundtree, "Meghan and Harry Are Living in Tyler Perry's $18 Million Hilltop Mansion," *Daily Mail* (UK), May 7, 2020; Caitlin O'Kane, "Tyler Perry Let Harry and Meghan Stay in His Home and Use His Security When the Royal Family Stripped Theirs Away," CBS News, March 8, 2021; James McClain, "Meghan Markle, Prince Harry Buy $14.7 Million Montecito Compound," *Variety*, August 12, 2020; Brooks Barnes, "Prince Harry and Meghan Sign Megawatt Netflix Deal," *New York Times*, September 2, 2020; Erin Vanderhoof, "Meghan and Harry Win a Battle in Their War Against Paparazzi," *Vanity Fair*, October 2020; "Harry and Meghan Not Returning as Working Members of Royal Family," BBC News, February 19, 2021; Mark Landler, "Harry and Meghan Going Public at a Tough Time for the Royals," *New York Times*, February 26, 2021; "Buckingham Palace to Investigate Claims Meghan Bullied Staff," BBC News, March 3, 2021; "Global Reaction to Harry and Meghan Interview Pours In," Associated Press, March 8, 2021; Caroline Linton, "Harry and Meghan Detail Royal Struggles, from Discussions of Baby's Skin Tone to Suicidal Thoughts," CBS News, March 8, 2021; Jennifer Hassan, "'What Have They Done?': Britain's Media Reacts in Horror to Meghan and Harry Interview," *Washington Post*, March 9, 2021; "Meghan and Harry Interview: Urgent Palace Talks over Claims," BBC News, March 9, 2021; Megan Specia, "In Britain, Meghan and Harry Talk Stirs Debate on Entrenched Racism," *New York Times*, March 9, 2021; Tom Sykes, "Prince William: My Family Is Not Racist, and No, I Haven't Spoken to Harry

Yet," Daily Beast, March 11, 2021; Benjamin Mueller, "Royal Rift Reveals Britain's Underbelly: 'A Very Big Silence Around Race,'" *New York Times*, March 12, 2021; Rob Picheta, "Meghan Reveals 'Concerns' Within Royal Family About Her Baby's Skin Color," CNN, March 14, 2021; Leah Asmelash, "Michelle Obama Says It 'Wasn't a Complete Surprise' to Hear Meghan Talk of Racism in the Royal Family," CNN, March 16, 2021; "Prince Philip Has Died Aged 99, Buckingham Palace Announces," BBC News, April 9, 2021; Marilyn Berger, "Prince Philip Died at 99 at His Home in Windsor Castle," *New York Times*, April 9, 2021; Anna Schaverien, "Two Tributes to Prince Philip, a.k.a. 'Grandpa'," *New York Times*, April 11, 2021; Rachel Elbaum, "All Eyes on Prince Harry, and Royal Rift, After His Return to U.K. for Prince Philip's Funeral," NBC News, April 16, 2021; Eliza Thompson, "Prince William, Prince Harry's Reunion at Philip's Funeral Was a 'Baby Step' in Healing Their Relationship," *Us Weekly*, May 7, 2021; Elizabeth Paton, "Losing Meghan, Prince Harry—and Potentially Billions of Pounds," *New York Times*, June 6, 2021; live coverage by the BBC, ABC, NBC, CBS, CNN, Fox News, MSNBC as well as extensive coverage by all other major media outlets of the wedding of Prince Harry and Meghan Markle at Windsor Castle on May 19, 2018; Meghan Markle and Prince Harry, interview by Oprah Winfrey, *Oprah with Meghan and Harry*, CBS TV news special, March 7, 2021; "William and Harry Unveil Diana Statue at Kensington Palace," Caroline Davies, *Guardian*, July 1, 2001; Mark Landler, "Unveiling of Diana Statue Reunites William and Harry, Briefly," *New York Times*, July 1, 2021.

BIBLIOGRAPHY

Allison, Ronald, and Sarah Riddell, eds. *The Royal Encyclopedia*. London: Macmillan, 1991.

Andersen, Christopher. *After Diana: William, Harry, Charles and the Royal House of Windsor*. New York: Hyperion, 2007.

———. *The Day Diana Died*. New York: William Morrow, 1998.

———. *The Day John Died*. New York: William Morrow, 2000.

———. *Diana's Boys: William and Harry and the Mother They Loved*. New York: William Morrow, 2001.

———. *Game of Crowns: Elizabeth, Camilla, Kate, and the Throne*. New York: Gallery Books, 2016.

———. *William and Kate: A Royal Love Story*. New York: Gallery Books, 2011.

———. *William and Kate and Baby George: Royal Baby Edition*. New York: Gallery Books, 2013.

———. *William and Kate: Special Wedding Edition*. New York: Gallery Books, 2011.

Anne the Princess Royal, with Ivor Herbert. *Riding Through My Life*. London: Pelham, 1991.

Arbiter, Dickie. *On Duty with the Queen: My Time as a Buckingham Palace Press Secretary*. London: Blink, 2014.

Aronson, Theo. *Royal Family: Years of Transition*. London: Thistle, 2014.

Barry, Stephen P. *Royal Service: My Twelve Years as Valet to Prince Charles*. New York: Macmillan, 1983.

Beaton, Cecil. *Beaton in the Sixties: More Unexpurgated Diaries*. London: Weidenfeld & Nicolson, 2003.

Berry, Wendy. *The Housekeeper's Diary*. New York: Barricade Books, 1995.

Blair, Tony. *A Journey: My Political Life*. New York: Alfred A. Knopf, 2010.

Boca, Geoffrey. *Elizabeth and Philip*. New York: Henry Holt, 1953.

Botham, Noel. *The Murder of Princess Diana*. New York: Pinnacle Books, 2004.

Bradford, Sarah. *Elizabeth. New York: Riverhead Books,* 1997.

———. *Diana*. New York: Viking, 2006.

Brander, Michael. *The Making of the Highlands*. London: Constable, 1980.

Bryan, J., III, and Charles J. V. Murphy. *The Windsor Story.* New York: William Morrow, 1979.

Burrell, Paul. *A Royal Duty*. New York: New American Library, 2004.

———. *The Way We Were*. New York: William Morrow, 2006.

Campbell, Lady Colin. *Diana in Private*. London: Smith Gryphon, 1993.

———. *Meghan and Harry: The Real Story*. New York: Pegasus Books, 2020.

Cannadine, David. *The Decline and Fall of the British Aristocracy*. New Haven: Yale University Press, 1990.

Cannon, John, and Ralph Griffiths. *The Oxford Illustrated History of the British Monarchy.* Oxford and New York: Oxford University Press, 1992.

Cathcart, Helen. *The Queen and Prince Philip: Forty Years of Happiness.* London: Hodder and Stoughton, 1987.

———. *The Queen Herself.* London: W. H. Allen, 1983.

Clarke, Mary. *Diana Once upon a Time.* London: Sidgwick & Jackson, 1994.

Clifford, Max, and Angela Levin. *Max Clifford: Read All About It.* London: Virgin, 2005.

Davies, Nicholas. *Diana: The Lonely Princess.* New York: Birch Lane, 1996.

———. *Queen Elizabeth II.* New York: Carol, 1996.

———. *William: The Inside Story of the Man Who Will Be King.* New York: St. Martin's Press, 1998.

Delderfield, Eric R. *Kings and Queen of England and Great Britain.* London: David & Charles, 1990.

Delorm, Rene. *Diana and Dodi: A Love Story.* Los Angeles: Tallfellow Press, 1998.

Dempster, Nigel, and Peter Evans. *Behind Palace Doors.* New York: Putnam, 1993.

Dimbleby, Jonathan. *The Prince of Wales: A Biography.* New York: William Morrow, 1994.

Dolby, Karen. *The Wicked Wit of Queen Elizabeth II.* London: Michael O'Mara Books, 2015.

Edwards, Anne. *Diana and the Rise of the House of Spencer.* London: Hodder and Stoughton, 1999.

Ferguson, Ronald. *The Galloping Major: My Life and Singular Times.* London: Macmillan, 1994.

Fisher, Graham and Heather. *Elizabeth: Queen & Mother.* New York: Hawthorn Books, 1964.

Foreman, J. B., ed. *Scotland's Splendour.* Glasgow: William Collins Sons, 1961.

Fox, Mary Virginia. *Princess Diana*. Hillside, N.J.: Enslow, 1986.

Goldsmith, Lady Annabel. *Annabel: An Unconventional Life*. London: Phoenix, 2004.

Goodall, Sarah, and Nicholas Monson. *The Palace Diaries: A Story Inspired by Twelve Years of Life Behind Palace Gates*. London: Mainstream, 2006.

Graham, Caroline. *Camilla—The King's Mistress*. London: John Blake, 1994.

———. *Camilla and Charles: The Love Story*. London: John Blake, 2005.

Graham, Tim. *Diana: HRH the Princess of Wales*. New York: Summit, 1988.

———. *The Royal Year 1993*. London: Michael O'Mara, 1993.

Gregory, Martyn. *The Diana Conspiracy Exposed*. London: Virgin, 1999.

Hardman, Robert. *Her Majesty: Queen Elizabeth II and Her Court*. New York: Pegasus Books, 2012.

Hewitt, James. *Love and War*. London: John Blake, 1999.

Hill, Duncan, Alison Guantlett, Sarah Rickayzen, and Gareth Thomas. *The Royal Family: A Year by Year Chronicle of the House of Windsor*. London: Parragon, 2012.

Hoey, Brian. *All the King's Men*. London: HarperCollins, 1992.

Holden, Anthony. *Charles*. London: Weidenfeld & Nicolson, 1988.

———. *The Tarnished Crown*. New York: Random House, 1993.

Hough, Richard. *Born Royal: The Lives and Loves of the Young Windsors*. New York: Bantam, 1988.

HRH the Prince of Wales. *Charles in His Own Words*. Edited by Rosemary York. London: W. H. Allen, 1981.

———. *Harmony: A New Way of Looking at Our World*. New York: HarperCollins, 2010.

———. *The Old Man of Lochnagar*. London: Hamish Hamilton Children's Books, 1980.

———. *A Vision of Britain: A Personal View of Architecture*. London: Doubleday, 1989.

———. *Watercolours*. London: Little, Brown, 1991.

HRH the Prince of Wales and Candida Lycett Green. *The Garden at Highgrove*. London: Weidenfeld & Nicolson, 2000.

HRH the Prince of Wales and Charles Clover. *Highgrove: Portrait of an Estate*. London: Chapmans, 1993.

Hutchins, Chris, and Peter Thompson. *Sarah's Story: The Duchess Who Defied the Royal House of Windsor*. London: Smith Gryphon, 1992.

Jephson, P. D. *Shadows of a Princess*. New York: HarperCollins, 2000.

Jobson, Robert. *Harry's War*. London: John Blake, 2008.

———. *The New Royal Family: Prince George, William and Kate, the Next Generation*. London: John Blake, 2013.

———. *William's Princess: The Love Story That Will Change the Royal Family Forever*. London: John Blake, 2006.

Joseph, Claudia. *Kate*. New York: Avon, 2009.

Junor, Penny. *Charles*. New York: St. Martin's Press, 1987.

———. *The Firm*. New York: Thomas Dunne Books, 2005.

———. *Prince William: The Man Who Will Be King*. New York: Pegasus Books, 2012.

Knatchbull, Timothy. *From a Clear Blue Sky: Surviving the Mountbatten Bomb*. London: Hutchinson, 2009.

Lacey, Robert. *Battle of Brothers: William and Harry—The Inside Story of a Family in Tumult*. New York: HarperCollins, 2020.

———. *Majesty*. New York: Harcourt Brace Jovanovich, 1977.

———. *Queen Mother*. Boston: Little, Brown, 1986.

Lathan, Caroline, and Jeannie Sakol. *The Royals*. New York: Congdon & Weed, 1987.

Lloyd, Ian. *William & Catherine's New Royal Family: Celebrating the Arrival of Princess Charlotte*. London: Carlton Books, 2015.

Lorimer, David. *Radical Prince*. Edinburgh: Floris Books, 2003.

Maclean, Veronica. *Crowned Heads*. London: Hodder & Stoughton, 1993.

Marr, Andrew. *The Real Elizabeth: An Intimate Portrait of Queen Elizabeth II*. New York: St. Martin's Press, 2012.

Martin, Ralph G. *Charles & Diana*. New York: Putnam, 1985.

Mayer, Catherine. *Born to Be King: Prince Charles on Planet Windsor*. New York: Henry Holt, 2015.

Montgomery-Massingberd, Hugh. *Burke's Guide to the British Monarchy*. London: Burke's Peerage, 1977.

Morrah, Dermot. *To Be a King: A Privileged Account of the Early Life and Education of H.R.H. the Prince of Wales, Written with the Approval of H.M. the Queen*. London: Hutchinson, 1968.

Morrow, Ann. *The Queen*. London: Granada, 1983.

Morton, Andrew. *Diana: Her True Story*. New York: Simon & Schuster, 1997.

———. *Diana: In Pursuit of Love*. London: Michael O'Mara, 2004.

———. *Inside Buckingham Palace*. London: Michael O'Mara, 1991.

———. *Meghan: A Hollywood Princess*. New York: Grand Central, 2018.

Nicholl, Katie. *Harry: Life, Loss, and Love*. New York: Hachette, 2018.

———. *William and Harry: Behind the Palace Walls*. New York: Weinstein Books, 2010.

Pasternak, Anna. *Princess in Love*. London: Bloomsbury, 1994.

Pimlott, Ben. *The Queen: A Biography of Elizabeth II*. New York: John Wiley & Sons, 1996.

Reese-Jones, Trevor, with Moira Johnston. *The Bodyguard's Story*. New York: Warner Books, 2000.

Rhodes, Margaret. *The Final Curtsey*. London: Umbria, 2011.

Sancton, Thomas, and Scott Macleod. *Death of a Princess: The Investigation*. New York: St. Martin's Press, 1998.

Sarah, the Duchess of York, with Jeff Coplon. *My Story*. New York: Simon & Schuster, 1996.

Scobie, Omid, and Carolyn Durand. *Finding Freedom: Harry and Meghan and the Making of a Modern Royal Family*. New York: William Morrow, 2020.

Seward, Ingrid. *The Queen and Di*. New York: HarperCollins, 2000.

———. *William & Harry: The People's Princes*. London: Carlton Books, 2009.

Simmons, Simone, with Susan Hill. *Diana: The Secret Years*. London: Michael O'Mara, 1998.

———. *The Last Word*. New York: St. Martin's Press, 2005.

Smith, Sally Bedell. *Diana in Search of Herself*. New York: Times Books, 1999.

———. *Elizabeth the Queen: The Life of a Modern Monarch*. New York: Random House, 2012.

———. *Prince Charles: The Passions and Paradoxes of an Improbable Life*. New York: Random House, 2017.

Snell, Kate. *Diana: Her Last Love*. London: Granada Media, 2000.

Spencer, Charles. *The Spencers: A Personal History of an English Family*. New York: St. Martin's Press, 2000.

Spoto, Donald. *The Decline and Fall of the House of Windsor*. New York: Simon & Schuster, 1995.

———. *Diana: The Last Year*. New York: Harmony Books, 1997.

The Operation Paget Inquiry Report into the Allegation of Conspiracy to

Murder Diana, Princess of Wales, and Emad El-Din Mohamed Abdel Moneim Fayed. London: Great Metropolitan Police Service, December 14, 2006. http://downloads.bbc.co.uk/news/nol/shared/bsp/hi /pdfs/14_12_06_diana_report.pdf.

Thornton, Michael. *Royal Feud*. London: Michael Joseph, 1985.

Thornton, Penny. *With Love from Diana*. New York: Pocket Books, 1995.

Vickers, Hugo. *Alice Princess Andrew of Greece*. New York: St. Martin's Press, 2002.

———. *Elizabeth the Queen Mother*. London: Arrow, 2006.

Wade, Judy. *The Truth: The Friends of Diana—Princess of Wales, Tell Their Stories*. London: John Blake, 2001.

Warwick, Christopher. *Princess Margaret: A Life of Contrasts*. London: Andre Deutsch, 2000.

Wharfe, Ken, with Robert Jobson. *Diana: Closely Guarded Secret*. London: Michael O'Mara Books, 2003.

Whitaker, James. *Diana v. Charles*. London: Signet, 1993.

Wilson, Christopher. *A Greater Love: Prince Charles's Twenty-Year Affair with Camilla Parker Bowles*. New York: William Morrow, 1994.

———. *The Windsor Knot*. New York: Citadel Press, 2002.

Ziegler, Philip. *Queen Elizabeth II*. London: Thames & Hudson, 2010.

INDEX